e Style

D0858882

TOWARD A SELF-MANAGED LIFE
STYLE

WILLIAMS, ROBERT L. & LONG, JAMES D.

Toward a Self-Managed Life Style

Robert L. Williams
The University of Tennessee

James D. Long
Appalachian State University

Houghton Mifflin Company **Boston**
Atlanta   Dallas   Geneva, Illinois   Hopewell, New Jersey   Palo Alto   London

Chapter-opening cartoons by Ed Fisher.

Library of Congress Catalog Card Number: 74-15400
ISBN: 0-395-18922-5

Contents

Prologue

This book is designed for students who wish to use behavior modification techniques in changing their own behavior. Instead of the traditional emphasis on how individuals *react to* their environment, the focus of this book is on how individuals *act upon* their environment to produce desired behavioral changes. We think self-modification is the ultimate application of behavior management concepts. By teaching individuals how to modify their own behavior, we have a permanent impact. If *we* assumed responsibility for modifying people's behavior, the quality of that behavior might continue to depend on our presence and support. The overriding purpose of this book is to produce self-responsibility for behavior and the ability to achieve desired behavior changes within oneself.

The text is divided into three sections: The Essence of Self-Management, Applications to Self, and Applications to Self and Others. The Essence of Self-Management (Chapters One and Two) explains how the concept of self-modification evolved within the field of psychology and outlines a comprehensive model for self-control. Applications to Self (Chapters Three to Seven) applies the self-control model to various personal domains, that is, health problems, sports skills, study behavior, career planning, and internal unrest. Applications to Self and Others (Chapters Eight and Nine) focuses on improving interpersonal relationships and getting assistance from others with self-management. Now, let us look specifically at the content of each chapter.

Chapter One (An Emerging Life Style: Foundations of Self-Management) identifies the benefits of self-management and its evolution within the field of psychology. Basic behaviorism and applied behavior modification are presented as the experimental foundations of self-management. Since self-management is more an integrated life style than a set of disparate techniques, its philosophical foundations, basic premises, and goals are also examined.

Chapter Two (The Less Traveled Road: A Model for Self-Control) describes the basic operations for producing desired changes in one's behavior. It explains why self-control ordinarily is difficult to attain, it distinguishes between self-management and will power, and it outlines the steps for achieving self-control. These steps include stating personal goals in behavioral terms, recording the quantity and circumstances of target behaviors, changing the setting events related to the target behaviors, establishing effective consequences for the target behaviors, focusing on these consequences, and mobilizing covert support.

Chapter Three (An Apple a Day: Controlling Health Problems) deals with such health menaces as excessive eating, smoking, and drinking. The chapter includes an analysis of the variables that maintain these self-destructive behaviors and a description of procedures for changing them. The self-control model outlined in Chapter Two is applied step-by-step to each problem area.

Chapter Four (The Rites of Passage: Developing Sports Skills) is meant for people who wish to make sports activity an integral part of their lives. This chapter focuses on the acquisition of sports skills in general rather than on specific skills. Among the issues treated are (1) when to practice, (2) how long to practice, (3) what to emphasize in practice, (4) how to make practice reinforcing, (5) how to use role models, (6) how to maximize feedback, and (7) how to transcend slumps. This chapter is based on the assumption that participation in sports can fundamentally enhance our lives.

Chapter Five (Panic in the Stacks: Managing Study Behavior) has four major sections: using the self-control model for increasing study behavior, enhancing reading comprehension, completing long-term projects, and behaving more creatively. In each domain, the self-management approach is contrasted with the more conventional mode of operation.

Chapter Six ("Life's Inmost Secret": Career Planning) first identifies behaviors that a college student should exhibit in making career plans. These include systematically analyzing one's interest patterns, appraising one's aptitudes, acquiring information about vocations, determining vocational choices, and selecting appropriate training experiences. The chapter then identifies setting events and reinforcement contingencies for producing these behaviors.

Chapter Seven ("The Inner Sanctum": Changing Internal Unrest) takes a somewhat different approach from the preceding chapters. Instead of focusing on overt behaviors, this chapter deals with such internal responses as anxiety, obsessive thoughts, mood states, and happiness. The strategies proposed for altering these internal reactions are self-directed relaxation, thought-stopping, positive self-verbalizations, and daily reinforcing activities.

Chapter Eight (Wealthier than Kings: Enhancing Interpersonal Relationships) is not another "how to win friends and influence people" discussion. Instead, the emphasis is on how to establish authentic and mutually reinforcing relationships with others. This chapter describes procedures for establishing reciprocal liking, for conveying sincere approval to others, for establishing reciprocal love (particularly with members of the opposite sex), and for resolving interpersonal conflicts. The development of assertive behavior receives special attention.

Chapter Nine ("Hold Me": Getting Help from Others) defines the principal strategies for enlisting others' help with personal problems. The chapter explains how to elicit candid feedback from others, how to formulate reciprocal contracts with others, how to get professional assistance, and how to use group support to strengthen appropriate behaviors. Among the self-help groups discussed are Alcoholics Anonymous, Weight Watchers, and activist organizations.

Recognizing that some of the terms used in this book may be new to you, we have provided a Glossary of major concepts. Each concept is identified with an asterisk when it is introduced in the text. If you have had a recent course in psychology, you should have little trouble following the explanations given in the text. But if you have had no background in psychology, the Glossary will enable you to acquire quickly the necessary concepts for understanding the text.

While we are pleased that you are reading our text, we hope that you will do a bit more than just read it. Since the real test of the book's worth will be seen in your behavior, we have included a number of self-management projects in the various chapters. You should count on doing at least one of these projects in each area of personal concern. But only you can make the decision as to which dimensions of your life should be changed.

As with most self-management projects, this book was completed with considerable assistance from others. Several people read portions of the manuscript and offered their editorial comments: Terry Alderman, Kamala Anandam, Pat Ball, Marty Begalla, Mike Blachly, Basil Johnson, Kevin King, Lib Long, John McCabe, and Tom Snipes.

Others gave extensive assistance in typing, editing, and proofreading the manuscript: Linda Clark, John Edgerly, Kay Hamilton, Ben Layne, Liz Mattice, Bob Walker, and Jackie Williams. Your contributions were significant, and they are deeply appreciated.

Robert L. Williams
James D. Long

The Essence of Self-Management

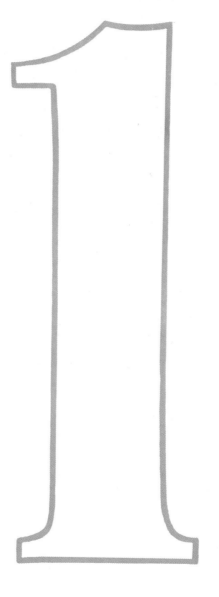

one

An Emerging Life Style:
Foundations of Self-Management

The impetus to change a behavior usually begins with others' reactions to that behavior . . . .

Ours is a time of much discussion about life styles, especially the differences among life styles. Roles and stereotypes are out, while freedom and uniqueness are in. We agree with this change in thinking because we believe roles have had a restrictive effect on personal development. Role expectations frequently prevent people from acting in ways that would bring great personal fulfillment. We would prefer that every person be allowed to pursue what makes sense to him/her. Only behavior that infringes on the rights of others would be restricted. But in everything else, each person's behavior would be governed more by personal values than by social and cultural norms.

We believe that one can best achieve a self-directed life style in an environment that is accepting and supporting of differences. Perhaps a college setting is the closest thing to a free and open society that many of us will experience. Even in this setting, what passes for freedom and uniqueness may simply be the adoption of another set of social norms. For most of us, there is still a major discrepancy between what we are and what we would like to be. We are not suggesting that behaving like others is always bad. Accepting social norms is questionable only when that acceptance undermines individual goals. However, we fear that in too many cases social conformity is achieved at the expense of important personal pursuits.

The objective of our book is to help you achieve behavior goals* that are important *to you*. These goals may be similar to those of others or totally unique. The fact that they are *your* goals is what matters. These goals may range from physical concerns (stopping smoking, losing weight, engaging in exercise) to social and career objectives (talking in group situations, re-establishing a friendship, making a career choice). Some goals may deal with private dimensions (for example, reducing guilt feelings), while others may focus on behaviors visible to all (e.g., decreasing stuttering).

The self-management approach described in this book involves the identification and control of specific environmental events that affect specific behaviors. Both *identification* and *control* are key terms in this definition. We are sometimes acutely aware that we have a problem, but quite unaware of the events contributing to that problem. When pressed for an explanation of our behavior, the best we can offer is "I simply don't know why I behave like that." Self-management provides the technology for identifying the contributors

*Defined in Glossary.

to your unwanted behaviors. Only after you have identified those contributors can you make the environmental changes that will produce behavior changes. But even more important, self-management allows you to identify and control those environmental factors that would produce desirable responses. It is the presence of these responses, rather than the mere absence of negative behavior, that leads to an enriched life.

Note that our definition of self-management speaks of *specific* environmental events and *specific* behaviors. Self-management does not attempt a total transformation of one's environment, but it does involve the changing of certain key events in that environment. Nor does self-management attempt to change one's entire personality; its focus, rather, is certain target behaviors.* Certainly, these target behaviors may be considered part of what is commonly called personality. If you change enough of these specific behaviors, it will appear that you have undergone a major personality change.

Since this book may represent only the beginning of your exploration into self-management, we would like to provide an appropriate background for your study. You need to have some awareness of the origins of self-management in psychology (the experimental background) and the objections that are usually voiced against self-management. We shall refer to the latter as the philosophical issues of self-management. These questions are considered for good reason, since self-management is more than a set of techniques extracted from empirical research. It represents an approach to life in which individuals assume responsibility for their behavior and then attempt to produce desired behavior changes. What are the major ethical problems that confront this self-management approach to life?

Experimental Foundations

Self-management has its roots in the field of behavior modification. Behavior modification, in turn, evolved from the behavioristic school of thought in psychology. So the lineage of self-management can ultimately be traced to behaviorism.

Behaviorism

The birth of experimental psychology is usually dated as 1879. In that year, Wilhelm Wundt established the world's first laboratory for the experimental study of psychology in Leipzig, Germany. As a result of his research and writings, Wundt came to be recognized as the world's first bona fide psychologist. Wundt focused on the mind, thereby following Descartes' distinction between mind and body. Wundt viewed the mind as that which separates humans from animals, and the unique task of psychology as the description of the elements that constitute the mind. The basic elements were assumed to be *sensations.* To identify these elements and their interrelationships, Wundt and his associates employed the method of introspection. A subject was presented a stimulus (e.g., a tone, odor, light), and then asked to describe precisely the sensations he experienced in response to that stimulus. The objective was to reconstruct all the sensations associated with that particular environmental event.

While Wundt was conducting his research in Germany, a somewhat different orientation was emerging in America. Influenced by the Darwinian doctrine of evolution, the American scholars—notably William James and John Dewey—emphasized the adaptive value of behavior and mental processes. Their principal question was, "What function does a behavior or a mental process serve in one's adjustment to one's environment?" Thus, their viewpoint, commonly called functionalism,* differed from Wundt's in two major respects: (1) it considered both mind and behavior; (2) it sought to identify the functions of mind and behavior, not just their structures. These researchers also went beyond Wundt's methodology by using behavioral observation as well as introspection.

In the 1910s the behavioristic school of psychology began to take shape. Its spokesmen, principally John B. Watson, contended that psychology could not attain scientific status without focusing on publicly observable events. That meant studying behavior rather than such internal events as feelings and thoughts. Introspective methods were shunned. Since subhumans (particularly the white rat) exhibit behavior, are quite accessible, and can be extensively controlled, many behaviorists turned to the study of animal behavior. From 1930 to 1960, behavioral psychology was dominated by animal experimentation. Much to the disdain of other psychologists, behaviorists contended that there were no absolute differences between humans and lower animals.

The building blocks of behavior were identified as conditioned reflexes. These were discrete responses that could be modified through specific environmental manipulations. Although human beings might possess a greater number of conditioned responses, and perhaps more complex conditioned responses, than animals, the basic principles of behavior change were assumed to be applicable to both. Subsequent behavioral research has shown that human and animal behaviors are not that dissimilar (chimpanzees are now being taught complex communication skills) and that humans respond in much the same fashion as animals to environmental manipulations. The all-time champion of the behaviorist school is the internationally known Harvard psychologist, B. F. Skinner. Many principles of conditioning* that are now being used in education, therapy, social programs, and self-management were first formulated in Skinner's animal laboratory.

Behavior Modification

Skinner's work on programmed instruction* and his description of a behavioral utopia in the best seller *Walden Two* (1948) set the stage for the dramatic shift in emphasis that took place in behavioral psychology in the 1960s. With the publication of Ayllon and Michael's article (1959), "The Psychiatric Nurse as a Behavioral Engineer," behaviorism began a double life. Laboratory research with animals continued while a new and vigorous phase of work applied to human settings came into existence. The widespread rumor that Skinner and his followers could communicate only with laboratory animals was proven false.

The principles of behavioral control, which had been generated by four decades of laboratory research with animals, were now being used in the real world. The application of behaviorism to real problems was variously known as behavior modification, behavior management, behavior technology, applied behavior analysis, and behavior therapy. Perhaps the most commonly used label was behavior modification. At first the concepts were applied to individuals classified as severely ill or mentally deficient. The applied analysts were able to reinstate verbal behavior in psychotic patients, condition social isolates to exhibit cooperative behavior, eliminate phobic reactions, instill self-care behaviors in the chronically ill, suppress self-destructive responses of autistic children, restore eating behaviors in fasting patients, re-establish vision in hysterically blind patients, reverse sexually impotent responses, and eliminate multiple tics.[1]

One of the more colorful examples of the early work in applied behavior management was reported by Ted Ayllon (1963), then at the Saskatchewan Hospital in Canada. He used the concept of stimulus satiation* or flooding to eliminate the towel-hoarding behavior of a patient who had exhibited the problem for nine years. The technique of stimulus satiation involves providing such excessive amounts of a stimulus that a person tires of it. Although nurses removed the towels from this patient's room about twice weekly, she usually had anywhere from twenty to thirty towels in her room at a time. During Ayllon's treatment program, retrieval of the towels was discontinued. Instead, the nurses would periodically deliver towels to the patient's room. She was given an average of seven towels per day during the first week of treatment and a daily average of sixty by the third week. In the early days of treatment, the patient was frequently observed rubbing the towels against her cheeks. Obviously towels were still quite enjoyable to her. As the quantity of towels rose to the hundreds, the patient spent much of her time just folding and stacking the towels. At first, she expressed appreciation for the generous supply of towels, but by the second week of treatment she was requesting that no more towels be delivered to her. During the third and fourth weeks, she began insisting that the towels be removed from her room and by the sixth week was removing the towels herself. A one year follow-up revealed that the towel hoarding had not returned.

Perhaps the classic treatise on the use of behavior modification in the mental hospital setting was Ayllon and Azrin's *The Token Economy* (1968). This document describes how applied behavior analysis can be applied to entire wards of patients. It suggests that mental patients continue to emit "sick" behaviors because they are rewarded for those behaviors, even by nurses, psychologists, and psychiatrists. Many of these rewards are probably inadvertent, coming in the form of social payoffs; that is, the individual exhibiting the most bizarre behaviors receives the most extensive clinical attention. Ayllon and Azrin demonstrated that seriously disturbed individuals could learn to take care of themselves, assume work responsibilities within the hospital, and behave in a generally sane fashion. This feat

---

[1]A representative sampling of the early work in applied behavior analysis is provided in L. P. Ullman and L. Krasner, *Case studies in behavior modification* (New York: Holt, Rinehart and Winston, 1965).

was achieved by making positive consequences dependent upon the emission of desired behaviors. Privacy, social contact, extra snacks, participation in religious services, and special kinds of reading materials were among the consequences used as rewards.[2] Each reinforcement privilege cost a specified number of tokens,* and each appropriate behavior earned a particular number of tokens. These reinforcement conditions were maintained twenty-four hours a day, seven days a week. The behaviors produced by their token economy* were the kinds of responses that would likely be rewarded and, therefore, maintained outside the hospital setting.

After mental institutions, the next major proving ground for applied behavior analysis was the educational environment. At first the behavior modifiers worked almost exclusively with young children. Various kinds of disruptive and immature behaviors were changed—kicking, screaming, crying, regressed crawling, and isolate behavior. The principal technique used in changing those behaviors was conditional social attention. Behavior modifiers discovered that undesirable behavior was usually followed by some type of social reaction; for example, the teacher reprimanded the child or other children laughed at the child's antics. Conversely, desirable behavior was often taken for granted and ignored. By reversing the contingencies* of social attention—that is, attending to the child when he behaved appropriately, and ignoring him when he behaved inappropriately—the behavior analysts were able to modify most types of undesirable behavior.

In the late 1960s and early 1970s, behavior modifiers began using complex token systems in the classroom, similar to what Ayllon and Azrin had instituted in the mental hospital setting. Token systems could be used with larger numbers of students, sometimes an entire school, and often produced higher levels of appropriate behavior than had been attained through teacher attention. Students earned tokens (e.g., poker chips or points) for a wide range of classroom behaviors, including academic achievement. These tokens could periodically be cashed in for free-time privileges (games, art work, comic books), tangible payoffs (money, trinkets, food), and even good grades. The payoffs for appropriate classroom behavior had become notoriously extrinsic.*

[2] The more technical term for reward is *reinforcer.* * A reinforcer is any event that strengthens the behavior immediately preceding it, e.g., an enjoyable activity following completion of work.

Classroom management research has also seen a change in the kinds of subjects used. The initial research efforts focused on young children and students in special education settings. This emphasis was so pronounced that some educators concluded that behavior modification was only applicable to young children or students with special problems. However, later research (Anandam and Williams, 1971; McAllister et al.,1969; Williams and Anandam, 1973) has demonstrated that the behavior modification strategies are equally effective with junior and senior high school students in typical settings. One current emphasis of classroom mangement is the application of token economies at the college level. For example, if students meet specified behavior objectives, they earn a predetermined number of points, which are then cashed in for grades.

The early 1970s saw a proliferation of behavior modification programs in diverse social settings—day-care centers, national parks, nursing homes, prisons, movie theaters, rehabilitation agencies, and private homes. An example of the social impact of behavior management is Achievement Place, a treatment center for delinquent boys in Lawrence, Kansas (Phillips et al., 1973), where six to eight boys live together in a large farmhouse with two teaching parents. Since Phillips and his colleagues view delinquency as resulting primarily from behavioral deficiencies, they identified and rewarded appropriate social, domestic, and academic behaviors. Their major treatment program has been a token economy in which students earn points that are exchangeable for tangible objects and privileges. The points are gradually phased out so that an individual eventually operates on a merit system in which all privileges are free. In addition to points, instruction, demonstration, practice, feedback, and approval are used in producing desirable behaviors. The success of Achievement Place exemplifies what behavior management can contribute to the solution of societal ills.

Self-Management

Self-management research emerged rather quietly within the field of behavior modification. One of the first studies to stimulate discussion of self-management was Israel Goldiamond's (1965) application of self-control procedures to personal behavior problems. His research set forth the array of problems that can be altered through self-modification and some of the basic operations involved in self-management. Goldiamond's conception of self-control depended mainly on stimulus control*—changing the factors that precipitate desired or undesired behavior.

Another group of the pioneering self-controllers (Bandura, Kanfer, Marston) compared self-administered consequences with externally administered consequences. Bandura and his associates at Stanford determined that self-administered contingencies could be as potent as externally administered contingencies (Bandura and Perloff, 1967). In other words, rewarding yourself is sometimes as effective as being rewarded by others. Kanfer's research group demonstrated that we reinforce ourselves in a way similar to the way we have been reinforced by others (Kanfer and Duerfeldt, 1967). Their research also indicated that teaching an individual to administer self-reinforcement* can prevent the loss of a response that is no longer externally reinforced. So if you have been very dependent on external rewards, self-management offers a means of accomplishing behavior change by self-administered rewards.

A number of self-management researchers have focused on the role of internal events* in self-management. Lloyd Homme (1965) was perhaps the first researcher to define formally the role of such internal events as feelings and thoughts in modifying overt behaviors. His approach is especially useful in subduing problem behaviors at the moment of temptation. The use of covert events to modify behavior has also been researched by Joseph Cautela, who contends that imagined behavior and imagined consequences can significantly affect the incidence of actual behavior. This approach suggests that the resources for managing one's behavior are to be found as much within oneself as in the external environment.

Homme's and Cautela's approaches use internal events to alter the probability of overt behaviors.* Other researchers have attempted to change internal reactions per se, such as anxiety, obsessive thoughts, and depression. Joseph Wolpe is perhaps the most notable of these researchers. Although Wolpe's conventional model for reducing anxiety (systematic desensitization*) makes extensive use of the therapist, his strategy for inducing relaxation can be adapted to self-management. Among the behavior modifiers who have attempted to alter mood states and self-esteem are Johnson (1971), Mahoney (1971), and Velten (1968). Their major strategy is self-verbalization* of positive statements. They assume that what people say about themselves is fundamental to mood states and self-regard, and their findings suggest that personal tranquility and self-respect are highly attainable goals.

Research on self-management is in a formative stage of development. Although several of the major behavior modification journals—*Behavior Therapy, Behaviour Research and Therapy, Behavior Therapy and Experimental Psychiatry, Journal of Applied Behavior Analysis*—are publishing increasing numbers of studies on self-management, the apex of this research has not yet been reached. In our opinion, self-modification represents the wave of the future in behavior modification. Such personal domains as interpersonal relationships, academic achievement, sports skills, health menaces, sexual behaviors, and internal mood states are being affected by self-modification procedures. Although we have seen no published research on the subject, self-management procedures may also be quite useful in altering sex-role behavior. While sex-role stereotypes are presently being de-emphasized, most of us have already been conditioned to behave in "masculine" or "feminine" ways. Changes in these traditional behavior patterns do not come easily or painlessly, but self-management strategies may prove effective in acquiring non-sexist behaviors.

Philosophical Foundations

Self-management has emerged as an important dimension of behavior modification; it could make quite an impact on society as a whole. The tone of self-management is consistent with our society's ethic of self-responsibility. We are held responsible for our behavior because we are assumed to be in control of that behavior. Thus, any orientation that increases the possibility of self-control ought to be highly acceptable.

In spite of our enthusiasm for self-management, you may still have reservations about its potential in your life. Some of these reservations can only be resolved through careful study of the remaining chapters in this text. Until you know more specifically what can be accomplished through self-management, you can hardly make a judicious decision about its utility. However, some reservations are primarily of a philosophical nature. You may take issue with some of the underlying premises of self-management, or you may question the goals of self-management. Before we attempt to describe the mechanics of self-control (Chapter Two), we must discuss the philosophical concerns.

Self-Control vs. External Control

Many behavioral psychologists, especially Skinner, contend that there is no such thing as true self-control. In his discussion of self-control, Skinner (1953) makes an important distinction between controlling responses and controlled responses. Controlled responses* are the target behaviors that we want to change through self-management strategies. For example, eating, exercising and talking might be controlled responses. The behaviors we emit in order to change the target behaviors are the controlling responses.* Buying a limited amount of food, making a reward contingent on a certain amount of exercise, and arranging a social situation to facilitate talking are illustrative of controlling responses.

In the preceding analysis, the controlled responses result from the controlling responses. The question now is, what controls the controlling response? In other words, what determines whether we will buy a limited amount of food? Most behaviorists would assume that controlling behavior is ultimately determined by genetic endowment and environmental events. A person may appear to be inner-directed, but his controlling behavior is actually controlled by variables outside himself. For example, a person may do something about his obesity because of negative input received from others. That negative input, not some autonomous inner force, is what precipitates weight-controlling behavior.

If the argument of the last paragraph is valid, how can anyone truly manage his own behavior? In the absolute philosophical sense, perhaps people do not manage their behavior. In a more pragmatic sense, a person can apply the same behavior modification strategies to his own responses as to those of others. For example, he can control his own reinforcement contingencies in the same way he controls reinforcement contingencies for others.[3] However, a person can only apply the strategies he has learned. Individuals exposed to faulty environments will probably lack the skills to manage their own responses effectively. The content of this book will soon become a part of your environmental history and may significantly alter your self-management skills.

[3]Perhaps the most useful distinction between external control and self-control has been suggested by Thoresen and Mahoney (1974). If a person has free access to reinforcers and yet does not partake of them until he meets certain behavioral criteria, he is said to be exhibiting self-control. If the reinforcement contingencies are controlled by others, the individual is assumed to be operating under external control.

Desire to Change

Some people feel that altering a behavior requires nothing more than *wanting* to change that behavior. Failure to change presumably results from insufficient motivation. Admittedly, desire to change is a crucial component of self-management. A person may be quite knowledgeable about self-management and yet do nothing to modify his behavior. However, we disagree with the idea that desire alone will produce behavior change. A person may want to change very badly but fail because of ill-designed self-control strategies. We contend that desire and knowledge are both indispensable to self-control.

If desire to change is indispensable to self-management, where does that desire originate? The impetus to change a behavior usually begins with others' reactions to that behavior. When a behavior is consistently ignored or criticized, we probably want to change that behavior. Being ignored or criticized produces a desire to change only in an environment in which rewards are available for other behaviors. If you are ignored or criticized for exhibiting behavior A but consistently reinforced for emitting behavior B, you will be motivated to emit less A and more B.

The negative feedback mentioned in the preceding paragraph does not have to be real or overt. Thinking that others dislike a behavior may be a sufficient impetus to change that behavior. Our perception of others' reactions is obviously affected by previous interactions. If we have frequently been criticized by others, we might assume that an individual is critical toward us when that is not the case. The point is that desire to change usually results from the perception that others are dissatisfied with our behavior, even when that perception is inaccurate.

What effect will this book have on your desire to change your behaviors? Clearly, it cannot motivate you in the traditional fashion, by providing negative feedback. Nonetheless, some of the reinforcement possibilities to be described may indeed affect your desire to change. Self-management presents potential for personal fulfillment that is not frequently realized. The conception of self-management presented here is far different from the conventional will-power approach. The Williams-Long orientation emphasizes immediate rewards rather than rewards that come after six months of pain and deprivation. Both the long-term and the short-term payoffs from self-management provide inducements to change. This text may also generate renewed hope for changing certain of your behaviors. The procedures described are mainly simple, enjoyable, and workable.

Presumably you have the desire to change at least some of your behaviors or you would not be reading this book. (It is most nonreinforcing for us to assume that you are reading the book simply to fulfill a course requirement.) If you are presently behaving exactly as you wish, there is no need to read further. However, most of us would probably say, "Well, my life is not so bad, but there are some behaviors that need changing." A critical problem in self-management is finding ways to change these behaviors without jeopardizing the "not so bad" part of your life. When people become entrenched in a particular life style, they are extremely reluctant to try alternatives that might upset their present balance of reinforcers. If your beloved screams at you twelve times a day, at least he/she is noticing you. You may be unwilling to jeopardize that attention by exhibiting new behaviors, even if they eventually could lead to a higher quality of attention. If you are like most people, you want to change your behavior only if the proposed change will not result in the loss of existing reinforcers. That is a reasonable expectation and one that we shall attempt to accommodate.

Potential for Change

Although self-management has proven effective with a wide range of behaviors, we do not assume that all behaviors are subject to self-modification. Some behaviors may be controlled primarily by biological factors and/or by environmental variables over which you have no control. Genetic endowment, physiological injury, and societal constraints may profoundly limit one's behavioral potential. Although we recognize that certain behaviors may be impervious to change, we do not know what those behaviors are—even in our own lives. We caution you against accepting the "I'm just that way" philosophy. Each of us has experienced personal changes that would have seemed impossible a few years ago. The prospect of writing a text on self-management would have been unthinkable ten years ago. (We presume that it is now quite thinkable!) While self-management strategies will not allow you to change behaviors ad infinitum, they may help you to change some behaviors that you presently view as practically unchangeable.

Not only are certain behaviors resistant to self-management; some problems may not even be definable in behavioral terms. Some of our most important concerns are internal in nature; but anxiety, depression, and obsessive thinking are not that easy to describe in precise, measurable terms. A person may have a feeling for what it means to be anxious or depressed, but his subjective frame of reference may fluctuate considerably from one situation to the next. In addition, there is no way for others to verify whether his introspective analysis is accurate. From a scientific perspective, it is almost impossible to work with private, internal events. But because these events are important to you, we will attempt to analyze how they can be changed (see Chapter Seven).

Sometimes even behavioral goals defy precise definition. One example is the goal of creativity. Because creativity involves novel activity, you simply cannot know in advance what form that novel activity should take. You may be able to recognize novel responses when they occur, but you can not predefine them. The best that you can do is arrange situations and consequences that others have used in facilitating creativity activity (see Chapter Five).

Effect on Personality

Some contend that self-management changes only superficial behaviors, not fundamental personality characteristics. The implication is that the *real* you remains intact. But how can the real you be assessed apart from your behaviors? The term *personality* is misleading because it implies that a person has underlying characteristics that will cause him to behave in similar ways across time and situations. Behavior, however, is quite situation specific. How an individual behaves at home, in a classroom, in an ice-cream parlor, on a remote beach, and in church can be significantly different. This is not to say that there are no overriding principles guiding our behavior across time and situations, but how we apply those principles can be vastly different in dissimilar settings.

Many clinical psychologists assume that a person's maladaptive behaviors are symptomatic of larger, hidden difficulties. The problem of obesity is sometimes said to reflect a need for affection. In fact, numerous disorders are attributed to a need for affection. Remember the woman who hoarded towels? She had previously been diagnosed as needing affection. So the argument runs, "Remove the symptom* (towel hoarding) and the real problem (a need for affection) will be expressed in other ways." Affection is undeniably important for emotional well-being. Nevertheless, it is our opinion that behavior problems do not generally reflect a need for affection or an underlying personality disorder. A person may have many problems, some internal and some external, but there is little evidence that changing one maladaptive behavior will cause another to appear. Individuals should concern themselves with altering what they say, think, and do; they should not presume that behavior problems reflect mysterious, deep-seated personality disorders. If several shortcomings exist simultaneously, a person will most likely need to analyze the determinants of each and formulate a self-management strategy for each. It is true that some responses appear to be interrelated, so that changing one response may indirectly alter other responses in the same class. However, many behaviors seem to operate independently of each other, so that each must be changed through separate environmental control.

Effect on Spontaneity

Some people object to any kind of systematic behavior control, including control of self. These individuals fear that a systematic effort to manage their own behavior might reduce spontaneity and authenticity. Such an orientation fails to recognize that many behaviors that presently seem very natural are the result of earlier, deliberate learning. Think of how awkward people are when first learning to dance, drive a car, introduce people to each other, perform the responsibilities of a new job, and so on. Even showing pleasure over a nice gift, or a not so nice gift, probably required conscious effort on the first few occasions. Being friendly with others, discharging social obligations, or engaging in other forms of self-directed behavior may initially seem mechanical and superficial; however, people become more spontaneous with practice. You eventually will be able to emit the desired behaviors without having to tell yourself what to do. The adage, "Practice a virtue though you have it not and soon it will be yours," surely holds true here.

Continuation of Self-Management

People may begin self-management projects with the greatest of enthusiasm, but soon find themselves cheating on self-management procedures. Before too many days have passed, the project has become extinct. How can this depressing fate be averted? A central component in self-management is providing systematic reinforcement for desired changes in the target behavior. But what about reinforcement for the self-management behaviors, e.g., collecting data on the target behavior, arranging an appropriate setting, administering specified consequences? Chapter Two will describe procedures for rewarding those behaviors and maximizing their occurrence. These suggestions will not be exhaustive or infallible. The fact remains that you may design a self-management program today and junk it tomorrow. The best predictor of the longevity of a self-management program is its quality. Many attempts at self-management go by the boards because of ill-designed self-management strategies. If that has been the fate of your previous self-management efforts, do not despair. Help is just a few pages away.

In Summation

Many treatises have been written on the topic of self-control. Philosophers, theologians, educators, and poets have spilled a considerable amount of ink on this topic. The distinction between this book and others that have dealt with the subject lies in the specificity of the procedures described. This text, rather than speaking in nebulous and moralistic terms, will attempt to describe specific procedures that can be interpreted and implemented with a minimal amount of confusion.

Self-management will not solve all your problems. We have explored numerous philosophical, religious, ethical, and social systems and have yet to find one that resolves all human difficulties. There are some problems that we believe to be inherent to human existence, problems that cannot be solved through self-management or any other approach. The tremendous problems created by physical illnesses, tragedy, old age, and death cannot be eliminated through self-management. But self-management has something to offer even in these areas. Beyond these profound existential concerns, there is a multiplicity of everyday experiences that contribute fundamentally to the quality of life. It is with these experiences that the impact of self-management can be felt most keenly.

References

Anandam, K., and Williams, R. L. 1971. A model for consultation with classroom teachers on behavior management. *School Counselor 18*, 253-259.

Ayllon, T. 1963. Intensive treatment of psychotic behaviour by stimulus satiation and food reinforcement. *Behaviour Research and Therapy 1*, 53-61.

Ayllon, T., and Azrin, N. 1968. *The token economy: A motivational system for therapy and rehabilitation.* New York: Appleton-Century Crofts.

Ayllon, T., and Michael, J. 1959. The psychiatric nurse as a behavioral engineer. *Journal of the Experimental Analysis of Behavior 2*, 323-334.

Bandura, A., and Perloff, B. 1967. Relative efficacy of self-monitored and externally imposed reinforcement systems. *Journal of Personality and Social Psychology 7*, 111-116.

Goldiamond, I. 1965. Self-control procedures in personal behavior problems. *Psychological Reports 17*, 851-868.

Homme, L. E. 1965. Control of coverants, the operants of the mind. Perspectives in psychology, XXIV. *Psychological Record 15*, 501-511.

Johnson, W. G. 1971. Some applications of Homme's coverant control therapy: two case reports. *Behavior Therapy 2*, 240-248.

Kanfer, F. H., and Duerfeldt, P. H. 1967. Motivational properties of self-reinforcement. *Perceptual and Motor Skills 25*, 237-246.

Mahoney, M. J. 1971. The self-management of covert behavior: a case study. *Behavior Therapy 2*, 575-578.

McAllister, L. W., Stachowiak, J. G., Baer, D. M., and Conderman, L. 1969. The application of operant conditioning techniques in a secondary school classroom. *Journal of Applied Behavior Analysis 2*, 277-285.

Phillips, E. L., Phillips, E. A., Fixsen, D. L., and Wolf, M. M. 1973. Behavior shaping works for delinquents. *Psychology Today 7*, 74-79.

Skinner, B. F. 1948. *Walden two.* New York: Macmillan.

———. 1953. *Science and human behavior.* New York: Macmillan.

Thoresen, C. E., and Mahoney, M. J. 1974. *Behavioral self-control..* New York: Holt, Rinehart and Winston.

Velten, E., Jr. 1968. A laboratory task for induction of mood states. *Behaviour Research and Therapy 6*, 473-482.

Williams, R. L., and Anandam, K. 1973. The effect of behavior contracting on grades. *Journal of Educational Research 66*, 230-236.

two

The Less Traveled Road: A Model for Self-Control

Some of the more intimate moments of life do not lend themselves to on-the-spot behavior recording.

When Robert Frost wrote "The Road Not Taken," he may not have had self-management in mind. Yet, the message of his poem surely applies to our present quest. In describing the mechanics of self-control, we are presenting you with a choice—a choice between a self-managed life style and whatever your present orientation might be. The self-managed life style is by all criteria the less traveled road. It is our opinion that most people do not even approximate their potential for self-management. They engage in behaviors that are hazardous to their health, fail to attain important personal goals, and generally experience much unnecessary frustration. Effective self-management is simply not the prevailing life style in this culture. This chapter will describe what self-management entails; you can then decide which path to pursue.

Although self-management research is relatively young, the concepts of will power* and self-control are not. They have frequently been used by lay persons as explanations for human behavior. The individual who responds calmly to an emotionally charged situation is said to have a high degree of self-control. The chain smoker who abruptly gives up the habit after years of smoking is revered for his remarkable will power. The average person tends to believe that behavior can be changed merely by "putting one's mind to it." Unfortunately, these lay explanations are seldom illuminating. They seem to imply that people possess some inner repository of strength that allows them to transcend problems. If this were so, it would make sense to tell an individual, "Just don't worry about it," "Don't let yourself get upset," "Pull yourself together," or "You must get better organized." But these suggestions usually are profoundly ineffective.

We are not denying the effectiveness of will power. On the contrary, we are searching for its ingredients. We suspect that what people often label as will power is simply a set of unspecified, yet workable, self-management procedures. The ingredients usually remain unspecified because most people do not have the skills to analyze systematically what influences their behavior. Consequently, they talk about will power without knowing how it is developed or how it can be exerted. The objective of this chapter is to specify the unspecified, thereby providing some useful tools for exercising will power, self-control, self-management, or whatever you prefer to call it. Let us begin by considering why self-control poses so much difficulty for many of us.

*Defined in Glossary.

We believe that the difficulty in achieving self-control is primarily related to conflict between long-term and short-term consequences of behavior. Very frequently a desired change would produce great dividends over an extended time period. An obese individual, for example, might resolve to lose fifty pounds in the next year. Imagine what rewarding benefits would result from attaining such a goal: the individual would be more attractive to others, might enjoy a substantially increased sex life, and would be able to pursue physical activities not engaged in for years. The payoff for losing fifty pounds would obviously be worthwhile. But after dieting for three-fourths of a day and doing a couple of sit-ups, the individual gives up on the long-term goal and once again becomes resigned to obesity. He or she may periodically reaffirm the intention to lose weight but always to no permanent avail.

This example epitomizes what happens to many attempts at weight control. In contrast to the long-term benefits of losing weight, the immediate consequences seem to favor weight-producing behaviors. Eating usually produces immediate gratification, while not eating may produce hunger pangs, headaches, and grouchiness. In addition, attempts to exercise probably result in immediate exhaustion and physical discomfort. So the long-range payoff cannot counteract the impact of immediate rewards and punishment. Control over a weight problem can be achieved only by altering the immediate consequences.

Effective self-management primarily involves the rearrangement of behavioral consequences so that desired behavior is *immediately* reinforced. Since unwanted behavior often produces immediate reinforcement of its own, the individual must either eliminate those rewards, administer immediate self-punishment for behaving inappropriately, or provide greater reinforcement for the desired response than for the undesired. This chapter provides an overview of the procedures used in accomplishing these objectives. Specifically, we shall discuss (1) selecting a goal, (2) recording the quantity and circumstances of behavior, (3) changing setting events for behavior, (4) establishing effective consequences, (5) focusing on contingencies, and (6) applying covert control. Some of these terms may be new to you; they will be explained thoroughly in the sections that follow.

The model presented on the following pages is not the only avenue to effective self-management. However, it does represent the brand of self-management that we have found to be most effective both personally and professionally. You may find the entire model suited to your personal life style, but more probably you will find certain features useful and others inappropriate. It is not necessary to go through all six steps in solving every problem. In fact, steps one through three will be adequate for modifying many behaviors. When a particular behavior reaches the level you desire, there is no need to continue with other components of the model.

Selecting a Goal

Selection of a goal is the first step in self-management and perhaps the most critical. Many self-management attempts go awry because of inappropriate goals. You can probably think of many dimensions of your life that you would like to change, but you cannot deal with all of them simultaneously. It is almost always best to establish one goal at a time. Working on a single goal maximizes your chances of success and increases the probability of your moving on to other goals. Factors you should consider in formulating your first self-management goal are (a) importance of the goal, (b) measurability of the goal, (c) internal vs. external nature of the goal, (d) level of the goal, and (e) positive vs. negative quality of the goal.

Importance of the Goal

A primary consideration is to select a goal that you care about attaining. Self-management involves doing things that may be foreign to you. You are not going to expend much effort unless you are working toward something that really matters. If a behavior is causing you pain (anxiety, guilt, fear, embarrassment, depression), then you will probably work to change it. Any sign of progress will be reinforcing to you and will provide further impetus to your self-management efforts. However, it is quite possible to care *too* much about a problem. Effective self-management demands a high degree of objectivity, something difficult to achieve while overwhelmed by a problem. Therefore, an initial focus of self-management should be something that is causing you pain but is not the most excruciating problem in your life. Getting to work on time would probably be a better first goal than re-establishing a badly strained relationship.

You also must be cautious about selecting an initial goal that requires the elimination of long-standing behaviors. One of our students almost became a self-management dropout by virtue of choosing such a goal. Her objective was to reduce the frequency of her sarcastic, one-upmanship remarks. On the surface her goal seemed reasonable, but in reality it jeopardized a well-honed mechanism for producing subtle social reinforcement. For quite some time, her sarcasm had been eliciting reactions, such as laughter, that she found to be reinforcing. In attempting to attain her self-management goal, she inadvertently began to withdraw from social situations and/or to remain silent when otherwise she would have contributed cutting remarks. As a result of achieving her goal, she felt she had lost her spontaneity and fighting spirit. Now that is not the way self-management is supposed to work. Her mistake was choosing a goal that took away a powerful source of social reinforcement and left nothing in its place but grim virtue.

Measurability of the Goal

Another consideration in formulating an initial self-management goal is to define that goal in measurable behavioral terms. As noted in Chapter One, *behavioral* refers to an overt act that others can readily see. Talking, smiling, walking, crying, smoking, and eating are examples of overt behaviors. In contrast, "becoming less anxious," "developing a more positive attitude," and "being a better person" are not behaviorally stated goals. These goals are unwieldy and defy precise assessment of progress. All are certainly worthwhile considerations, but they must be translated into measurable, behavioral terms before they will be amenable to self-management. To illustrate the point, suppose your problem is excessive anxiety. Ask yourself, "What are some ways in which I manifest my anxiety?" or "What kinds of things does my anxiety prevent me from doing?" It might, for example, keep you from participating in class discussion. Let us say that you presently make few, if any, comments during class. A possible first goal might be to make at least one comment per class period in a particular course. By stating your goal in these terms, you identify something that can be measured unequivocally. Had you said that your goal was to remove pangs of anxiety, there could be considerable confusion, even in your own mind, as to exactly what constitutes a pang of anxiety—one heart flutter? a twinge? two gulps? a combination? You can see the mess—and the anxiety—this method would create. Objectively measuring the frequency of goal-related behavior is fundamental to self-management. Confusion as to the meaning of a goal can strike a death blow to that objectivity.

Internal vs. External Goals

At this point, you may protest that the real problems of life are internal in nature. Your contention is that speaking up in class will not make you a less anxious person inside. Do not be too sure. We generally assume that behaviors are a product of feelings, but things often work in reverse; that is, feelings can result from behaviors. People reduce fear by behaving as if they are unafraid—the old whistling-in-the-dark method. In the same vein, speaking up in class may very well reduce internal manifestations of anxiety. Your anxieties probably relate to many behaviors other than participating in class. If you are willing to identify and change these behaviors one by one, you may find that most of your anxiety eventually disappears.

Some internal responses seem to transcend changes in overt be-havior. You may learn to comment in group situations and still feel shaky whenever you speak up. Because of this possibility, a later chapter will be devoted to strategies for changing covert responses. In our opinion, however, it is highly unwise to formulate your initial goals in terms of internal responses. Let us bolster your skills in dealing with overt behaviors before attacking the covert.

Level of the Goal

You can identify a goal that is important to you, state that goal in measurable terms, but still have an inappropriately defined goal. Many self-management neophytes get too bold in the formulation of goals. Instead of shooting for one comment per class period, they aspire to be the class orator. Your first goal should be set only slightly higher than your present level of operation. If you never comment in class, your initial goal might be one comment per week. It is impera-tive to begin with a goal that is readily attainable. When you can consistently meet that goal, you can move your expectations up a notch (e.g., a comment every two class sessions). People do not change their whole being in one dynamic, creative moment. What we call personality includes a multitude of overt and covert reactions. Therefore, the effective method for producing change is to deal with these small units of behavior. When enough bits and pieces have been changed, possibly the whole person will be transformed.

Positive vs. Negative Goals

It is usually best to state goals in terms of positive behaviors. What we are aiming for is not just the absence of negative events but the presence of positive responses. You could refrain from many negative behaviors and still have an unsatisfactory existence. Besides, one of the best ways to eliminate negative behavior is to strengthen positive behavior that is incompatible* with the negative. A teacher who was attempting to reduce her use of the expression "okay" made a list of comments that could be used instead of "okay"; for example, "excellent," "great," "not real good, but better," "you're improving," "remarkable," "fantastic," and "I like that." By increasing the frequency of these responses, she decreased the likelihood of saying, "okay." If you cannot identify a positive response that is incompatible with the negative, perhaps you can initially replace the negative response with a behavior that is not quite so undesirable. For example, one girl reduced the frequency of scratching her skin disorder by substituting stroking and then patting for the scratching behavior (Watson et al., 1972).

Another reason for stating goals in positive terms will become clearer as you explore the section on recording behavior. The act of recording must be reinforced in order to be sustained. It is much more likely that you will find this act inherently reinforcing if you log positive events than if you record negative. You may be eager to record the days you get to work on time but disinclined to record the times you are tardy. If your record-keeping system focuses primarily on negative behaviors, it is more likely that you will allow that record-keeping to slip.

Recording Quantity and Circumstances of Behavior

Importance of Recording

For several reasons it is important to appraise precisely the extent of your problem before attempting to solve that problem. People frequently launch massive self-management attempts without making provisions for monitoring the target behavior. A major reason for recording behavior prior to the initiation of self-management is to provide a reference point for evaluating progress. You may feel that you can recognize changes in your behavior without elaborate record-keeping. However, behavior does not usually change abruptly. Change may evolve so gradually that you become habituated to that change. But these slight day-to-day changes can add up to significant improvement over extended time periods. For example, you might reduce your smoking rate by one or two cigarettes per day, which would not give you an overwhelming sense of accomplishment. But continuing this reduction rate for several days would produce a substantial decrement. Keeping precise records of the target behavior maximizes your awareness of progress.

In some instances it is important to record not only the baseline* frequency (the original amount) of a behavior but also events that immediately precede or follow occurrences of that behavior. Information concerning those circumstances may dictate where to begin in altering the behavior. You might initially be oblivious to the fact that certain events consistently trigger an undesirable response. Smokers, for example, may not be aware that they light cigarettes more frequently when drinking or conversing. We may be equally unaware of what is producing certain of our social behaviors. Gestures, comments, or noncomments may be consistently tied to particular environmental events. You may have had the experience of expecting to behave in one way (laughing, conversing) in a social situation but actually behaving in an opposite manner. Perhaps you went to a social event expecting to be the life of the party, but wound up hardly saying a word. Perhaps the subdued laughter to your first joke, the involvement of your favorite people in conversation with others, someone's comment about your not looking well, and even the temperature of the room contributed to your depressed response. As you will see in later sections, identifying the specific stimuli that precede or follow a behavior makes it easier to do something about that behavior. As long as you do not know what is setting the stage for an undesired behavior or what might be reinforcing that behavior, you have little capability for modifying it.

Methods of Recording

Behavior records tend to be most accurate when responses are recorded as they occur. Attempting to reconstruct your behavior several hours later will introduce an intolerable degree of subjectivity into your self-management efforts. People selectively remember and forget. Failure to record behavior immediately may negate any possibility of precisely determining the effects of a self-management program. Naturally, you have reservations about the feasibility of recording behavior immediately after it occurs. You cannot imagine always having paper and pencil conveniently available or being able to record behavior unobtrusively in all situations. Some of the more intimate moments of life certainly do not lend themselves to on-the-spot behavior recording. However, many situations do. For example, most academically related behaviors occur in situations where paper and pencil are available. The number of times you speak up in class, the amount of time you devote to study, and the number of assignments completed are quite easily recorded. All you need is a sheet on which to record instances of the behavior and the events preceding and following those instances.

You might be surprised at the versatility of paper-and-pencil recording strategies. One of our students (Gilmore, 1973) set as his self-management goal the consistent buckling of his seat belt whenever he entered his car. (This project was done before mechanization forced us to buckle our seat belts.) To establish the baseline level of his behavior and the circumstances (besides just getting in the car) that might be contributing to that behavior, he devised a card on which to indicate the time of seat belt application or nonapplication, whether family or friends were in the car with him, and the mileage traveled (a mileage counter mounted on the front dashboard was used for this purpose). This card was placed on the console of the car and thus was readily accessible for recording data.

In situations where paper-and-pencil recording would be impractical or obtrusive, alternative strategies are available. Two of these are a wrist counter and a knitting-stitch counter. Both of these can be manipulated without interrupting other activities. With the wrist counter, you can record three behaviors concurrently, or you can record occurrences of a particular behavior plus opportunities for that behavior.[1] For example, you might record the times when you behave assertively plus the times when you should behave assertively. If you want to know how frequently a specific behavior is occurring in different situations, you can use the separate dials to record instances of the behavior in those situations. At a party, you might record your

---

[1]A wrist counter with three separate recording dials can be obtained from Behavior Research Company, Box 3351, Kansas City, Kansas 66103, for approximately $4.00.

frequency of swearing when you are talking with different people. We have found the knitting-stitch counter most useful when working with teachers. It fits snugly over the end of a pencil and allows the individual to continue teaching functions while recording behaviors.

Perhaps even more versatile than either of these counters is a bead counter presently being used at the University of Tennessee's Counseling Center. As shown in Figure 2-1, the bead counter is worn around the wrist and allows you to monitor up to eight behaviors at once. The beads are tightly strung so they will not accidentally slip back and forth. Each strand has twelve beads, but the number of strands and beads per strand can be increased. Students have reported that they can use the bead counter in a less obtrusive manner than the conventional wrist counter.

Types of Records

Our discussion of modes of record-keeping has perhaps suggested that there are three major types of behavior records that can be used in self-management: (1) frequency count,* (2) time duration, and (3) product assessment.* A frequency count involves nothing more than tabulating the number of times a particular behavior occurs. This is the easiest and most widely used method of assessing behavior. Any behavior that can be defined in terms of discrete instances can be assessed by a frequency count. Comments in class, sit-ups, nasty remarks to your spouse, and obscene gestures can all be subjected to

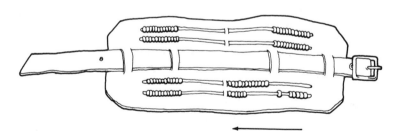

Figure 2-1 Bead counter used in the self-recording of behavior. (This particular counter allows you to monitor eight behaviors concurrently. When a particular behavior occurs, a bead is moved to the opposite end of that strand. In the drawing, six of the eight behaviors have not occurred, one has occurred twelve times, and one six times. The arrow indicates the direction the beads are moved when behavior occurs.)

frequency count assessment. If a behavioral episode occurs over a short time period and has a definable beginning and end, frequency-count assessment is an appropriate method of recording that behavior.

Many behaviors, such as crying, sleeping, and studying, tend to occur over extended time periods and, therefore, cannot be differentiated into discrete behavioral events. In this case, the most accurate way of assessing the behavior is to record the amount of time invested in the behavior. The simplest way to accomplish this objective is to use a stopwatch, activating it each time the behavior starts and deactivating it when the behavior stops.[2] If the stopwatch approach reminds you too much of your track coach, an alternative strategy would be to use a regular watch and jot down starting and stopping times for different episodes of a behavior. From this information, total time devoted to a behavior could later be computed. This procedure is more laborious than the stopwatch approach, but it does indicate the times during the day when the specified behavior occurred— information that may be important in determining where to begin in modifying a behavior.

In many cases an accurate record of a behavior can be achieved by examining the products of that behavior. Completed assignments, a clean room, and weight on the scale are products that can be used to establish the efficacy of a self-management strategy. In fact, products usually provide the ultimate verification that a self-management program has worked. However, products do not usually tell us where to begin in changing our behaviors. Finding out that you turned in only one homework assignment last week or that you have weighed 312 pounds for ten consecutive days does not tell you how to solve your problem. Instead, you first have to identify behaviors that are interfering with completion of assignments or contributing to excessive weight and then change those behaviors. In other words, your behavior change strategies (rewards, punishments) should be applied to the process* behaviors (eating, napping) that contribute to the behavior product (overweight, incomplete assignments) rather than to the behavior product itself. For example, one of our students aspired to lose five pounds over a two-week period. She hypothesized that between-meal snacking was the principal barrier to reaching that

[2]Helbros manufactures a chronograph, which can simultaneously be used as a regular watch and as a stopwatch.

goal. Therefore, her reinforcement contingencies were primarily tied to nonsnacking behavior (process) rather than to loss of weight (product). As normally happens with this arrangement, the process behavior evidenced a change before the behavior product. This result is shown in Figure 2-2.

Regardless of which recording system you use, you will find that graphing behavior helps to clarify the current status of your actions and provides a reference point for evaluating future performances. Graphing can also serve as significant reinforcement for your self-management endeavors. There are few things more reinforcing than seeing desired behavior begin to increase or undesired ones decrease. Some researchers (Broden et al., 1971; Johnson and White,

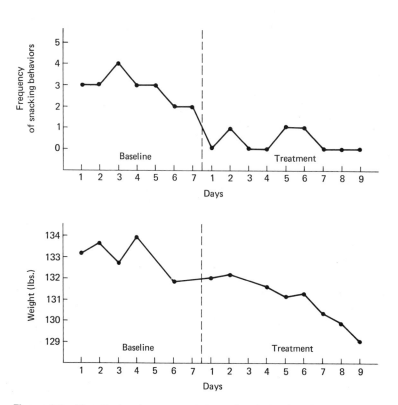

Figure 2-2 Magnitude of process and product behavior changes across baseline and treatment days. (Kornrumph, 1973.)

1971; Kanfer, 1970; Mahoney et al., 1973) report that the mere act of recording and graphing a behavior frequently leads to improvement in that behavior. This is especially true of behaviors that you are highly motivated to change. Graphing can also help a person transcend those inevitable plateaus in self-management programs. Assuming that one is able to get past the first plateau, the graph will demonstrate that it sometimes pays to continue a program when that program is ostensibly producing no further improvement. The vertical axis on a self-management graph generally denotes level of behavior (frequency, duration, amount, or percentage) and the horizontal axis baseline and treatment days (see Figure 2-2).

Hopefully, this section has given you a general overview of procedures for recording behavior. It must be emphasized that the recording of behavior is begun prior to implementing other self-management procedures and continued during the application of those procedures. Only by following this course can you determine the precise impact of your self-management strategies. As we deal with different types of personal and academic problems in subsequent chapters of the book, we shall identify specific behaviors to record and procedures for recording them. For the time being, remember that objectively measuring your behavior may reveal something far different from what you subjectively believe to be the case. Objective measurement may, in fact, be the answer to Robert Burn's plea:

> O wad some Pow'r the giftie gie us
> To see oursels as others see us!
> It wad frae monie a blunder free us . . .

Changing Setting Events

Avoiding Situations

Most behaviors are triggered by certain situations or certain events within those situations. Psychologists refer to these precipitating stimuli as setting events. One of the quickest ways to modify behavior is to alter the situation in which the behavior usually occurs. Perhaps the easiest way to deal with a troublesome situation is to avoid it. One overweight student reported that a weight problem was partially related to passing a particular restaurant on the way to and from school each day. The delectable aroma from the restaurant invariably led to a short snack. The suggestion that a different route to school be taken does not seem profound—but it largely solved the problem.

If you are protesting that avoiding situations does not solve anything, you have a point. It would be a pathetic individual who dealt with all problems simply by avoiding difficult situations. That individual might eventually have a severely restricted sphere of activity and would epitomize the person who "should have stayed in bed." The avoidance strategy is recommended only for those problem behaviors that are practically certain to occur in given situations. We have to be honest with ourselves—in certain settings we are going to imbibe, eat, get upset, and so on. In fact, these behaviors may occur quite automatically without our even being aware of what is happening. If our objective is to avoid exhibiting those behaviors at all cost, we will initially have to avoid the situations in which they habitually occur. Note that we used the word *initially*. A number of strategies that will be described later can help you defuse vexing circumstances. But at the onset of your self-management endeavors, the only way to avoid some undesired behaviors may be to avoid certain situations. For example, if you are seized with an anxiety attack every time you attend an athletic contest, the most obvious way to prevent these attacks is to stay home.

Altering Troublesome Situations

Effective self-management primarily entails the modification of bothersome situations, not the complete avoidance of those situations. Many problem behaviors have a wide range of stimuli that evoke them and that serve to increase their immediate reinforcement value. Sitting down to watch TV, picking up a magazine, and turning on the stereo all may lead to snacking behavior and make snacking more reinforcing. Self-management in such situations should be directed toward accomplishing three major changes: (1) The circumstances should be arranged so that you are forced to think about the problem behavior before it occurs; the intent is to prevent behaviors from occurring reflexively and automatically. (2) The range of stimuli that produce the undesired behavior should be reduced. (3) The cues associated with the nonproductive behavior should be made as nonreinforcing as possible.

Becoming aware of behavior Cognizance of what one is about to do can be achieved by arranging circumstances so that a series of actions must be taken before the problem behavior is emitted. For example, overweight individuals might purchase only food that requires considerable preparation before it can be consumed. This would preclude the reflexive consumption of cookies, chips, and candy. If overweight people posted pictures of obese and slender persons on their refrigerator door, they would be even more inclined to think about what they are doing. A person with a smoking problem might store his cigarettes in a location difficult to get to—say, in a metal safe, with the combination known only to his best friend . . . who is presently out of the country. If part of your problem is sinning before you realize what you are doing, the stategy suggested in this paragraph is a beginning step toward self-management.

Limiting the precipitating stimuli   A second step is to limit the range of stimulus situations associated with the problem behavior. Suppose you have been inclined to light a cigarette while watching TV, reading, or engaging in conversation. You should not initially demand a complete abdication of smoking. In all probability, that demand would quickly fall by the wayside. A far more realistic expectation is to limit the situations in which you smoke. You might identify one locale at home and one at work where you can continue to pollute yourself. That locale should be a non-TV, nonreading, and nonconversation setting. Remember the student who aspired to lose five pounds in two weeks? She allowed herself to snack only while sitting at her dressing table in the bedroom. As a consequence, she had to carry the food from the kitchen (her usual snacking locale) and look at herself in the mirror as she ate.

Eliminating additional reinforcers   By following the strategy outlined above, you will discover that more time is required to get environmentally situated for the target behavior, thus causing the behavior to lose some of its reinforcement potential. You will also find that the absence of niceties such as TV, books, and conversation will further diminish the enjoyment you derive from the target behavior. The approach is quite simple: think of all the attending stimuli (food, drink, sex) that embellish the undesired behavior; then require that the target behavior occur in the absence of these stimuli. Subsequently, the undesirable behavior will decrease in frequency because of its reduced reinforcement value.

Providing Supportive Stimuli

If your problem can best be described as the absence of a particular behavior, you need initially to make the environmental setting as optimal as possible for the desired response to occur. If the difficulty is the inability to talk in group settings, do not place yourself before a throng of thousands and expect to be loquacious. Put yourself in a small group situation, among the warmest, most accepting people you know. If you have difficulty talking to person A but can talk to person B forever, attempt first to talk to A in B's presence. Some of the warmth and acceptance that you feel from B should make it easier to talk to A. After establishing a high frequency of desired behavior under the most favorable circumstances, you can then move up one notch in difficulty, that is, attempt to exhibit the behavior in a slightly less favorable situation (talk to A with B some distance away). By moving very gradually to increasingly difficult situations, you eventually may be able to speak freely even before that throng of thousands.

Optimizing setting events is not necessarily a highly complex operation. The student who was attempting to increase his frequency of seat belt applications simply made certain that the seat belt and shoulder harness were clean, that they were properly adjusted for use, and that they were appropriately hung after each use. Students attempting to get to work on time usually have to arrange setting events the previous evening. These may include changing the location of the alarm clock, altering the temperature of the room, laying out clothes for the next day, getting work materials together, packing lunch, and putting the breakfast cereals on the table. There may be some equally simple changes in setting events that would facilitate the behaviors you have been aspiring to emit.

Establishing Effective Consequences

Our previous discussion shows that we consider self-control to begin with the identification of a target behavior, monitoring the occurrence of that behavior, and then arranging optimal setting events for the desired behavior. If you stopped at this point, you would have a modestly effective strategy for altering many behaviors. However, the most powerful technique for producing behavior change is yet to be discussed.

Most of our behaviors are governed by their consequences. Those consequences that strengthen behaviors (make them more likely to occur) are called reinforcers* and consequences that weaken behavior, punishers.* You can immediately identify some events that are reinforcing or punishing to you. Perhaps praise, money, athletic activities, and fine wine are reinforcing to you. (They certainly are to us.) What is reinforcing or punishing varies from person to person and from situation to situation for the same person. There is probably no event that would be reinforcing for all persons across all situations. When we speak of reinforcement and punishment, you should think in terms of how environmental consequences affect you. If an event is highly reinforcing to you, it matters not that it has a neutral impact on most of the rest of us. We caution only that you do not choose reinforcers that would create other problems for yourself. A slightly overweight undergraduate used ice cream and chocolate mints as the immediate reinforcers for nonsmoking behavior. She reduced her smoking but she also gained 0.25 pounds by the end of the third week of treatment!

Identifying Reinforcers

The identification of reinforcers and punishers can be more elusive than you think. For example, we have found that primary and junior high school students have considerable difficulty in predicting how particular consequences will affect their behavior (Atkins and Williams, 1972; Runyon and Williams, 1972). This is espcially true of consequences that they have not encountered frequently. We suspect that adults are equally unaware of many potential reinforcers. A principal component of your self-management quest is to expand the list of consequences that can be used as reinforcers. This will require some systematic investigation. One possibility is to carry a note pad with you for a few days and jot down the especially pleasant or unpleasant events that occur. Ordinary actions may be significant reinforcers. Consuming a cold drink of water, having a cup of coffee, looking through a magazine, eating ice, reading a newspaper, going on evening walks, and sitting in a particular chair are some of the short-term consequences used by our students as reinforcers for appropriate behaviors. Among the long-term reinforcers used by our students, new phonograph records, stereotapes, and items of clothing have been the most frequent payoffs.

Establishing Reinforcement Contingencies

Having formulated a list of consequences that are reinforcing to you, you are now ready to use these consequences in modifying your behavior. The strategy for accomplishing this objective is straightforward—require yourself to exhibit the desired target behavior before you partake of the reinforcing consequences. If failing to work on assignments is your sin, a highly reinforcing privilege should be made conditional upon working on assignments. But there are behaviors other than the target that should also be reinforced. These behaviors are what Skinner called controlling responses, that is, the behaviors involved in implementing a self-management strategy. Recording behavior and rearranging setting events are nontarget behaviors that are fundamental to the success of self-management. Therefore, these behaviors should be rewarded, regardless of what is happening to the target behaviors. For example, you would earn certain privileges simply by recording behavior and making specified changes in setting events (e.g., buying low-calorie foods). This means that you would be earning some reinforcers from the very beginning of your self-management efforts, even before the target behavior began to change.

Although you have identified target and nontarget behaviors to reinforce and privileges to use as reinforcers, your excursion into self-management can still be less than ecstatic. Two things can bring your self-management to naught: (1) not applying the reinforcers immediately after the desired behaviors occur, and (2) setting the requirements for reinforcement too high.

Immediacy of reinforcement   Suppose you have identified attending a movie as the principal reinforcer for completing academic assignments. Attending a movie immediately after completing each assignment probably would not be a feasible arrangement. What would be possible is a credit system in which you reward yourself with points or tokens whenever you complete an assignment. For example, you might decide that you will earn five points for eaeh completed assignment, and that when you have earned twenty points, you can attend a movie of your choice. Five immediate points will not be as potent as an immediate movie. But because of association with movies, points will assume increasing reinforcement value as you proceed with self-management. Most importantly, points will allow you to transcend the delay between target behaviors and certain reinforcement privileges.

In addition to using points to bridge this delay, some students use visual representations of the desired long-term reinforcer. One student was earning points toward extra serving pieces for her china and silver. To enliven her quest, she prominently displayed pictures of these pieces in the locale where the undesired behavior (snacking) was likely to occur. Another student, who had gained fifty pounds in two-and-a-half years, placed a picture of herself at 118 pounds on the table where she ate. Since these pictures served as prompts for good behavior, they would technically be classified as setting events. Nevertheless, they served their purpose by giving immediate relevance to long-term reinforcers.

Do not interpret the preceding paragraphs as meaning that most rewards will be of a long-term nature. Where possible, actual rewards should be applied immediately after the desired behavior. Our student with the seat-belt problem applied four types of reinforcement to seat-belt application. He placed a bag of large jelly gumdrops on his car console and immediately ate one as soon as he applied the seat belt. He also placed a bag of dimes totaling $5.00 on the console and immediately took a dime each time he put on his seat belt. The dime was to be used for coffee during his midmorning break—no dime, no coffee. Money that remained at the end of the treatment phase was given to his wife. Another contingency involved turning on his cool-air vent after he had applied his seat belt (the research was done during the hottest period of the year). Finally, he received a kiss from his wife each time he attached the seat belt. Since his wife walked to the car with him each morning, he received an immediate kiss for applying the seat belt in the morning. Whenever he applied the seat belt away from home, reinforcement of this type was deferred until his return home in the afternoon. Following the study he reported that he found the candy and the immediate kiss from his wife the most reinforcing consequences. He attributed their strength to their immediacy. The money could not be used until midmorning and the air vent generated no cool air until the car was moving.

Requirements for reinforcement   With the very best of intentions, newcomers to self-management often impose exceedingly stringent reinforcement requirements upon themselves. The rationale is that a difficult goal will increase their motivation to change. Unfortunately, things usually work in the opposite direction. In your virgin attempts at self-management, it is imperative that you experience success early and frequently. The more success you have, the more likely you will be to maintain your program. The probability of success can be directly altered by manipulating the criteria of success. The initial criterion for reinforcement should be only slightly above your present level of operation. If you are presently accomplishing nothing on your assignments, doing perfect assignments every day of the week would not be an appropriate initial criterion for success. Rewarding yourself for just getting out your academic materials would be a better starting point. The next criterion level might be the completion of some small part (any part) of an assignment. By very gradually raising your criterion for reinforcement, you may eventually reach the point of completing assignments every night. In all probability, you will never achieve that degree of productivity if perfect performance is the initial criterion for success.

Mobilizing Social Reinforcement

Thus far we have identified fun activities and tangible payoffs as possible reinforcers for appropriate behavior. It is readily apparent that some of the more potent reinforcers are social in nature. A compliment or criticism from a significant person can change the course of the day's events. If the circumstances of your life could be arranged so that you received social support for appropriate be-havior, your self-management efforts would be markedly enhanced. In attempting to accomplish this objective, you should first be careful not to establish reinforcement contigencies that are aversive* to others, because that will invariably result in nonsupport for your efforts. If what is ecstatically reinforcing to you is excruciatingly abrasive to others (for example, playing acid rock throughout the night), you will not experience profound social approval from your neighbors.

A reinforcement contingency may involve something that you or-dinarily do with someone else. (Yes, even sexual interaction.) Sup-pose for the last several months you have taken the family to a movie on Saturday night, which has proven to be a reinforcing event for one and all. You now decide that the Saturday night movie will be contin-gent upon your engaging in a certain amount of exercise during the week. Your contention is that the added social pressure will provide additional impetus for your exercise routine. Good point, but what happens if one week you fail to meet your behavior criterion? You may catch so much hell from the family that you decide to forego the reinforcement contingencies and go to the movie anyway. That would probably be a lethal blow to your self-management program. If you want to use family privileges as reinforcers, insist that the family go without you when you do not meet the reinforcement conditions.

Some personal problems seem to result from a pervasive lack of social approval. Most of us probably would behave more confidently if we could increase the amount of approval received from others. Since procedures for accomplishing this will be described specifically in Chapter Eight, we need emphasize here only that one increases social reinforcement *received* by increasing social reinforcement *given*. Learning to respond to others in a more reinforcing fashion usually results in receiving more reinforcement from others.

In addition to providing social support for your appropriate behaviors, others can assist you in applying tangible consequences to those behaviors. A major problem in self-management is cheating on the contingencies. You may say, "I will give myself a dollar only if I do such and such," but when the critical moment comes, completely disregard that contingency. If that is likely to occur, it may make sense to put your payoff in the hands of someone else and let that person provide reinforcement at the appropriate time. Several of our students have employed this strategy in getting to work on time. They give a specified amount of money to a colleague and ask him or her to provide money for the coffee break only if they have arrived on time that day. If they have not, the money for the day goes to the other person. The major hazard of this arrangement is that you may come to dislike the other person if he/she has to withhold a great many payoffs.

Applying Aversive Consequences

Pain   Positive events are not the only type of consequences that can be used in modifying behavior. Some people attempt to alter their behavior by applying aversive consequences to their undesirable responses. For example, one of our persistent nail-biters applied a commercial preparation of cayenne pepper to his nails upon arising from bed each morning. When this came in contact with his lips, it produced a burning sensation, which led to immediate removal of the fingers. This strategy resulted in complete elimination of nail-biting. Despite the success of our nail-biter, we have many ambivalent feelings about using pain to modify behavior. Unless you are a masochist, you will not find the act of self-inflicting pain enjoyable. There will have to be powerful external reinforcers to maintain that behavior. If the target behavior changes drastically or if you receive international acclaim for your self-administered punishment, perhaps your program of aversive conditioning will be sustained. Otherwise, a strategy that entails flipping yourself with a rubber band, shocking yourself, or slapping yourself could cause you to give up on the concept of self-management before achieving good results.

Social reproval   A type of aversive consequence that, in our opinion, is more acceptable than physical discomfort is social reproval. To mobilize this form of social pressure, people sometimes make public announcements regarding their behavioral goals and concomitant reward and punishment contingencies. Peace treaties signed in public, for example, are probably honored more frequently than are private agreements. A nation or an individual would lose face by failing to honor a public announcement. Everyone at one time has lamented, "I wish I had not told _____ that I would . . . " Such public statements could be made when a person feels that he might relent on what he presently intends to do when the time to act finally arrives. By telling your closest friend that you are going to reward yourself with such and such when you have accomplished so and so, you increase the probability that you will stick to that contingency and that the contingency will have an effect on your behavior. This works especially well on behaviors that are obvious to others, such as smoking and swearing.

Stimulus satiation   Satiation* is another type of aversive consequence that can be used to alter undesired behavior. In using this approach, the individual repeatedly emits the target behavior until he simply tires of whatever made the response reinforcing. (Remember the towel hoarder?) Everyone is familiar with the idea of tiring of a good thing or of keeping so much company with a friend that the friendship wanes. Forcing yourself to continuously think compulsive thoughts, to smoke one cigarette after another, or to consume several bowls of banana pudding could cause you to become sick of those activities. Presumably, you would eventually choose to do something else. The major hazard of a satiation strategy is that if satiation does not occur, the behavior becomes more firmly instilled as a result of all those reinforcing occurrences.

Focusing on the Contingencies

The refrain, "I wasn't thinking," is frequently offered as an explanation for some rather stupid behaviors. The best-planned contingencies are sometimes ineffective because they are not considered at the moment of behavior. Many unwanted behaviors appear to be impulsive in nature, that is, they are emitted before the individual really thinks about what he is doing. The problem is to identify procedures that will cause you to think about your responses *before* you act. As described previously, this problem can be solved partially by arranging the setting events so that you have to emit several requisite behaviors before emitting the target behavior. If you purchase only food that requires considerable preparation before consumption, you are more likely to consider what you are doing than if you keep the candy and cookie jars overflowing.

Another procedure that has proven quite effective in reducing impulsivity is the verbalization of contingencies. Research (Blackwood, 1970) has shown that behavior modification approaches work best with people who verbalize the consequences of their actions before they act. In contrast, individuals who are unresponsive to behavior modification tend not to verbalize contingencies. Blackwood eventually achieved control over the unresponsive students' behavior by training them to verbalize fluently the consequences of their behavior. These students first read a paragraph describing their behaviors and the attending consequences, then they copied the paragraph, then paraphrased it, then wrote it in their own words from memory, and finally orally described the content of the paragraph. Other researchers (Meichenbaum and Goodman, 1971; Palkes et al., 1968) have found self-verbalizations to be highly effective in helping hyperactive children become less impulsive. In the Meichenbaum and Goodman study, the children were trained to verbalize step-by-step instructions (including corrections of errors) while performing a task and to praise themselves for completing the task. Over the course of training, the overt verbalizations were faded to a covert level without loss of behavior control.

It has often been facetiously claimed that "talking to oneself" is the last step before insanity. It now appears that self-verbalizations may contribute to rational, sane behavior. You might think that covert statements would be just as effective as overt. That is not the case initially, because you are much more likely to exhibit the right behavior if you state aloud what that behavior is. If the overt verbalizations lead to significant improvement in the target behavior, you can gradually make the shift to covert statements. The key to whether you are making the shift too rapidly is level of behavior control. If the improvement in the target behavior begins to erode, go back to a higher frequency of overt statements.

Applying Covert Control

The last step in our self-management model, applying covert control, requires some preliminary explanation. First, most problems will be solvable without the use of covert control. If an overt strategy (any combination of the five steps just described) will solve your problem, you will not need covert control. Second, covert strategies are considerably more complex than overt procedures. Consequently, they are generally more difficult to implement by yourself than are overt techniques (changing setting events, altering reinforcement contingencies). In spite of these reservations, there are two major reasons why covert control should be considered in our analysis of self-management: (1) a covert reaction may be an important link in a stimulus-response chain* leading to an overt behavior; and (2) overt behaviors may be changed by visualizing specified behaviors and consequences.

Certain behaviors seem to be highly correlated with identifiable thoughts or emotional reactions. You might say to yourself, "I think I'll fix a snack," "I'd like a cigarette," or "I've got to have a drink." In these cases, the self-verbalization constitutes a link in a behavior chain that will ultimately lead to the undesired response. There are two features of behavioral chains that are relevant to the present discussion: (1) as each link is completed, the probability increases that you will complete subsequent links; and (2) when one link is broken, the entire habit (behavioral chain) may be disrupted. This means that if you applied a covert strategy immediately after thinking, "I'd like dessert," you might prevent the consummatory behavior—eating the dessert—from occurring.

In some cases, you will have to use the initial steps of self-management before you can interject a covert response into the behavioral chain. Suppose a behavior occurs so automatically that you are unaware of what you are doing until you have done it. You first need to slow down the behavior so that you become conscious of your ongoing responses. As suggested earlier, this might be achieved by arranging setting events so that you have to emit several requisite responses before you get to the target behavior. This procedure allows you to think about the fact that you are getting ready to have a cigarette, drink, or snack. Having introduced thought into the process, you are in a position to use covert control as a deterrent to completing the behavioral chain.

There are two major ways to use covert events in modifying overt behavior. First, you can employ a covert strategy when the unwanted behavior is about to occur. The covert strategy thus counteracts the effect of immediate environmental stimuli. Second, you can use a covert strategy when you are removed from the situation where the behavior is likely to occur. The purpose of the covert exercises is to decrease the probability of the unwanted behavior when you again encounter the actual situation.

Coverant Pairs

We begin our discussion of covert models by describing what can be done at the moment of temptation. The major strategy that can be used under the pressure of immediate temptation is Homme's (1965) coverant model.[3] To illustrate, an individual might see a food commercial on TV and immediately start thinking about snacking. What immediate action can he take to counteract that sudden lust for food? According to Homme, the individual would first emit a thought that is incompatible with his desire to snack, for example, "Snacking makes me fat," "I'll feel depressed if I snack." In other words, this covert response would focus on the negative consequences of snacking. A second covert response should emphasize the positive benefits of *not* snacking; "I'll lose weight if I don't snack," "I'll feel good about myself if I don't snack." The coverant pair* is intended to be a new link in the stimulus-response chain, a link that presumably would prevent the target behavior from occurring.

The sequence of negative-positive coverants would be followed by an overt reinforcing activity, such as looking through a magazine, listening to a favorite record, or sitting in a favorite chair. Ideally, the reinforcing activity should be unrelated to the target behavior and take you out of the situation where the problem behavior is likely to occur. For example, having a cup of coffee might not be a good reinforcer for emitting snacking-related coverants. The activity would probably generate many prosnacking cues and put you in a situation—e.g., the kitchen—where snacking stimuli are often most rampant.

[3] The term *coverant* is a contraction for *covert operant. Operant** is a term in behavioral psychology referring to behavior that has an effect on the environment (e.g., causing good things to happen).

Covert Reinforcement

Homme's coverant model has been extended by Cautela (1970). Cautela views covert events as approximations of overt events; therefore, altering a covert response ought to have an effect on the parallel overt response. For example, you may wish to talk more in group situations. That can be accomplished by imagining that you are interacting in group settings and that this interaction is followed by reinforcing consequences (people are responsive and friendly). A major strength of Cautela's covert reinforcement exercises is that they can be practiced at any time, not just when the actual situation is imminent.

The imagined reinforcement need not always be naturally related to the target behavior. In other words, you could use any kind of reinforcing imagery* to strengthen any kind of covert response. A given covert behavior might be reinforced by visualizing yourself walking through the forest, swimming on a hot day, skiing down a mountainside, taking a shower, or engaging in sexual activity. Where possible, however, you should visualize a reinforcing event that might naturally follow the target behavior. If you have difficulty imagining events, it might help to assemble a group of pictures or slides representing the relevant events. You could have slides portraying the desired behavior and slides depicting the reinforcing consequences.

Cautela has also used covert negative reinforcement* in strengthening behaviors. Negative reinforcement involves the strengthening of behavior by means of the termination of an unpleasant event. In other words, a behavior that terminates an aversive stimulus will be strengthened, or negatively reinforced. Covert negative reinforcement requires the individual to imagine himself in a horrifying situation. For example, he is about to be bitten by a poisonous snake and is struggling to escape. He then abruptly focuses his imagery on the desired behavior (e.g., talking in group situations). Visualizing the desired behavior thus becomes the means of escaping from the unpleasant imagery. Although there is some fairly strong evidence (Ascher and Cautela, 1972) that this approach is effective, we think you will find this strategy less enjoyable than covert positive reinforcement. Therefore, if a specified covert response can be strengthened by either covert positive reinforcement* or covert negative reinforcement, we suggest the former.

Covert Sensitization

Covert sensitization* is the major strategy used by Cautela (1969) in dealing with undesirable eating, drinking, and smoking behaviors. The individual first visualizes the desired object or event—cigarette, food, or liquor. He makes his imagery of the pleasurable stimulus as realistic as possible, including all the visual, auditory, olfactory, and tactile sensations associated with that stimulus. He then imagines the typical sequence of events leading to the target behavior—pouring the drink, holding the drink in his hand, looking at the drink, smelling the drink, bringing the drink to his lips. In the past, these behaviors have been followed by immediate reinforcement, that is, the consumption of the pleasurable stimulus. His goal is to replace that immediate reinforcement with something immediately aversive. Cautela generally recommends nausea as the aversive event. Although any event that is highly aversive to you—feces, open wounds, spiders—could be used, nausea is the reaction that is most directly opposite to the consummatory behavior. Whatever type of noxious imagery you employ, be sure to apply that imagery immediately before the anticipated consummatory response. Your purpose is to prevent the latter (eating, drinking, smoking) from occurring.

Covert sensitization appears to be one of the most clearly delineated covert strategies. Several published reports (Ashem and Donner, 1968; Cautela, 1966; Cautela, 1967; Janda and Rimm, 1972) provide exact imagery to use with various kinds of undesirable approach behaviors. Cautela suggests that covert sensitization exercises be practiced in two daily sessions of ten to twenty trials each. With such frequent covert nausea, you might expect some persons to develop actual stomach problems. Although that has in fact happened (Ashem and Donner, 1968), Cautela minimizes the likelihood of its occurrence. Of course, if there is any reason to believe that you are vulnerable to such stomach problems as ulcers, we recommend that you not employ covert sensitization. But if you have a healthy stomach, continue the covert sensitization exercises until the very suggestion of the desired object makes you nauseated. Like covert reinforcement exercises, covert sensitization can be practiced any time—not just when you are faced with an immediate temptation.

In Summation

After this rapid excursion through the mechanics of self-management, you may be quite concerned about the difficulty of it all.

Sometimes our students ask, "Wouldn't it be easier just to change your behavior than to do all the things you recommend?" It would certainly be easier to tell yourself that you are going to change than to do many of the things we recommend. But how far does "telling" usually take you? A major difference between self-management and the conventional "telling" approach is that self-management does not require you to change a behavior directly. With self-management, you modify the factors that are controlling the behavior. Once these factors are altered, the behavior changes automatically.

Students are sometimes distressed by the sheer multiplicity of techniques included in our model. No self-management project ever involves all of these procedures, or even a majority of them. The mere identification of a problem (Step 1) is occasionally sufficient to produce behavior change. The individual may become so sensitized to his difficulty that he behaves differently. Appreciable changes in behavior may also occur when individuals begin recording a behavior and get their first objective look at that behavior. In certain cases, therefore, Step 1 or a combination of Steps 1 and 2 is all that you need to alter a behavior.

Most problems, however, require more than the application of Steps 1 and 2. Our third strategy—changing setting events—should be especially useful in coping with such problems as inadequate weight control and poor study habits. Step 4 recognizes that individuals behave for a reason, that is, they seek rewards and attempt to avoid punishment. Most problems cannot be solved without altering the consequences of problem and nonproblem behaviors. By emphasizing self-verbalization, Step 5 (focusing on contingencies) should help an individual internalize self-management behaviors. The final step (applying covert control) should be useful in changing those overt behaviors that are difficult to modify by using only overt manipulations. (See Table 2-1 for a flow chart of our self-management model.)

Regardless of which combination of steps you use, having strategies to help you become self-directive in one endeavor should move you toward greater control in other areas. This chapter is talking about more than solving just one problem through self-management. That is the beginning point, but our long range hope is that you will develop a self-management orientation to life. Instead of acquiescing to self-pity, the self-manager looks for the factors that contribute to a problem and then alters those factors. Not many of us

Table 2-1 Self-Management Model

Step 1 Selecting a goal	Step 2 Monitoring target behaviors	Step 3 Altering setting events	Step 4 Arranging consequences	Step 5 Focusing on contingencies	Step 6 Using covert control
		continue recording the target behavior			
A. Establish one goal at a time.	A. Start recording target behaviors before behavior change strategies are implemented.	A. Initially avoid situations that are certain to produce undesirable behaviors.	*maintain changes in setting events*		
B. Goal should be:	B. Record behavior immediately after it occurs.	B. Alter situations so as to:	A. Identify consequences that would be reinforcing or punishing.	*maintain consequences*	
1. important	C. Use paper and pencil, wrist counter, bead counter, stop watch, or wrist watch to record behavior.	1. become aware of what you're doing;	B. Arrange reinforcement contingencies such that:	A. Purpose is to make yourself aware of behavioral consequences at the moment of behavior.	*continue*
2. measurable		2. limit the stimuli that evoke the bad behaviors;	1. appropriate behavior is immediately reinforced;		A. Use covert strategies only after Steps 1-5 have been completed.
3. external				B. Awareness of contingencies may be attained by:	B. Overt behaviors may be altered through three
4. attainable					
5. positive					

D. Do a frequency count, time duration, or product assessment of the behavior.

3. eliminate additional reinforcers for bad behaviors;
4. make it easy to emit desired behaviors.

2. criteria for reinforcement are readily attainable;
3. significant other people will support attainment of behavioral goals.

C. Three types of aversive consequences may be used if reinforcement contingencies fail to produce desired changes in behavior:
1. mechanically induced pain
2. social reproval
3. stimulus satiation

1. rearranging setting events;
2. self-verbalizing contingencies.

major covert strategies:
1. coverant pairs
2. covert reinforcement
3. covert sensitization

manage our lives this way. But you are not averse to taking the less traveled road this time, are you?

References

Ascher, L. M., and Cautela, J. R. 1972. Covert negative reinforcement: an experimental test. *Journal of Behavior Therapy and Experimental Psychiatry 3*, 1-5

Ashem, B., and Donner, L. 1968. Covert sensitization with alcoholics: a controlled replication. *Behaviour Research and Therapy 6*, 7-12.

Atkins, J., and Williams, R. L. 1972. The utility of self-report in determining reinforcement priorities of primary school children. *Journal of Educational Research 65*, 324-328.

Blackwood, R. O. 1970. The operant conditioning of verbally mediated self-control in the classroom. *Journal of School Psychology 8*, 251-258.

Broden, M., Hall, R. V., and Mitts, B. 1971. The effect of self-recording on the classroom behavior of two eighth-grade students. *Journal of Applied Behavior Analysis 4*, 191-199.

Cautela, J. R. 1966. Treatment of compulsive behavior by covert sensitization. *Psychological Record 16*, 33-41.

————. 1967. Covert sensitization. *Psychological Reports 20*, 459-468.

————. 1969. Behavior therapy and self-control: techniques and implications. In *Behavior Therapy: Appraisal and Status*, ed. C. M. Franks, pp.323-340. New York: McGraw-Hill.

————. 1970. Covert reinforcement. *Behavior Therapy 1*, 33-50.

Gilmore, G. D. 1973. Report of a self-management project. Unpublished manuscript, University of Tennessee.

Homme, L. E. 1965. Control of coverants, the operants of the mind. Perspectives in psychology, XXIV. *Psychological Record 15*, 501-511.

Janda, L. H., and Rimm, D. C. 1972. Covert sensitization in the treatment of obesity. *Journal of Abnormal Psychology 80*, 37-42.

Johnson, S. M., and White, G. 1971. Self-observation as an agent of behavioral change. *Behavior Therapy 2*, 488-497.

Kanfer, F. H. 1970. Self-monitoring: methodological limitations and clinical applications. *Journal of Consulting and Clinical Psychology 35*, 148-152.

Kornrumph, C. 1973. Self-management of snacking behavior. Unpublished manuscript, University of Tennessee.

Mahoney, M. J., Moore, B. S., Wade, T. C., and Moura, N. G. M. 1973. Effects of continuous and intermittent self-monitoring on academic behavior. *Journal of Consulting and Clinical Psychology 41,* 65-69.

Meichenbaum, D. H., and Goodman, J. 1971. Training impulsive children to talk to themselves: a means of developing self-control. *Journal of Abnormal Psychology 77,* 115-126.

Palkes, H., Stewart, M., and Kahana, B. 1968. Portues maze performance of hyperactive boys after training in self-directed verbal commands. *Child Development 39,* 817-826.

Runyon, H. L., and Williams, R. L. 1972. Differentiating reinforcement priorities of junior high school students. *Journal of Experimental Education 40,* 76-80.

Watson, D. L., Tharp, R. G., and Krisberg, J. 1972. Case study in self-modification: suppression of inflammatory scratching while awake and asleep. *Journal of Behavior Therapy and Experimental Psychiatry 3,* 213-215.

Applications to Self

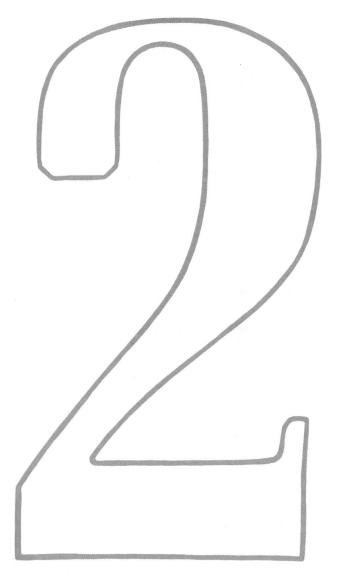

three

An Apple A Day:
Controlling Health Problems

One strategy known to reduce spontaneous smoking is changing the place where you normally carry your cigarettes.

As children, we often heard the expression, "An apple a day keeps the doctor away." While this adage probably overstates the medicinal value of apples, it does make an exceedingly important point: one can do something to promote good health. Most individuals can control most behaviors that fundamentally affect their health. This statement does not preclude the possibility of serious illness for the individual who has faithfully observed the standards of good health, but it does minimize that possibility.

When it comes to health, life in America is something of a paradox. In spite of the near-famine conditions that exist in many parts of the world, millions of Americans suffer from too much, rather than too little, to eat. Countless others disregard medical research and shorten their lives with cigarettes. Millions more suffer excruciating misery from the alcoholic beverages that once brought them pleasure. Some Americans have been able to effect change in these problem areas. For example, some people drastically modify their eating, smoking, or drinking behavior in order to salvage interpersonal relationships. But as soon as those relationships have been reaffirmed, such individuals often revert to their old ways of doing things. Can we solve these riddles? Not entirely. But we can identify the self-management procedures that others have found effective in modifying eating, smoking, and drinking behaviors. Although we can make no promises, we have great confidence in the success of these techniques.

Excessive Weight

While you may not weigh three hundred pounds, you still may have an interest in losing weight. Of course, only you can decide whether you wish to lose fifty pounds, ten pounds, or zero pounds. Looking in a mirror or gathering a fold of skin on your side may generate enough motivation to keep you with us for the next several pages.

Although genetics, hormonal imbalances, emotions, and injury to the hypothalamus have been studied as possible causes of obesity, no ultimate causes have been identified. However, two common characteristics have been observed in obese persons: the tendency to overeat and the tendency to underexercise (Stuart, 1967). Behavioral attempts to reduce weight, therefore, have concentrated on changing eating behavior and/or activity level. But before we deal with either eating or physical activity, we must briefly consider an essential factor in any weight program: calories.

A calorie is a basic unit of measurement that tells you how much energy you get from food. For every 3500 calories you get that you do not use up, you gain approximately one pound. That pound is stored in the form of fat. You can lose that pound of fat by eating less (getting fewer calories), by increased activity, or both. For example, if your present weight is maintained by eating 2800 calories each day, you would have to go to 2300 calories a day in order to lose one pound per week, unless you also increased your physical activities. A precise, systematic attempt to lose weight makes some calorie counting almost inevitable. We suggest, therefore, that you obtain a chart which shows the caloric value of foods and a chart giving the approximate number of calories required to perform various physical activities.[1]

Controlling Eating Behavior

Behavioral attempts to change eating behavior have usually involved some effort to control setting events. These attempts have evolved from the early work of Ferster, Nurnberger, and Levitt (1962), and Goldiamond (1965), who demonstrated that overeating is maintained by a wide range of stimuli. The basic approach is to decrease eating behavior by reducing the range of stimuli that precipitate eating. Additional control has been achieved by altering the consequences for appropriate and inappropriate eating behavior and identifying procedures that ensure concentration on those behaviors. Most studies stop here. However, a few studies have attempted to control eating behavior through covert strategies. Since these various procedures fit so nicely into our basic self-control model, we shall apply the model, step by step, to the problem of weight control. Perhaps you will then be able to use the model more easily with other problems.

Selecting a goal   If you have a serious weight problem (e.g., 25 percent body fat) we recommend that you consult a physician before undertaking any weight reduction program. Your physician can help you determine how much weight you should lose. Most physicians emphasize percent body fat, measured by skin calipers, rather than height and weight charts. Your physician can also determine whether there is any organic basis for your excessive weight. In a word,

[1]Excellent calorie and exercise charts are provided in R. B. Stuart and B. Davis, *Slim chance in a fat world: Behavioral control of obesity* (Champaign, Ill.: Research Press Company, 1972).

he/she can help you decide on a weight-reduction plan that will not jeopardize your health. Remember that a weight-watcher needs the same kind of food as anyone else. This means that you regularly need food from the four basic food groups—dairy, meat, vegetable and fruit, and bread and cereal. You also need at least twelve hundred calories daily. Because of these basic needs, your physician would probably not suggest losing more than one to two pounds per week.

Seldom does one have to starve to produce substantial weight reduction. Starvation can undermine your health permanently. A person who reduces his weight too rapidly through dieting probably loses more muscle mass than body fat. The purpose of a weight-reduction program is obviously to lose body fat, not muscle mass. Besides, why go on a crash diet, lose a few pounds, and then return to your old eating habits? A more sensible approach—one that your physician will probably suggest—is to establish eating habits that you can continue even after you have lost weight. Establishing these eating habits is where self-management comes in.

So far we have suggested that selecting a weight-control goal should include consultation with a physician (if your problem is extreme), and we have implied that a plan of losing one to two pounds per week might be desirable. We now recommend that you state your goal in behavioral terms. You may already recognize that losing one or two pounds per week is not a behavior, it is a product. We raise the point only to emphasize that your behavior is what must be changed if you are to lose weight. You certainly should keep track of the product, but not to the point that you lose track of your behavior, the important variable. Weight gain or loss results from what you do or fail to do. Your initial goal, therefore, might be to reduce between-meal snacking. By devising ways to control snacking, the weight loss will take care of itself. Another goal might be to reduce consumption at each meal. You might decide to give up your usual habit of having an extra helping of dessert. One researcher (Stuart, 1967) recommended as a very first step that subjects interrupt their meals by putting down their utensils and sitting for two or three minutes without eating. His rationale was that sitting briefly without eating teaches some self-control and demonstrates that eating behavior can in fact be altered.

Recording quantity and circumstances of behavior   Accurate recording of the quantity and circumstances of eating behavior is extremely important, for only through accurate recording can you hope to establish the relationship between your behavior and your weight.

	Conditions					
	Food Eaten	Time	Place	Mode of Preparation	Calories	Weight
Breakfast						
Lunch						
Dinner						
Snacks						

Total Daily Calories _____

Figure 3-1   Daily Food Chart.

You should not take this point lightly. For example, if you fail to record everything you eat, you might mistakenly convince yourself that your weight problem is not due to your behavior. We will not speculate as to why some overweight individuals underrecord their eating behavior, but evidence does point in that direction. Schachter (1971) found three studies in which obese individuals reported eating considerably less food than normal. Observations show, however, that while obese individuals may eat fewer meals than others, they eat far more food per meal. Furthermore, when obese persons are fed what they claim to have been eating, they steadily lose weight. The point is: do not underrecord.

Now that we have stressed the importance of accurate recording, precisely what is it you are to record? Four records may be helpful in controlling eating behavior. These are (1) a record of everything you eat, (2) a record of the caloric value of what you eat, (3) a record of conditions of your eating (time, place, mood, mode of food preparation), and (4) a record of your weight. The records of what you eat and its caloric value will help you see the direct relationship between your eating habits and your weight.[2] Recording the conditions of your eating behavior should provide important clues as to how to change that behavior (more about this under Changing Setting Events). A chart similar to Figure 3-1 can be used for recording all the informa-

[2]Amount of food consumed is sometimes established by counting mouthfuls. A simple supermarket expense counter would be suitable for this purpose (Stuart and Davis, 1972).

tion in one place. You can then take your four basic records and construct graphs that will immediately tell you how changes in your behavior are affecting your weight. For example, you might graph the amount you eat, your caloric intake, and your weight. By placing your graph in a conspicuous spot (on the kitchen cabinet or refrigerator door, for example), you will find that it serves not only to reinforce appropriate behavior but also to remind you of when, what, and how much to eat.

Let us examine briefly how your four basic records can be helpful with different goals. If you are attempting to reduce snacking behavior, you may question the relevancy of recording everything you eat, caloric value, and so forth. Such records, however, should clarify how and to what extent snacking behavior is contributing to your weight. If you cut out snacks and simultaneously increase consumption at meals, you probably will not lose weight. Only by recording *everything* you eat can you determine whether other eating is remaining constant as you reduce snacking. Also, recording calories in your snacks will give you valuable information on how long it will take you to lose a specific number of pounds once snacking is reduced. For example, if your present weight is maintained on 3300 calories per day and 1000 of those calories come from snacking, you could lose two pounds per week by eliminating snacks, assuming that your activity level and other eating behaviors remain unchanged. You will also find the four basic records exceedingly useful in managing your regular meals. For instance, a record of the caloric content of foods plus information on such conditions as mode of preparation might indicate that another selection of food from the same basic food group or just a different mode of preparation for the same food would result in fewer calories.

How long should these basic records be maintained? Your baseline records should be maintained until you see a regular eating pattern emerge on your graph. You certainly do not want to attempt any behavior changes until you know exactly what you are trying to change; to do otherwise would be to invite misinterpretation of subsequent behavior changes. A one-week baseline would probably give you an accurate picture of your eating. Once you have established a baseline, we recommend that you maintain your records until you have reached your weight goal and the control of energy intake and output has become automatic.

Changing setting events   After you have established a record-keeping system, you should be in a better position to determine ways in which your behavior can be changed by altering the environment. Should you learn from your records that you snack rather freely throughout the day, you may decide to remove snack items from your house or place of work. The point is: why deliberately subject yourself to constant temptations? Get your weight down and perhaps then you can turn down that "second" potato chip. Obese persons seem to be stimulus bound with respect to eating. When food and food-related cues are available, they are far more likely to eat excessively than are individuals of normal weight. In contrast, obese persons are disinclined to expend effort in preparing food. Not keeping ready-to-eat snack items around the house should dramatically alter their snacking behavior.

Should your records reveal that your snacking is associated with TV, reading, study, or other activities, you will want to limit the range of places where you snack. Goldiamond (1965) describes the slimming of one young man following this procedure.

> He was instructed to eat to his heart's content and not to repress the desire. He was, however, to treat food with the dignity it deserved. Rather than eating while he watched television or while he studied, he was to devote himself to eating when he ate. If he wished to eat a sandwich, he was to put it on a plate and sit down and devote himself exclusively to it. Thus, reinforcing consequences such as watching television or reading would be withdrawn when he engaged in the behaviors of preparing the food, eating, and cleaning up. Responding to the refrigerator in between meals resulted in withdrawal of such consequences, as did going to the refrigerator while watching television. Television, studying, and other stimuli would lose their control of initiating the chain of behaviors and conditions that terminated in eating. Within one week the young man cut out all eating between meals. "You've taken all the fun out of it," he said to me.[3]

Your records will probably reveal that you are far more likely to snack at certain times than others. One major contributor to snacking appears to be boredom. You may find that you are most inclined to

[3]Reprinted with permission of author and publisher: Goldiamond, I. Self-control procedures in personal behavior problems. *Psychological Reports,* 1965, 17, 855.

snack when you are alone and have nothing to do. Having identified the hazardous periods of the day, you are then in a position to schedule high-priority activities during those times. Contrary to what you might expect, eating is not the most preferred activity of obese persons. According to an outstanding authority on the behavioral control of eating, (Stuart, 1967), obese individuals rank socializing, work, affectionate and/or sexual encounters, and personal nonfood pleasures ahead of eating. Snacking behavior might therefore be replaced by any of these activities. By this time you should have an accurate idea of your own list of preferred activities. If you are inclined to snack at certain times during the day, deliberately plan nonfood-related high-priority activities for those periods. What you are attempting to do is to condition noneating responses to stimulus events that generally have produced eating.

In addition to helping the snacker, changing setting events can help reduce consumption at each meal. Some individuals have found that preparing smaller portions of food at each meal reduced their temptation to eat large amounts. If you use this strategy, make the portions of food appear as large as possible by spreading out the food on the plate. Some people find that eating from smaller plates is helpful in reducing food intake. (A child's tea set might be overdoing it.) Perhaps you have learned that you need to lengthen the time it takes you to consume a meal. Obese persons generally eat rapidly and consume large amounts of food in short periods. Stuart's suggestion about putting down the eating utensils for brief periods would be one way to slow the pace of eating. Maybe you could learn to savor your food by tasting it carefully before swallowing. What about conversing between bites? You might also try different modes of preparing food as a way of reducing caloric intake. A baked potato may be quite as desirable as french fries, and it contains considerably fewer calories. Even if the amount and kind of food that you eat per day remains unchanged, there is some evidence that spreading that food out over several small meals is more facilitative of weight loss than eating two or three large meals (Derby et al., 1968).

Clearly, arranging setting events for appropriate eating behavior cannot be divorced from your shopping behavior. The amount and kinds of food you buy will affect your eating behavior at home. Having determined the types and amounts of food that would contribute to weight reduction, you should head your shopping list with these foods. If you are shopping for a family, you may have to purchase some foods that are not conducive to your weight-reduction goals. Even then, shop from a list and take only enough money to cover that list. This will prevent you from impulsively purchasing unnecessary items. Parking your automobile some distance from the store may serve as an additional deterrent to buying huge amounts of food. It may also be helpful to do your shopping just after consuming a full meal.[4] Generally speaking, the more removed you are from your next eating opportunity, the more control you can exercise over your behavior. It is easier to behave rationally in the grocery store than at the dinner table. Similarly, you can exercise greater control when making out a shopping list at home than when facing an array of attractive possibilities in the store.

Establishing effective consequences   You may be inclined to think that altering setting events is all that is necessary to reach your weight-reduction goals. It is true that this strategy can produce substantial changes in your eating behavior. However, effective consequences can facilitate changes in setting events. If you were attempting to alter setting events, you probably would be more likely to make the appropriate changes if an immediate payoff were granted for that behavior. Marked changes in weight are not going to occur immediately. Unless some immediate consequence is available for your initial efforts, you may fail to sustain appropriate setting events. Even the establishment of a record-keeping system and daily recording should be the subject of effective consequences. Recall our recommendations in Chapter Two about reinforcing controlling behavior as well as controlled behavior.

In addition, effective consequences can maintain desired behavior changes produced through changes in setting events. Your behaviors, once changed, have to be reinforced if they are to remain changed. How many weight-watchers have lost weight only to regain every pound that was lost, plus a few more? Stunkard and McLaren-Hume's review (1959) of weight-control research showed that most obese individuals do not keep off the weight they lose. We suspect that this results from not receiving continued reinforcement after

[4]There is some indication, however, that obese persons may buy *less* food when they shop on an empty stomach than on a full stomach. Remember the eating behavior of obese persons seems to be tied more to environmental cues than to actual hunger. After eating a full meal, the obese person may feel more resigned to his obesity (and thus purchase more food) than when he has not eaten.

desired changes have occurred. When you are attempting to lose weight, others may compliment you on your progress, you may receive reinforcement from observing the downward slope of your behavior graph or weight chart, or you may receive reinforcement from weighing yourself each day. If these reinforcers were no longer available to you once you changed your eating habits and have lost some weight, extinction of the behaviors that led to the weight change could occur. It is possible that other natural reinforcers (e.g., ability to engage in more sports activities, sex, social outings) may take over and maintain your appropriate behavior. You may get slim and stay slim. But we suggest that you continue some potent reinforcers until you know that natural reinforcers are working for you.

The kinds of reinforcers that can be applied to controlling and controlled behaviors are numerous. Some of our students have set up self-administered token economies in which they earned or lost tokens (usually in the form of points) for specified behaviors.[5] When enough tokens were earned, they were cashed in for such back-up reinforcers* as a new dress, a new drill press, or a weekend trip. Some students have sustained their initial weight-reducing efforts by enlisting reinforcement from others. One woman persuaded her husband to wash the morning and evening dishes whenever she limited herself to only one serving of each food. (Of course, the quantity of the serving should be predefined.) Others have found that calling a friend or engaging in a fun activity following a specified behavior was sufficient to strengthen that behavior. Applying such consequences will provide added incentive to do the things that lead to weight reduction.

Focusing on contingencies   Some individuals establish judicious consequences for eating behaviors but still fail to alter those behaviors. This failure may be a function of not thinking about those consequences whenever the eating behaviors are emitted. We mentioned in Chapter Two that eating behavior can occur reflexively, without our really being conscious of what we are doing. Awareness of behavior and the consequences of that behavior can sometimes be

---

[5]Some weight-watchers place pieces of pork fat in their refrigerator and they remove one piece for each pound lost (Penick et al., 1971). That is a rather symbolic consequence!

*Defined in Glossary.

achieved through rearrangement of setting events. When you re-move snack foods from the house, purchase foods that require con-siderable preparation, and place high caloric foods on the rear of cabinet shelves, you decrease the probability of unthinking eating behavior.

We also mentioned in Chapter Two that another way to focus on contingencies is to verbalize the consequences of a specified be-havior whenever you are about to emit that behavior. However, the reflexive eater is not likely to remember to verbalize. In that case, reminders can be placed on those stimuli that typically lead to eating behavior, such as the kitchen cabinet and refrigerator. The reminders would simply state the desired (or undesired) response and its con-sequences. With this arrangement, one is forced to deal with the consequences of behavior before emitting it.

Achieving covert control   Homme's coverant pairs (Horan and Johnson, 1971) and Cautela's covert sensitization and covert positive reinforcement (Manno and Marston, 1972) are the principal covert procedures that have been used in altering eating behavior. As you will recall from Chapter Two, Homme's coverant model requires the subject to verbalize the negative consequences of the undesired be-havior and then the positive consequences of the desired response. The consequences visualized under the model are typically those of an immediate nature. However, some of the early researchers of eating behavior (Ferster, Nurnberger, and Levitt, 1962) contend that focusing on the ultimate consequences of obesity is essential to weight control. By pairing thoughts of those consequences with pro-eating thoughts, you may develop an aversion to certain types of eating behavior. In developing their list of consequences, Ferster et al. had weight-watchers draw primarily from personal experiences. These experiences, often related to social rejection and humiliation, were more aversive than the use of statistical information on dia-betes, heart disease, and high blood pressure. One of our students told us recently that he had gotten so overweight that he could hardly engage in sexual activity. Surely, that would qualify as an ultimate aversive consequence!*

Manno and Marston's (1972) covert sensitization strategy was de-signed to produce nausea in response to certain foods. This nausea was programmed to occur at progressively earlier stages in the eating process. Initially, each subject was asked to visualize the following sequence of events: seeing a specific food item, picking it up, being tempted to eat it, bringing it to the lips, and then feeling nauseated. The next sequence of images was seeing the food, picking it up, (but not bringing it to the lips), wanting to eat it, feeling nauseated, putting the food down, and feeling better. The third sequence was seeing the food, reaching for it, feeling sick, pulling hand away from food and feeling better (thus preventing vomiting). The last sequence of images was seeing the food, wanting to eat it, feeling ill, saying "I don't want it," and feeling much better.

Manno and Martson's covert positive reinforcement followed essentially the same sequence of images as the covert sensitization procedure but without the feelings of nausea. At the critical moment, the subjects simply imagined putting the food down and turning away. As a consequence they felt very good about themselves and were applauded by their friends. In other words, they imagined positive social consequences for resisting temptation. Manno and Marston found the covert sensitization and covert reinforcement strategies to be about equally effective in producing weight loss. Both were significantly superior to a control condition.

Physical Activity

Since the next chapter is devoted to sports activity, we will comment only briefly on the role of exercise in weight control. Diet control plus regular exercise definitely leads to faster weight reduction than dieting alone. Lest you think exercising makes dieting more difficult, research (Mayer, 1968) has shown that individuals who lead a sedentary life eat more than those who regularly participate in moderate activity. Overweight persons have much to gain from physical activity because they burn more calories per minute than individuals of normal weight engaged in the same activity. Unfortunately, the obese person is typically not as physically fit as the lean person and is therefore not as likely to engage in exercise. The first route to increased activity is to be found within one's work and domestic chores. You could readily increase the amount of standing and walking that you do in your work. For example, you may choose between the elevator and the stairs several times a day. Over the course of a year, those choices could make a difference of several pounds.

Admittedly, most of us need more physical exercise than we can incorporate into our work. (Jogging around the classroom might be distracting to other students.) While involvement in sports is probably the best way to get that exercise, we are not opposed to sit-ups, calisthenics, and jogging. However, because these activities are not inherently reinforcing to most of of us, external reinforcement is needed to maintain them. Perhaps the single most important requirement for these activities is to pursue them with someone else. That not only makes the activity more reinforcing; it also allows each person to remind the other to engage in the activity. Beyond this social support, we recommend a liberal use of tokens and high-priority activities in your exercise program.

In Summation

We do not expect our analysis of excessive weight to produce a generation of slender Americans. In fact, we suspect that our model would be most effective for individuals who are only moderately overweight (ten to twenty pounds). People who are significantly overweight (fifty to one hundred pounds) would obviously have to stay with a program for an extended time period to get their weight to an acceptable level. When programs are extended over many months, the probability of things going awry becomes much greater. We always recommend that an obese person see a physician before initiating an ambitious weight-reduction program. A medical solution may constitute the only workable solution to some weight problems.

A Self-Management Exercise

Before moving on to other issues, let us see how our self-management model could be applied to one specific problem.

1. *Selecting a goal*: To reduce the frequency of snacking.
2. *Recording quantity and circumstances of behavior:* Maintain a daily record of everything eaten, conditions, calories, and weight.
3. *Changing setting events:* Eat all snacks at the kitchen table. Remove all candies, cookies, and chips from the house. Keep only foods that require preparation.
4. *Establishing effective consequences:* Establish a point system. Earn points for appropriate record-keeping, eating snacks at the kitchen table, and not surpassing a specified level of snacking behavior. Lose points for eating in front of the TV and eating while studying. Cash in a specified number of points for a special weekend privilege. (No, not wining and dining.)

5. *Focusing on contingencies:* Attach notes describing the desired behavior and its consequences to places where food is kept.
6. *Achieving covert control:* Use Homme's coverant pairs each time you get the urge to snack. Don't forget to include some "ultimate aversive consequences."

Smoking

Cigarette smoking is perhaps the most widespread health problem in this society. According to recent figures released by the National Center for Health Statistics, about 43 percent of adult men and 31 percent of adult women in the United States smoke regularly. That means that approximately forty-five million adults in this country face a potential health problem from smoking. About 26 percent of the male smokers and 18 percent of the female smokers consume more than a pack a day. Their per capita consumption is about four thousand per year. While the figures for smokers are discouraging, the data for ex-smokers are quite encouraging. About 26 percent of the men and 11 percent of the women in this country are former smokers. This means that approximately twenty-two million have been successful in giving up cigarettes. Cigarettes therefore do not represent an unbeatable foe.

Some people believe that the frequently discussed correlation between cigarette smoking and various health problems is unsubstantiated. However, evidence from hundreds of medical studies clearly associates cigarette smoking with some of our most dreaded diseases. Smoking greatly increases the probability of coronary heart disease, emphysema, chronic bronchitis, and cancer of the lungs, larynx, oral cavity, esophagus, and urinary bladder; and it is associated with an increase in the prevalence of peptic ulcers (*The Health Consequences of Smoking*, 1973). Overall, the risk of death in any given year is about 70 percent greater for a male smoker than for a nonsmoker. Table 3-1 further clarifies the deleterious consequences of smoking. Notice that a 25-year-old male who has never smoked can expect to live an additional 48.6 years, while the smoker who uses two or more packs a day can expect to live an additional 40.3 years. In other words, the nonsmoker can expect to live 8.3 years longer than the heavy smoker.

To what extent can the risks produced by cigarette smoking be reversed by the termination of smoking? Individuals who have not

Table 3-1 Life Expectancy (Additional Years) at Various Ages, Estimated for United States Males

Age	Never smoked regularly	Cigarettes smoked by daily amount			
		1-9	10-19	20-39	40+
25	48.6	44.0	43.1	42.4	40.3
30	43.9	39.3	38.4	37.8	35.8
35	39.2	34.7	33.8	33.2	31.3
40	34.5	30.2	29.3	28.7	26.9
45	30.0	25.9	25.0	24.4	23.0
50	25.6	21.8	21.0	20.5	19.3
55	21.4	17.9	17.4	17.0	16.0
60	17.6	14.5	14.1	13.7	13.2
65	14.1	11.3	11.2	11.0	10.7

Hammond study. Reprinted by permission of Public Health Service, Department of Health, Education, and Welfare.

already developed a serious smoking disorder can expect an almost total reversal, substantially lowering the risk of death from heart disease, emphysema, chronic bronchitis, and cancer. Their life expectancy will eventually approach that of people who have never smoked. Other immediate benefits usually include a reduction in coughing, increased sensitivity to the taste of food, and loss of smoker's breath.

Since the noted 1964 Report of the Advisory Committee to the Surgeon General of the Public Health Service, which linked smoking to numerous diseases, a host of behavioral strategies have been used to alter smoking behavior. These range from intense electric shock to muscle relaxation. Unfortunately, there is no clear-cut evidence as to which procedure is best. Most studies show mixed results: the methods are effective with some individuals but not with others. A number of previously used strategies will be included in our model and offered now for your consideration. You must be the judge as to which combination of procedures will work best for you.

Selecting a Goal

Selecting a goal relative to smoking poses a problem because the ultimate goals—not contracting cancer or coronary heart disease—cannot readily be assessed on a daily or weekly basis. A far more manageable goal is to reduce the frequency of smoking behavior. For example, a person may say, "I want to smoke ten cigarettes today, eight cigarettes tomorrow, and six cigarettes day after tomorrow."

The major consideration in defining a goal is to establish one that is readily attainable. For that reason, your initial goal should *not* be to quit smoking, cold turkey. Although thousands of people do this every year, thousands more fail miserably in their pursuit of this goal. If your goal is the total cessation of smoking, what will happen if you unconsciously light a cigarette one day (perhaps in a moment of stress)? You may see your efforts as totally negated and thereafter resume smoking at full strength. In other words, all incentive to deal with your smoking behavior is lost. So you end up making the all too familiar statement, "I've got to die some way, so why not do it enjoying myself." (We really doubt that anyone enjoys dying from lung cancer.) As we suggested in Chapter Two, it makes more sense to set your initial goal only slightly above (or in this case, below) your present level of behavior. Gradually increasing the stringency of the goal is the most painless way to quit smoking and the surest.

Monitoring Target Behavior

Before implementing treatment procedures, you should log the number of cigarettes you smoke, the amount of each cigarette smoked (e.g., one half, one quarter), and the conditions of smoking (time and place). This will give you a basic idea of the extent of your problem and where to begin to deal with that problem. Your records will probably reveal some surprising relationships between your smoking behavior and setting events. For example, one student discovered that his highest frequency of smoking occurred when driving his automobile. You may also find that the initial record-keeping itself will alter your behavior. McFall (1970) found that students smoked less once they began monitoring their smoking. Prior to self-monitoring, the students' frequency of smoking had been unobtrusively recorded by classmates. This reactive phenomenon may well exist when you start recording any behavior, because you become more aware of the unwanted behaviors you are emitting.

Following implementation of treatment, you should record not only the target behavior but also behaviors related to implementation of treatment (controlling responses). In what ways have you changed the setting events and consequences, focused on contingencies, achieved covert control? How often have you used these strategies? Logging the treatment procedures and recording the number and amount of cigarettes smoked should reveal the relationship between changes in your behavior and the product (number of cigarettes consumed).

Changing Setting Events

You will undoubtedly want to make some changes in setting events as you attempt to control your smoking behavior. Since much smoking is spontaneous, you may want to arrange circumstances that prevent reflexive lighting up. One strategy known to reduce spontaneous smoking is changing the place where you normally carry your cigarettes. If you normally carry your cigarettes in a left shirt pocket, switch to the right pocket one day and a coat pocket the next. Make it difficult to find a cigarette. You could also try keeping your cigarettes in a case if that is unfamiliar to you. Or you might deliberately not carry matches or a lighter, so that you have to ask for others' assistance to light a cigarette. The objective is to alter setting events so that it is difficult to smoke without realizing what you are doing. Reducing your spontaneous smoking can assist you in applying other strategies. For example, if you wanted to pair an aversive thought with lighting a cigarette, your strategy would fail unless you could control spontaneous smoking.

Another appropriate change in setting events is reducing the range of stimuli associated with smoking. Think of all the stimuli with which smoking is associated: smoking and eating, smoking and drinking, smoking and parties, smoking and conversation, smoking and studying, smoking and worrying, smoking and sex. It is no wonder that some people smoke heavily! Breaking these associations can reduce the tendency to smoke. We suggested earlier that you identify one place at work and one place at home to smoke. This suggestion is based on the concepts of self-control set forth by Ferster, Nurnberger, and Levitt (1962) and Goldiamond (1965). Once you reduce smoking to one or two locations, you have a less intense (and probably less reinforcing) habit to break. However, reaching this point may require some programming of setting events. Sachs et al. (1970) had people rank the situations in which they would be most inclined to smoke. The subjects first gained control over the easy situations, and then over the more difficult ones. The subjects could smoke if they wished, but they were to remove themselves from the specified situation (e.g., reading) before they smoked. The strategy substantially reduced smoking for the group.

It may not be sufficient simply to restrict smoking to one or two locales. You might also associate smoking cues with nonsmoking activities. Some people substitute a piece of candy or chewing gum for a cigarette. (This may provide some semblance of the oral gratification previously provided by cigarettes.) One of the most noble attempts to alter the stimulus value of smoking cues was reported by Musick (1974). He had been inclined to follow his meals with coffee and cigarettes. When he initiated his self-management project, he would immediately leave the table after eating and start doing something that required physical activity. He began taking evening walks around the neighborhood instead of smoking. In addition, he carried a litter bag and started picking up debris along the street. As a result of his self-management efforts, he has stopped smoking, is getting his exercise, and is cleaning up the neighborhood. Who could possibly ask for more?

In addition to eliminating the control that certain stimuli have over smoking behavior, you may want to create control for other stimuli. Upper and Meredith (1970) have provided an ingenious demonstration of this strategy. A smoker was trained to keep a daily record of smoking behavior and to compute the average baseline time between cigarettes. A small portable timer, which the smoker wore, was initially set to buzz whenever the average time between cigarettes had transpired. The subject smoked only when the timer buzzed. As you might guess, the intercigarette interval was gradually increased until smoking was practially eliminated. Essentially the same approach could be used with an ordinary watch or clock. You might initially allow yourself to smoke every fifteen minutes, then every thirty minutes, then on the hour, until you are smoking very infrequently. This approach not only controls the frequency of smoking but also supplants a host of cues (meals, conversation, stress) that previously elicited smoking.

Establishing Effective Consequences

Altering the consequences of smoking is one of the most widely used means of controlling smoking. You can apply consequences not only to smoking behavior but also to the maintenance of record-keeping and appropriate setting events. A variety of stimuli can be employed as consequences. Electric shock following smoke inhalation has been used with some degree of success. McGuire and Vallance (1964) found that six out of ten subjects still refrained from smoking one month after receiving shocks for smoking. However, Powell and Azrin (1968) report that half of their participants dropped out of an experiment that involved use of a portable electric shock apparatus. Smoking behavior of all subjects returned to baseline once the shock condition was removed. We have never had a student use shock to control smoking behavior, but we do not rule out that possibility. If you choose to go this route, you may want to use the portable shocker described in Chapter Seven.

A consequence that you would probably find more palatable than shock is stimulus satiation. Resnick (1968) found that having subjects double or even triple their smoking during treatment sessions was effective in reducing smoking and holding it at a low level. Marston and McFall (1971) found that having the subject smoke three cigarettes each time they smoked was effective in reducing smoking. (The three-for-one treatment also included self-recording of cigarettes smoked and several changes in setting events.) Six months later the group showed a relapse but was still below baseline. Although this process may work for you, you could find yourself smoking more than ever if it fails.

Some people enlist the aid of others in delivering consequences. For example, you could contract to quit with another person, who would provide approval and tangible rewards for nonsmoking behavior. Tooley and Pratt (1967) have used this technique as a final strategy for reducing the smoking of a husband and wife. Tighe and Elliot (1967) got subjects to make a cash deposit (fifty to sixty-five dollars) and sign a behavior contract that provided for a weekly refund of a portion of their money for abstaining from smoking. Maybe you could strike a bargain with a friend who also wants to quit. Such a public commitment gives some people a strong incentive to reduce smoking. If interpersonal contracts are unappealing to you, contract with yourself. One of our subjects altered setting events as the primary means of reducing smoking, and purchased phonograph records with the money saved on cigarettes. Failure to adhere to specified setting events meant less money for records.

Focusing on Contingencies

In discussing setting events, we mentioned some ways to focus on the relationship between your behavior and its consequences. You might also increase awareness by changing behaviors that accompany smoking. For example, you could hold your cigarette differently. If you are right handed, try holding the cigarette in your left hand. Two researchers (Marston and McFall, 1971) have suggested holding the cigarette continental style—between thumb and forefinger, palm toward face. You could also change your way of lighting your cigarette, the way you stand or sit when you smoke, the way you hold the cigarette in your mouth, or the way you exhale smoke—anything to disrupt the series of responses that habitually accompanies smoking.

As we suggested for controlling eating, you could use written reminders to focus your attention on the contingencies of smoking. Reminders could be placed in strategic places, but they would have to be read to be effective. For example, thoro is a warning on the side of every pack of cigarettes. Some people know it is there but do not look at it; others have become habituated to it. The warning has therefore become ineffectual to these people. We think the warning would be more effective if it were different on every pack. Perhaps a remark that is personally meaningful would eventually appear on everyone's pack. In the meantime, you could print your own warning on each pack, or even on each cigarette. One of our students printed her children's names on her cigarettes. She looked at each cigarette and the name before lighting the cigarette. She said that she tried to concentrate on the 8.3 years she might be cutting from her life and how she would not be around to spend them with her children. Gruesome, but effective for her. Perhaps statistics on health mean something to you; perhaps they do not. Find some consequences that have personal relevance to you and portray these (by writing or pictures) in places where you usually smoke.

Achieving Covert Control

Several covert processes have been evaluated for controlling smoking. Homme (1965) has achieved modest success with use of his coverant pairs. Tooley and Pratt (1967) used Homme's model, Cautela's (1970) covert sensitization, and a contract with the same couple. This may represent the most judicious use of covert control, i.e., as an adjunct to the manipulation of the overt environment. Of the various covert approaches, Cautela's covert sensitization may offer the greatest potential for modifying smoking behavior. In using this strategy, Cautela first has his clients imagine scenes in which presmoking behavior leads to nausea. The individual escapes from this nausea by putting down his cigarette and declining to smoke. Eventually the self-controlling response comes earlier in the sequence of presmoking behaviors:

> You are at your desk working and you decide to smoke, and as soon as you decide to smoke you get this funny sick feeling at the pit of your stomach. You say to yourself, "The hell with it; I'm not going to smoke!" As soon as you decide not to smoke you feel fine and proud that you resisted temptation.[6]

Some people report that they smoke in response to anxiety. Since attempts to reduce smoking may heighten that anxiety, the best method of dealing with it may be the procedure for self-directed relaxation described in Chapter Seven. By using this strategy, you can learn to relax in situations where you typically smoke.

In Summation

There are few areas of self-management where the stakes are higher than in the one just discussed. The long-range benefits of not smoking are irrefutable. Recognizing the powerful control that setting events and immediate consequences have on smoking behavior, we have attempted to specify procedures for transcending these immediate causes. The most important part, implementing self-management strategies, we now leave with you.

Applied Exercise

Assume that you have a smoking problem, to be specific, you are presently smoking about one pack a day. The major symptoms you have experienced so far are shortness of breath and periodic coughing. You recognize the long-range hazards of smoking but have generally felt that you can beat the odds. However, social reactions to your smoking (e.g. other people's demand for clean air) have made you think twice about your habit. So you have committed yourself to smoking less, at least in certain situations. Let us see what you might prescribe for yourself.

[6]Reprinted with permission of author and publisher: Cautela, J. R. Treatment of smoking by covert sensitization. *Psychological Reports* 1970, 26, 417.

1. *Setting a goal:* Will your initial goal be to quit, cold turkey, or to reduce the frequency of cigerettes smoked by one or two a day, or to hold the number of cigarettes constant but to reduce the amount smoked per cigarette?

2. *Recording the quantity and circumstances of behavior:* Will you simply record the total number of cigarettes smoked per day or will you record the cigarettes smoked in various situations? Will you also record the events that precede and follow your smoking behavior? Will you record the amount smoked per cigarette?

3. *Changing setting events:* Will you identify one or two locales (nonsocial situations) in which to do your smoking? Will you attempt to arrange circumstances that would prevent reflexive smoking?

4. *Arranging consequences:* Will you use an aversive strategy, such as shock or stimulus satiation, or will you attempt to strengthen nonsmoking behavior through reinforcement? Will you administer all the contingencies yourself or will you formulate a mutual contract with someone else who has a smoking problem?

5. *Focusing on consequences:* Will you leave written reminders in places where you are most inclined to smoke?

6. *Applying covert control:* Will you use Homme's coverant pairs to interrupt the behavioral chain leading to smoking, or will you employ Cautela's covert sensitization to attach an aversive connotation to smoking?

Drinking

Whatever your views on alcohol, there is no denying that it is an integral part of American life. It is associated with religious rites, festivals, social gatherings of all sorts, and relaxation. It is used at least occasionally by some ninety-five million adults in the United States *(Alcohol and Alcoholism,* 1972). Unfortunately, the use of alcohol is a double-edged sword: intelligent use can be a source of pleasure, while misuse or abuse can be a source of grief. An estimated nine million adults in this country are considered to be alcoholics because of their extensive abuse of alcohol. We define abuse as drinking to the point where your well-being or others' well-being is jeopardized. When abuse becomes a regular part of a person's life, that person is said to be an alcoholic. You could be an occasional abuser without being an alcoholic, but you could not be an alcoholic without being an abuser. We have no bias against those who abstain from alcohol or against those who use it. Our concern is to assist those who want to *control* their drinking. Notice that we did not say, "quit."

Lest you think that what we have to say is relevant only to skid row residents, be assured that that group is a stereotyped minority. Only 5 percent of the alcoholics in this country are on skid row (*Alcohol and Health,* 1971). The remaining 95 percent come from all walks of life, college students not excluded. With the exception of tobacco, alcohol abuse is the biggest drug problem in the country (Fort, 1973). The drinking habits people establish undoubtedly have a substantial bearing on whether they become abusers or alcoholics. Controlling one's use of alcohol increases the chances that enjoyment, not unhappiness, will be the product of drinking behaviors.

Learning to drink

Any number of theories have been offered to explain alcohol abuse and alcoholism. Some contend that lack of self-esteem, lack of love, traumatic experiences, and genetic endowment are the sources of alcohol abuse and alcoholism. From a behavioral viewpoint, we believe that all drinking patterns—whether labeled as intelligent, abusive, or alcoholic—are learned. An individual with a drinking problem can conceivably learn to drink differently. The person who presently has no problem can control circumstances so that his drinking remains within acceptable standards.

How do people learn to abuse alcohol? Behaviorally oriented psychologists say that abuse of alcohol is learned from the consequences that follow drinking. For example, Sobell and Sobell (1973) contend that excessive consumption is often a function of stress reduction. They discuss three potential reinforcers for drinking under stress. First, alcohol is a sedative. An individual who finds himself in a stressful situation can reduce the physiological components of stress by drinking. If you think alcohol is a stimulant, you are mistaken. People make that mistake because alcohol appears to make them more uninhibited. Some people are more talkative and aggressive after drinking, but these reactions are thought to result from depression of brain centers that normally inhibit such behaviors. In fact, such individuals are less perceptive of what is happening around them. Second, excessive drinking may lead to physical debilitation and subsequent removal from an unpleasant situation. Third, intoxication may result in less chastisement for otherwise unacceptable behavior. A person's flirtatious, aggressive, or sexual behavior may be excused on the grounds of intoxication. Reduced chastisement plus the inherent reinforcement value of these behaviors may indeed serve to strengthen drinking behaviors.

Perhaps the foregoing rewards do not account for much alcohol abuse among college students. Other rewards, however, are available in abundance. College students are frequently pressured by peers to drink. Maybe you have been pressured to drink excessively or have been a party to pressuring others. People who succumb to this pressure win the approval of their companions. The college beer blast may offer social rewards to the individual who is able to drink the most. Some people find reinforcement in taking their friends to gaze at an array of empty beer cans accumulated from the previous night's fun. Excessive drinking may be learned at social gatherings where nothing but an evening of drinking has been planned; having fun is then equated with how much one drinks. Excessive drinking may lead to escape from the thoughts of failure associated with a particular college course. As you can see, many reinforcers are available to reward a pattern of drinking that may be highly detrimental to a person's best interests.

Controlling Drinking Behavior

Since drinking behavior is learned, it must be subject to change. Evidence is mounting that even individuals with severe drinking problems can alter their drinking patterns (Bigelow et al., 1972; Mills et al., 1971; Schaefer, 1972; Sobell and Sobell, 1973). If environmental manipulation can help confirmed alcoholics alter their drinking patterns, it surely can work for you—which leads us once more to our model for self-control. Since we have already been through the model twice in this chapter, we will make the present analysis short. (Frankly, we are worried about stimulus satiation.)

Defining target behaviors   Perhaps your goal is to decrease the frequency of drinking to reduce stress. This is probably the most hazardous form of drinking behavior. You may also desire to limit the occasions on which you drink. Drinking should be reserved for periods of relaxation, meals and good cheer. Even on those occasions, drinking should not be the top recreational priority. One important goal would be to restrict the amount you drink on any one occasion. A person might have ten cocktails over the period of a week without experiencing any deleterious effects, but condensing those ten cocktails into one evening may reduce the individual to less than a fully functioning person.

Monitoring target behavior   Whatever your target, you will probably want to keep track of your daily consumption of alcohol. You could use a form similar to Figure 3-2 for recording the type of drink, amount consumed, conditions (time and place), time taken to consume the drink, number of sips, and occasion for drinking. You might also attempt to log the degree of intoxication. (This is one of the few behaviors that you may have to record after the fact.) Your record should tell you when, where, and how much your drinking behavior needs to be altered. If you find yourself drinking high-proof liquors, gulping your drinks, or drinking on all occasions (e.g., to celebrate Washington's crossing of the Potomac), you should have some definite clues as to what needs changing. If your drinking is confined to wine, beer, or diluted beverages at dinner, an occasional drink with a friend, a moderate amount consumed at parties, and other forms of

Day	Type of Drink	Condition Time	Condition Place	Time to Consume The Drink	Number of Sips	Occasion for Drinking
1						
2						
3						
4						
5						
6						
7						

Figure 3-2 Drinking Record

socially accepted drinking, you probably will not need to alter your drinking at all. In addition to keeping a record of your drinking behavior, you should keep a record of the treatment procedures you are using. You should record how often you implement treatment strategies and whether they have the desired effect.

Changing setting events   There are any number of ways to alter setting events to control your drinking behavior. You could limit the type and amount of alcohol that you purchase at any given time. Rather than picking up a pair of six-packs in preparation for a ball game on TV, you could buy yourself only two cans. Shop for liquor when you are not in a drinking mood, so that you can affect the amount consumed when circumstances are conducive to drinking.

At home and in party situations, try having food available whenever you are drinking. Eating as you drink slows the absorption of alcohol into the blood, thereby reducing blood-alcohol level. You might also alter the way in which you drink. If you drink from a bottle, you could be developing a bad habit. Pour your drink into another container, dilute your liquors with water or noncarbonated mixers. If you have a bar, keep it stocked with mixers so that you do not have to take a straight drink. Lock your liquor cabinet after preparing each drink in a effort to control the number of drinks you consume. If you want to drink slowly, try setting a kitchen timer to ring after ten or fifteen minutes so that you become accustomed to holding a drink for a given amount of time. Keep nonalcoholic beverages in your home so that you have alternatives to alcohol. You might keep table wines on hand as alternatives to stronger drinks. If you go out for a drink with a friend, take only enough money for one or two drinks and ask your friend to do the same.

Another way to change setting events is to limit the occasions or circumstances when your drink. Restricting the situations in which you drink does not mean that you *always* imbibe at a particular time and place; time or place could then serve as a stimulus for drinking, regardless of what is happening on that occasion. You be the controller; do not permit trivial events to trigger unwanted drinking.

Controlling drinking behavior by means of setting events is more likely to be achieved by the social drinker than by the alcoholic. Research (Miller et al., 1974; Nathan and O'Brien, 1971) suggests that alcoholics are just as likely to drink in the absence of alcoholic cues as in their presence, whereas social drinkers are far more inclined to drink in the presence of alcoholic cues (e.g., being in a cocktail lounge or at a social gathering with others drinking). If your drinking is tied to certain environmental cues, you are a social drinker and your drinking behavior can be altered by changing those cues.

Establishing effective consequences   Establishing effective consequences should pose little problem for you. You should first establish effective consequences for all behaviors that contribute to the appropriate use of alcohol (the controlling behaviors). But most important, you should reward appropriate drinking behavior. A token economy, a contract calling for exchange of benefits with a friend or spouse, the elicitation of support from others, self-administration of subvocal words of praise, "fun" activities contingent upon nonabusive use of alcohol, or punishment (e.g., shock) for abuses—these techniques can contribute to control of your drinking behavior.

Focusing on contingencies   Signs or notes placed in conspicuous places, changes in the way you hold your glass, changes in the containers you drink from, changes in what you drink, and changes in the places you drink all can contribute to awareness of your drinking behavior. It is especially difficult to maintain that awareness in certain social situations. Others may do you the dubious favor of constantly refilling your half-empty glass, causing you to lose track of how much you are imbibing. Preoccupation with conversation can also make you oblivious to your drinking behavior. If these events are likely to occur, perhaps you can prearrange for assistance from another person. The two of you could work out a behavioral code (e.g., baseball coaching signs) so that you could be reminded unobtrusively of the quantity and rate of your consumption.

Achieving covert control   Covert sensitization is the principal covert strategy that has been applied to drinking behavior. It can be used in a variety of ways. For example, if you wanted to limit your drinking behavior to one or two drinks per occasion, you would apply sensitization to visualization of the third drink. If you have ever been nauseated from alcohol, you might call upon those memories when you attempt to visualize nausea. There is some evidence (Ashem and Donner, 1968) that this covert sensitization procedure can affect drinking patterns over a period of several months.

We indicated earlier that one of the payoffs for excessive drinking is the reduction of stress. If your behavior records show stress reduction to be your principal reason for drinking, the practice of relaxation exercises—focusing on those situations that make you tense—can preclude this source of reinforcement for drinking. (See Chapter Seven for a discussion of self-induced relaxation.)

Summary of drinking behavior   Although we have no bias against total abstinence, we feel that drinking can be a regular and problem-free dimension of your life. However, drinking to reduce stress or drinking heavily often definitely spells trouble. This is the beginning of a behavior pattern that could eventually annihilate your chances for a productive life. Even though you may discount the possibility of your having a drinking problem (most people do), no harm would be done by recording the frequency, quantity, and circumstances of your present drinking. In addition, you might seek some candid feedback from others as to how they perceive your drinking. Perhaps that input plus your behavior records will indicate the need for change. You can then attempt to restrict the range of stimuli that elicit drinking behavior, to have available only certain types and quantities of liquor, to identify both tangible and social reinforcers for nondrinking behavior, to arrange for written and social reminders about your drinking responses, and to apply covert sensitization to the visualization of drinking activity.

Concluding Comments

This chapter has by no means exhausted the application of self-management concepts to health-related problems. However, excessive eating, smoking, and drinking are the three problem areas to which self-management strategies have most frequently been applied. This trend holds true both in the research literature and in the individual projects conducted by our students. Self-management may also prove very useful in the area of drug abuse.

We believe that some individuals can realize their fullest potential for self-management in the areas of eating, smoking, and drinking problems. People sometimes reach a point where self-management in these areas becomes unattainable. But it is our hope that if you have such problems, you will not succumb to them without giving self-management an all-out try.

References

Alcohol and Alcoholism. 1972. Rockville, Md.: National Institute of Mental Health/National Institute on Alcohol Abuse and Alcoholism.

Alcohol and Health. 1971. Washington, D. C.: United States Department of Health, Education and Welfare.

Ashem, B., and Donner, L. 1968. Covert sensitization with alcoholics: a controlled replication. *Behaviour Research and Therapy 6,* 7-12.

Bigelow, G., Cohen, M., Liebson, I., and Faillace, L. A. 1972. Abstinence or moderation? choice by alcoholics. *Behaviour Research and Therapy 10,* 209-214.

Cautela, J. R. 1970. Treatment of smoking by covert sensitization. *Psychological Reports 26,* 415-420.

Derby, G., Rohr, R., Azouaou, G., Vassilitch, I., and Mottaz, G. 1968. Study of the effect of dividing the daily caloric intake into seven meals on weight loss in obese subjects. *Nutrito Dieta 10,* 288-296.

Ferster, C. B., Nurnberger, J. I., and Levitt, E. B. 1962. The control of eating. *Journal of Mathetics 1* (1), 87-109.

Fort, J. 1973. *Alcohol: our biggest drug problem.* New York: McGraw-Hill.

Goldiamond, I. 1965. Self-control procedures in personal behavior problems. *Psychological Reports 17,* 851-868.

The Health Consequences of Smoking. 1973. Washington, D. C.: United States Department of Health, Education, and Welfare.

Homme, L. E. 1965. Control of coverants, the operants of the mind. Perspectives in psychology, XXIV. *Psychological Record 15,* 501-511.

Horan, J. J., and Johnson, R. G. 1971. Covert conditioning through a self-management application of the Premack principle: its effect on weight reduction. *Journal of Behavior Therapy and Experimental Psychiatry 2,* 243-249.

McFall, R. M. 1970. Effects of self-monitoring on normal smoking behavior. *Journal of Consulting and Clinical Psychology 35* (2), 135-142.

McGuire, R. J., and Vallance, M. 1964. Aversion therapy by electric shock: a simple technique. *British Medical Journal 1,* 151-153.

Manno, B., and Marston, A. R. 1972. Weight reduction as a function of negative covert reinforcement (sensitization) versus positive covert reinforcement. *Behaviour Research and Therapy 10,* 201-207.

Marston, A. R., and McFall, R. M. 1971. Comparison of behavior modification approaches to smoking reduction. *Journal of Consulting and Clinical Psychology 36* (2), 153-162.

Miller, P. M., Hersen, M., Eisler, R. M., Epstein, L. H., and Wooten, L. S. 1974. Relationship of alcohol cues to the drinking behavior of alcoholics and social drinkers: an analogue study. *Psychological Record 24,* 61-66.

Mills, K. C., Sobell, M. B., and Schaefer, H. H. 1971. Training social drinking as an alternative to abstinence for alcoholics. *Behavior Therapy 2,* 18-27.

Musick, F. G. 1974. Thirty-year-smoker tells how he quit and retained his waistline. *Knoxville News-Sentinel,* March 2, p. 4.

Nathan, P. E., and O'Brien, J. S. 1971. An experimental analysis of the behavior of alcoholics and nonalcoholics during prolonged experimental drinking: a necessary precursor of behavior therapy? *Behavior Therapy 2,* 455-476.

Penick, S. B., Filion, R., Fox, S., and Stunkard, A. J. 1971. Behavior modification in the treatment of obesity. *Psychosomatic Medicine 33,* 49-55.

Powell, J., and Azrin, N. 1968. The effects of shock as a punisher for cigarette smoking. *Journal of Applied Behavior Analysis 1,* 63-71.

Resnick, J. H. 1968. Effects of stimulus satiation on the overlearned maladaptive response of cigarette smoking. *Journal of Consulting and Clinical Psychology 32,* 501-505.

Sachs, L. B., Bean, H. and Morrow, J. E. 1970. Comparison of smoking treatments. *Behavior Therapy 1,* 465-472.

Schachter, S. 1971. Some extraordinary facts about obese humans and rats. *American Psychologist 26* (2), 129-144.

Schaefer, H. H. 1972. Twelve-month follow-up of behaviorally trained ex-alcoholic social drinkers. *Behavior Therapy 3*, 286-289.

Sobell, M. B., and Sobell, L. C. 1973. Individualized behavior therapy for alcoholics. *Behavior Therapy 4,* 49-72.

Stuart, R. B. 1967. Behavioral control of overeating. *Behaviour Research and Therapy 5,* 357-365.

Stuart, R. B., and Davis, B. 1972. *Slim chance in a fat world.* Champaign, Ill.: Research Press Company.

Stunkard A., and McLaren-Hume, M. 1959. The results of treatment for obesity. *Archives Internal Medicine 103,* 79-85.

Tighe, T. J., and Elliott, R. 1967. Breaking the cigarette habit: effects of technique involving threatened loss of money. Paper presented at the meeting of the American Psychological Association. Washington, D. C., September.

Tooley, J. T., and Pratt, S. 1967. An experimental procedure for the extinction of smoking behavior. *Psychological Record 17,* 209-218.

Upper, D., and Meredith, L. 1970. A stimulus-control approach to the modification of smoking behavior. *Proceedings of the 78th American Psychological Association Convention 5,* 739-740. Washington, D.C.: American Psychological Association.

four

**The Rites of Passage:
Developing Sports Skills**

External feedback refers to information regarding your performance that is
supplied by an external source.

Why a chapter on athletic participation in a book devoted to self-management? Are not athletics relevant only to a certain age level (the pre-adult years), to a certain societal level (simple, primitive cultures) and to a certain sex (male)? Many primitive societies use tests of physical dexterity, strength, and endurance as their rites of passage into manhood. One can readily see how these physical criteria could be basic to survival in a primitive society. But in contemporary America, physical prowess appears quite unrelated to most professional pursuits. In spite of the nonphysical nature of our professions, we believe that sports participation is still a fundamental dimension of the "good life."

Athletic involvement can generate a host of reinforcers, not the least of which is good health. Practically everyone reports feeling better as a result of sports activity. People who participate regularly in sports appear to be less troubled with fatigue and minor physical ailments (e.g., colds and influenza) than those who do not. Sports enthusiasts also seem to recover faster from minor disorders than do nonparticipants. Perhaps most important is the role of physical exercise in preventing cardiovascular and respiratory diseases. Any person who is extremely sensitive to good health is likely to be significantly reinforced by sports activity.

Participation in sports can enhance one's self-image. The weight control and muscle tone resulting from sports activity can produce real changes in physical appearance. Sports activity should also increase your sensitivity to your physical self. In a sense vigorous activity awakens you to aspects of your body that sedentary living may leave undiscovered. Part of this awareness comes from experiencing your body in motion. Movement sharpens our body image, while sleep and inactivity dull that image (Harris, 1972). One of the more depressing facets of old age is the loss of body awareness resulting from immobility.

Sports activity is sometimes portrayed as having a positive impact on emotionality. An investigation at the University of Florida (Barger, 1968) found athletic activity to be the major avenue of stress relief for male students. Vigorous physical activity probably produces an actual reduction in muscular tension. (At least, we have little trouble sleeping after a spirited tennis match.) In addition, sports activities tend to command our total attention. For an hour or so, we can completely lose sight of professional and personal concerns, which previously seemed excruciatingly important. The impact of sports activity on emotionality has been most conclusively demonstrated by Ismail and Trachtman (1973). They found that four months of exercise (jogging and other athletic activity) significantly enhanced the emotional stability of middle-aged males who previously had been in poor condition. Sports might be good group therapy!

Sports activity may even affect mental productivity. Remember the Greek axiom about a healthy body and healthy mind? Physical educators (Hart and Shay, 1964; Weber, 1953) have found modest but statistically significant correlations between indices of physical fitness and achievement in college. Of course, one cannot assume cause and effect from correlational data, since both physical fitness and academic achievement may be functions of some third variable, such as achievement motivation. However, the Ismail and Trachtman report indicates that extended periods of exercise may contribute directly to increments in imagination. That physical exercise would enhance mental productivity is not an unreasonable physiological possibility. Exercise increases circulation to the brain, which in turn increases the quantity of glucose available for the brain's nutrition. Not that we are suggesting that you prepare for tomorrow's test by playing basketball all afternoon!

The social payoffs for participating in sports are significant. Few areas provide more opportunities for meeting new people and establishing friendships. Social interaction comes easily and naturally in the atmosphere of sports. Ismail and Trachtman suggest that sports participation can substantially improve social relationships even among old acquaintances. So if your social life is dull, consider sports as an avenue of rejuvenation. Warren (1970) affirms that sports may be the optimal domain for the "meeting" that, according to Martin Buber (1958), is the goal of all human experience.

Beyond these extraneous benefits of sports activity, a great deal of reinforcement may be inherent to the activity. The exhilaration that comes from rapid movement or from the correct execution of a skill is almost without parallel. This type of reinforcement is usually intensified as you progress in a sport. In the first place, your physical condition improves and you are thus able to move more vigorously. Second, your movements become more coordinated as a result of practice. Participation in sports can evolve into a genuinely aesthetic experience. This dimension is far more likely to emerge in some sports than in others. Aesthetic satisfaction can probably be found more readily on the basketball court than at the bottom of a football pile-up. However, aesthetic appeal varies with different value systems. The point is that experiencing rhythm and grace in one's movements can be a principal reinforcer for sustaining involvement in sports activity.

Although behavior modifiers are not particularly fond of the term, a person may experience a type of self-actualization through sports participation. Maslow defines self-actualized as becoming all that one is capable of being. In *Man, Sport, and Existence* (1967), Slusher contends that many persons find sports that sphere of life in which they come closest to realizing their full human potential. In the sports arena, your physical skills are obvious. Usually, it is also quite evident what must be done to improve those skills (e.g., better conditioning, more practice). So the stage is set in the sports domain for you to become the best that you can be.

Another issue is, who can enjoy the benefits of sports? Our discussion of sports activity is not intended primarily for football stars. Although college athletes may find some beneficial suggestions for improving skills, they are not the intended recipients of our message. We address our comments primarily to the individual who will *not* compete in college athletics and who will never sign with a professional team. This chapter is intended for people who want to make sports activity a secondary but permanent dimension of their lives. We contend that sports have their greatest value when they are pursued for personal pleasure and conditioning. Because the barriers to participation often become accentuated once an individual is out of college, we shall devote special attention to strategies for making sports activity a continuing part of your adult life.

This chapter is intended just as much for women as for men. Women can enjoy exactly the same benefits from sports as men do. We are past the era when participation in sports was viewed as antithetical to femininity, when femininity demanded that a woman be pale and fragile. Participation in sports activity enriches women's lives and relationships among men and women. Sports provide many opportunities for heterosexual socializing. Sports may even enhance the sexual dimensions of our relationships. We mentioned earlier that vigorous physical activity makes people more aware of their bodies. This increased awareness is likely to be felt in the sexual domain.

In this chapter we will present some general principles that can be applied to a variety of sports activities. The application of these principles can enhance both your skills and your enjoyment of sports.

Defining Target Behaviors

In Chapter Two we described the logistics of goal-setting in self-management. We emphasized that goals should be defined in measurable, behavioral terms, and we distinguished between process and product assessment. A product is the outcome of a behavior, e.g., the number of free-throws made, the number of games won. Processes are the behaviors emitted in producing a desired outcome, e.g., getting in position to shoot the basketball, watching the goal while shooting, and following through after releasing the ball. In the early stages of learning a sport, we recommend that you focus primarily on process behaviors. Gauging your progress according to the number of free-throws made or games won could seriously undermine your progress in a sport. We will elaborate on this point shortly.

Defining your initial targets in terms of process behaviors does pose some difficulties. Many behaviors that are generally treated as discrete units are actually chains* of smaller behaviors. Stroking a tennis ball may involve positioning yourself to run to the ball, running to the ball, getting your racket back, positioning your feet properly, bending your knees, watching the ball, and swinging through the ball. If you really want to be precise in defining your goals, you will divide sports skills into chains and define your goals in terms of the units that these chains comprise.

The concept of chaining has major implications for the relearning of skills. While a novice in a sport might have to learn every single unit in a chain, an established player might need to reshape only one or two of those units. Focusing on one unit at a time, while leaving other behaviors intact, is the most reinforcing way to rebuild a skill. If you have not been raising the basketball sufficiently high over your head as you shoot or have not been following through on your shots, you initially should attempt to change only one of these elements. You might begin with the link closest to the end of the chain (following through) and work backward. This approach seems to be less disruptive of the previously established response chain than beginning with an early link and working forward. Or, if one link is noticeably easier to change than another, you might begin with the easier link. The point is that you should focus on one thing at a time; do not try to rebuild a skill in a day.

Your behavior targets will change dramatically as you progress in a

*Defined in Glossary.

sport. Once you develop some proficiency in executing the fundamental process behaviors, you can begin thinking in terms of products, e.g., number of tennis serves in the service courts. You eventually should reach a point where the goals are exceedingly stringent.
For example, your goal might be to avoid double-faulting in an afternoon of tennis. Who knows, one day your goal may be to win at
Wimbledon.

Monitoring Target Behaviors

A primary hazard in attempting to monitor target behaviors is that the
logistics of monitoring can undermine your enjoyment of the sport. A
friend of ours who was trying to increase the velocity of his second
service in tennis attempted to establish a baseline by recording after
each of his service games the number of hard and soft second serves
that occurred during the game. However, he found this information
hard to remember while playing—to the point that his general concentration was diminished. Paper-and-pencil techniques are generally too cumbersome for self-recording in sports activity. Instead, we
recommend the bead or wrist counter described in Chapter Two,
which can be used to record your behavior without interfering with
the game itself.

Sometimes a straight frequency count (the number of times a
response occurs) can present a deceptive picture of a behavior. The
opportunities for a particular behavior may vary markedly from day to
day. In that case, you should log occurrences of the behavior plus
opportunities for the occurrence of that behavior. This can be accomplished easily with either the wrist counter or the bead counter.
You can then calculate the percentage of time a specific behavior
occurred when it should have occurred. This is equivalent to comput-
ing batting averages in baseball or shooting percentages in basketball.

You should also record playing conditions in order to interpret your
frequency data appropriately. A windy day will affect your skills in
tennis, a muddy field your skills in football, and choppy water your
skills in water skiing. Unless you record these conditions, you might
incorrectly assume that your skills had regressed—when in reality
you performed better than the last time you encountered such conditions.

Self-recording in sports often focuses on product behavior—"Did the ball go over the net?" "Did the ball go through the hoop?" "Did I make it through the slalom gates?" These are obviously much easier to self-record than process behaviors. Nevertheless, assessment of process behaviors are often more useful in improving your game. You need to know *how* you hit the ball when it did or did not go over the net. Many process behaviors are of a subtle nature, such as where you begin your acceleration in water skiing or when you watch the ball in racquet sports. You often may be completely unaware of what you are doing as you hit the ball. An external observer may be required to monitor accurately many process behaviors. Perhaps you can solicit the aid of a friend. Since your friend will not want to spend all of his/her time watching you play, identify a segment of your playing time (e.g., the last ten minutes of play) and have the observer monitor your behavior only during that period. Make sure the observation period is always during the same period of playing time, because a varying time of observation could drastically affect your evaluation of progress.

Arranging Setting Events

Making Time for Sports

Arranging setting events for sports participation begins with your schedule. There are two major ways to make time for sports activity. If you regularly participate in sports and find that participation highly enjoyable, you can use sports activity as a reward for completing less reinforcing tasks. But if you are not presently involved in sports, we recommend instead that you schedule sports on an unconditional basis. Presumably you have at least a mild affinity for sports, but that affinity gets buried under a multitude of work pressures. This will happen increasingly as you become involved in professional pursuits. You may think that life could never be more demanding than it presently is, but you will probably discover that professional pursuits are more time consuming than college work. Even with a love for sports, the only way to be assured of sports participation is to make that activity an unconditional part of your schedule.

Scheduling sports activity on an unconditional basis makes many achievement-oriented adults uneasy because of the time they are taking from their work. In dealing with this issue, we have come to think in terms of total living time. Other factors being equal, the individual who keeps himself in good physical condition will live longer and more fully than the individual who does not. Taking an hour a day for vigorous physical activity will probably result in more total time for your career. In addition, we have come to realize that time devoted to work is not the only variable that affects work output. People obviously attack their work more energetically on some occasions than others. What you expect to follow a segment of work can affect the zest with which you do your work. If we have tennis planned for a specific hour in the afternoon, we are far more likely to be productive up to that hour. Some people work better *after* a period of invigorating physical activity. Whatever your preference, you will find that you can accomplish just as much by taking an hour a day for sports activity as in working an uninterrupted twelve-hour day.

Choosing a Sport

The ease of scheduling sports activity is related to the kind of activity in which you wish to engage. Unless you are affiliated with an agency that organizes sports programs, you will obviously have more difficulty scheduling team sports than individual sports. Many of our sports efforts have floundered because of the difficulty in getting a group together to play. In choosing an activity, you must also consider the amount of time required to participate in that activity. While a round of golf might take an entire afternoon or water skiing a whole day, you can get a terrific workout in paddleball, tennis, or handball in an hour's time (even if you would prefer to play longer). Giving up an hour of your work day can be achieved with considerably less pain than giving up an afternoon.

The availability of various sports facilities should also affect your decision about which sport to pursue. Those of us who reside on a university campus usually have a variety of athletic facilities in close proximity. But as a student, you should also be thinking of the kinds of athletic facilities that will be most accessible outside the university setting. For example, public tennis courts will probably be more available than public gymnasiums or public golf courses. Whatever the case, identifying an athletic facility that is near your residence or place of work can simplify scheduling. Any extra time that you must spend in getting to an athletic facility will act as a deterrent to engaging in that activity.

Another factor that affects sports participation is the expense involved. If you are independently wealthy, skip this paragraph. Otherwise, you should be cultivating sports interests that will not demand a vast expenditure of funds. When you are in college, you can take a variety of physical education courses for essentially the same fee. But even then you should be asking, "Is this a sport that typically must be played in a country-club setting or can it be played in the back yard?" You know how golf and badminton score on that count.

Perhaps the most critical variable in choosing a sport is the exercise value of that sport. In our estimation the preferred sports are those that allow you to get lots of exercise quickly. We do not discount the therapeutic value of an afternoon on the golf course. The serenity of the setting undoubtedly enhances the reinforcement value of this experience. However, one should not count on golf for keeping in good physical trim. In contrast, paddleball, although played in a much less picturesque setting than golf, can exhaust you in thirty minutes.[1] Many sports can be played either as singles or doubles. You will get more exercise and develop your skills more rapidly if you choose singles.

Deciding When to Play

The time of day when you attempt to play can produce great satisfaction or considerable frustration. If possible, attempt to schedule sports activity at a time when the designated facilities are most accessible. The last thing you want to do is spend two hours waiting for a court to become available. If your work schedule prevents you from using recreational facilities at the optimal hours, and waiting is therefore inevitable, why not take something along to work on during the wait? Of course, if a recreational facility operates on a reservation basis, you can be spared much of the agony of waiting.

If you have a specified number of hours per week to devote to athletic activity, should you divide that time into several short periods or a few extended periods? That depends, first of all, on the time you must invest in getting prepared to play (e.g., travel time, waiting). If

---

[1]Kozar and Hunsicker (1963) have found that handball, paddleball, tennis, and badminton produce essentially the same mean and the same peak heart rates during thirty-minute participation periods. Volleyball and bowling produce significantly lower heart rates.

preparation time is negligible, more frequent playing periods are preferable. Scheduling six one-hour blocks of physical activity is ordinarily wiser than scheduling two three-hour blocks. The shorter, more frequent activity periods are superior both in exercise value and in skill acquisition. In lengthy practice sessions, fatigue tends to undermine the effective use of time; it can so completely undermine the appropriate execution of skills that you leave the session feeling that you have regressed. As you will see in the next section, it is imperative that you leave a playing session feeling good about your play. If your overall work schedule is conducive to longer periods of play, practice a variety of skills during each playing session. According to Rushall and Siedentop (1972), fatigue is less likely to be a debilitating factor if you intermittently practice different skills than if you focus on the same skill for the duration of the practice session.

Choosing a Playing Partner

One important setting event is the people with whom you play. You have undoubtedly heard that you should play with someone who is better than you in order to maximize your progress. Though that is true to a degree, a person can be so much better than you that your skills are rendered nonfunctional. For example, a highly skilled tennis player may hit the ball so hard or place it so well that you cannot hit it at all. (You would find that this arrangement has no reinforcing value whatsoever.) It is probably best to seek someone for a playing partner who is at approximately your skill level and who has a commitment to the sport similar to yours. If you can find a person who not only wants to improve his/her game but also wants to help you improve your game, you have the optimal pairing for enjoyment and improvement. Our discussion of reinforcement contingencies will show that external feedback is a major means of facilitating skill acquisition. Surprisingly, feedback from inexperienced players may be as accurate as feedback from skilled performers (Osborne and Gordon, 1972). Therefore, it is important to find a playing partner who is willing to give you feedback relative to your process behaviors.

Practicing Alone

You do not need a playing partner to practice many sports skills. In fact, practicing some skills independently may be preferable to working on those skills under game conditions. Examples are such activities as shooting a basketball, stroking a tennis ball off a wall, and serving a tennis ball. Independent practice gives you more opportunities to execute the skill than game conditions do. Independent practice also allows you to keep playing conditions more consistent than is typically possible under game conditions. This is especially important in the initial stages of skill acquisition. For example, it is very difficult to refine your tennis stroke when the ball is coming back to you in many different ways. A wall would give you a more constant return than would an inexperienced playing partner. A ball machine would be even better than a wall, but most of us cannot afford such luxuries.

Obtaining Instruction

As the final setting event, we recommend formal instruction in the sport of your choice, rather than going out and learning a sport on your own. While you can acquire many skills just by playing, you can also acquire a multitude of bad habits that are practically impossible to change. (We speak from first-hand experience.) Naturally acquired skills can limit your future development. So if you plan to get any instruction in a sport, the best time to get it is when you first get involved with the sport.

If formal instruction is not available, consider the possibility of programmed instruction.* Programmed materials have been developed for a number of sports, including gymnastics, tennis, golf, badminton, and basketball. Programmed materials are intended to be self-instructional. They usually identify the skills that are fundamental to a sport and then take you through those skills in an orderly sequence. For each skill directions are given regarding practice methods, behavioral chains that make up that skill, and procedures for evaluating your progress. Most programs make liberal use of diagrams in delineating the behavioral chains to be learned. Programmed instruction appears to be at least as effective as conventional instruction in producing sports skills (Locke and Jensen, 1971). In fact, it may be somewhat superior to conventional instruction in facilitating form (appropriate process behaviors). This is probably true because of the detailed description of process behaviors normally included in programmed materials.

You can sometimes improve your own skills simply by watching a skilled player perform. This is what psychologists refer to as modeling.* A demonstration of a skill is often much clearer than a verbal description of that skill. You can benefit most from watching a skilled performance after you have developed some fundamental skills of your own. Otherwise, you will not be sensitized to what the skilled performer is doing. You will only be aware that the performer is executing certain major skills. You will not see the behavior chains (e.g., positioning of the feet, back-swing, follow-through) that constitute those skills.

Summary of Setting Events

Unless sports already represent a high-priority activity in your life, you should schedule sports involvement on an unconditional basis. In choosing a sport, you should emphasize individual rather than team sports, sports that can be engaged in during relatively brief time periods, sports for which facilities will be readily accessible once you are out of college, sports that can be inexpensively pursued, and sports that have a high exercise value. When scheduling sports participation, select a time of day when the facilities are least used. If you have a set amount of time to devote to sports activity, it is usually best to spread that time over several short sessions. In looking for a regular playing partner, seek someone at about your own skill level and someone who is committed to both improving his/her own play and helping you improve your play. In attempting to learn a new sport, it is best to get formal instruction at the very outset. Also, take advantage of opportunities to watch skilled players perform.

The setting events recommended in this section can most easily be achieved through assistance from friends experienced in your sport. Friends can tell you where the most appropriate facilities are, the optimal time of day to play, the cost involved in playing, the acceptable playing attire, and appropriate equipment to use. Better still, they can take you with them when they play, show you the facilities, and introduce you to instructors or potential playing partners. This arrangement can minimize the awkwardness that one often feels in launching a new athletic venture.

Arranging Reinforcement Contingencies

Much of the reinforcement for participating in athletics will evolve quite naturally from the activity itself; however, natural reinforcement is not inevitable. We are all familiar with the person who goes out to play golf with the greatest of anticipation but ends up wrapping the clubs around a tree—or at any rate, feels that his/her game has totally deteriorated. This sense of frustration can be transcended. The major objective of this section is to describe procedures for maximizing the reinforcement value of athletic participation and for minimizing its frustration potential.

Winning as a Payoff

Our initial recommendation is that you *not* make winning the principal payoff for playing. Although it is nice to win now and then, there are other, more fundamental payoffs for athletic participation. If we make winning the primary reason for playing, we achieve our reinforcement at another's expense. You feel good because you won, but the other person feels bad because he/she lost. Emphasis on winning can also impede your progress in a sport. It keeps you from practicing skills that would eventually lead to a higher level of play, because pressure to win can cause you to retreat into a very conservative style of play. Winning is also too much of a one-shot kind of reinforcement. Normally, one is declared the winner only at the conclusion of the game. However, an individual ought to experience many instances of reinforcement during play. So the question is, how does one approach a sport in order to experience reinforcement during play rather than at the conclusion of play?

Exercise as a Payoff

Two major objectives should characterize participation in sports— exercise and execution of skills. No matter how badly you play, vigorous exercise can still make athletic activity worthwhile. Unfortunately, amount of exercise and proficiency of play tend to be highly correlated. This is particularly true if you consider the performance of all participants collectively. Poor performance on the part of one or more participants usually means that the ball is not kept in play long enough for anyone to get much exercise, except in chasing balls. There is another way that poor play diminishes the exercise value of athletic participation: When things go badly, you may stop attempting difficult shots and start sulking between points. This slows the pace of the game even more, accentuates your mood of self-pity, and further decelerates your performance level. There will be days when your muscular coordination simply is not as sharp as on other days.

This problem cannot be totally eradicated; however, you can control whether you attempt the difficult shots, and you can control the pace of your movements between shots. If those behaviors can be altered, you can still get a great deal of exercise even though you are not playing well. There are days when the primary satisfaction comes from being able to say, "I'm really playing hard," rather than, "I'm really playing well." If you have some way to objectify the amount of exercise you get, you can be more exact in reinforcing yourself for vigorous physical activity. A device that may be useful in this respect is a pedometer, an instrument about the size of a stopwatch that clips onto your belt or pocket. While pedometers are generally used to measure mileage run, they may have the potential for differentiating vigorous from mild activity [2]

Skill Execution as a Payoff

Intrinsic feedback   The second major source of reinforcement for participation in sports comes from the execution of certain skills. We use two types of feedback in evaluating performance level. First, there is what Rushall and Siedentop (1972) refer to as intrinsic information feedback.* This kind of feedback is inherent to a sport. You can readily determine whether you hit the ball over the net, in the court, or in the hole. This feedback affects your future attempts at that behavior. Skills that can be evaluated in terms of accuracy (e.g., whether you rounded all of the buoys on a slalom course, whether the ball went through the hoop) usually provide enough intrinsic feedback for you to improve your skills on your own. Through independent practice you learn to hit a higher percentage of your shots. However, some sporting events, such as swimming and dancing, initially provide little intrinsic feedback, thereby making external feedback fundamental to improvement. Even in sports that provide a great deal of intrinsic feedback, external feedback is valuable. Intrinsic feedback per se can shape a response that will later severely limit your performance potential. As suggested earlier, improving your skills demands that you focus more on process behaviors than behavioral products. While you can make some on-the-spot judgments about process behaviors ("Did I lean too far forward on the ski?" "Did I decelerate at the proper time?"), a more comprehensive evaluation of your per-

[2]A pedometer can be purchased from several companies (e.g., Amsterdam Company, Amsterdam, N.Y., 12010 and Hoffritz Company, 20 Cooper Square, New York, N.Y. 10002) for approximately $10.00.

formance would involve external feedback.

External feedback   External feedback refers to information regarding your performance that is supplied from an external source. For example, a coach may view your process behaviors (response chains) and then tell you what you are doing appropriately or inappropriately. One of the best ways to get this kind of feedback is to use videotapes of your performance. A videotape can give you immediate and accurate feedback about your responses—feedback that can be very useful in adjusting those responses. Videotape feedback is most useful in sports that provide little intrinsic information feedback, especially sports in which form is exceedingly important, such as gymnastics, horseback riding, archery, fencing, and slalom skiing.

An important question with respect to videotaping is whether external visual feedback can be translated into internal kinesthetic feedback.* Robb (1966) found that concurrent visual feedback (immediately after the behavior occurred) was the most effective kind of feedback in altering movement patterns. She also found that once a skill was established by means of visual feedback, it could be accurately judged and regulated through internal cues. DeBacy (1970) has also shown that viewing videotapes of one's behavior increases the accuracy of self-assessment when videotape replays are no longer provided.

Correct skill vs. correct execution   In evaluating your performance under game conditions, you must examine your behavior in highly specific terms. It is not sufficient simply to ask whether you are having a good or bad day. Instead, you must appraise your behavior in the different situations that occur during play. There are two questions that should be asked about each situation: (1) Was the correct skill attempted? (2) Was the skill performed correctly? When your performance goes awry, it may be that the skill was well executed but inappropriate for that situation. Or, you might have selected the right skill but executed it poorly. Unless you can answer these questions, you may attempt to change the wrong dimension of your behavior. You might have been waltzing beautifully, but the impact of your performance was diminished by the fact that the band was playing jazz.

Reinforcement on a Bad Day

A phenomenon known to all who participate in sports is the infamous bad day. Absolutely everything goes wrong and you become convinced that the gods are against you. It is this kind of day that can cause a person literally to give up on a sport. As mentioned earlier, your reflexes and coordination will be better some days than others. (Incidentally, both men and women seem to experience a time of the month when their coordination is diminished.) However, there are ways to find reinforcement even on the worst days. Contrary to what you might think, there is usually some aspect of your game that you are executing rather well. Capitalize on that skill—use it extensively enough to make the game interesting. In practically all sports, a sense of control is fundamental to enjoying the activity. When you can control the flight of the ball, you can have a wonderful time. By emphasizing a skill that you are executing fairly well, you can achieve some sense of control, even on bad days. For example, there are days when lob shots in tennis can keep an opponent from overpowering you. But there are other days when lob shots consistently fail to go over your opponent's head. That spells disaster. On those days, it is better to emphasize some other tactic (such as passing shots) in attempting to neutralize your opponent's net game. If all else fails, swearing is a possibility.

Summary of Reinforcement Consequences

Although some people make winning the primary reason for playing, we are opposed to this orientation. An emphasis on winning can prevent you from working on new skills (which initially have a high error rate) and can cause you to feel second-rate on the days you fail to win. Instead, seek your reinforcement from exercise and skill execution, sources of reinforcement that are available even when you are losing. When an attempted behavior goes awry, you should determine whether you used the appropriate skill and whether the skill was executed appropriately. Both intrinsic and external feedback can be used in evaluating skill execution.

Applying Self-Verbalization

There are few areas in which we have used self-verbalization more extensively than in sports. In learning new skills or attempting to re-establish old skills, we spend a lot of time talking to ourselves. Just before a behavior is to be executed, we say to ourselves, "Do this and that." It is imperative that your self-verbalization focus on process rather than product. Focusing on the product ("Get it over the net," "Hit it in the court") will cause you to anticipate the consequences of your actions, which often will cause you to lose sight of the immediate behavior to be executed. Self-verbalizations such as "Get in position," "Watch the ball," and "Swing through the ball" will focus your attention where it belongs. These verbalizations will also maximize the chances of the ball going over the net and into the court.

What we have just described is an operational procedure for concentrating. Lack of concentration is often posited as an explanation for elemental errors in athletic activity. But how does one learn to concentrate? We do not have the complete answer, but we believe that self-verbalization increases concentration. Verbally telling yourself to do something does increase the probability of doing it. The timing of this verbalization is of critical importance. Ideally, it should immediately precede the behavior to be emitted; otherwise, you may still forget to emit the behavior.

Earlier, we mentioned the bad day phenomenon. When your skills seem to be deteriorating, self-verbalization may reverse that trend. When things go badly, you have an increased tendency to anticipate the consequences of your behavior, thereby eroding concentration and making matters even worse. By self-verbalizing the behavior you are to emit, you can reclaim some portion of your skills. The behavior to which we return again and again in tennis is watching the ball, because that is the behavior that seems most fundamental to effective tennis and a behavior that we are least likely to emit when we begin making bad shots. Unless we deliberately direct ourselves to watch the ball, our anxiety about where the ball is going will completely negate ball-watching behavior.

Achieving Covert Control

The previous section suggested that concentration is a very elusive concept in sports. The concept of confidence is even more elusive. Whatever confidence is, it probably evolves primarily from success. We have described what we feel are the most appropriate norms for measuring progress, setting events that facilitate skill development, and procedures for reinforcing desired behaviors. Application of these strategies should contribute to the development of confidence. However, these strategies do not represent the whole story. As we construe the concept, confidence is a covert response which entails at least two dimensions: (1) absence of extreme muscular tension, and (2) belief that you can execute the skills required in the sport.

Unquestionably, extreme muscular tension adversely affects the performance of many sports skills. Muscular tension is most destructive to responses that require a high level of of muscle coordination, such as diving, executing a 360° wake turn on trick skis, hitting a tennis ball, and shooting a basketball. (Tension would not be quite so catastrophic to interior line-blocking in football.) The muscular relaxation exercises described in Chapter Seven could increase the quality of play in sports activities that demand a high level of muscle coordination. One might engage in those relaxation exercises just before going to play. If you could put muscle relaxation under the control of a single stimulus (e.g., the word relax), you could employ that strategy during play. Whenever you felt yourself tensing up, you could apply that stimulus immediately. By using these relaxation procedures, one of our students has not only allayed muscular tension but has also averted the ritual of regurgitation that he had frequently experienced just before important athletic events.

A second dimension of confidence is believing that you can execute the necessary skills. We wonder if Cautela's covert reinforcement concept is applicable to this belief. By visualizing (1) the execution of a certain skill and (2) favorable consequences resulting from that skill, you may enhance your ability to perform the skill. Modest support for this assertion is provided by Corbin (1967). He compared actual practice of a skill to mental practice and to no practice. Not surprisingly, actual practice produced more rapid acquisition than did the other conditions. However, mental practice was superior to no practice. Corbin also found that mental practice was most effective when it was preceded by actual practice. To visualize yourself accurately performing a task, you must have had some experience in executing that skill. Therefore, covert reinforcement is most useful as an adjunct to actual performance of skills. Covert reinforcement appears to be a systematic way to develop a positive approach to the correct execution of skills.

Your overall perception of yourself as an athlete can be enhanced through positive self-references. In sports, as in most spheres of life, we can focus too extensively on our negative attributes. There are undoubtedly many admirable features of your athletic participation (e.g., increasing the time that you can play without total exhaustion, executing new skills). By writing down these positive features and verbalizing them to yourself just before engaging in high probability behavior*you may enhance your perception of yourself as an athlete.

Concluding Comments

This chapter has identified some principles of sports participation that will facilitate your skill development and your enjoyment. Although we obviously have a strong bias toward tennis, our aim here is to prompt you to pursue regularly *some* type of physical activity, be it ballet or mountain climbing, in which you get vigorous exercise and enjoyment. Enjoyment is important because the reinforcement value of an activity will affect your tendency to engage in that activity and consequently the amount of exercise you get.

If sports activity is already an indispensable facet of your life, we encourage you to keep it that way. Vigorous physical activity should be a permanent aspect of living. However, if you are presently the paragon of inactivity, we hope this chapter will give you the impetus and technical expertise to begin an involvement with sports. We have seen many people at different ages discover a new life through physical exercise.

References

Barger, B. 1968. Some relationships of physical education to mental health. *Journal of School Health 38,* 65-68.

Buber, M. 1958. *I and thou,* 2d ed. New York: Charles Scribner's Sons.

Corbin, C. B. 1967. Effects of mental practice on skill development. *Research Quarterly 38,* 534-538.

DeBacy, D. 1970. Effect of viewing video tapes of a sport skill performed by self and others on self-assessment. *Research Quarterly 41,* 27-31.

Harris, D. V. 1972. Dimensions of physical activity. In *Women and sport: a national research conference*, ed. D. V. Harris, pp. 3-15. State College: Pennsylvania State University, College of Health, Physical Education and Recreation.

Hart, M. E., and Shay, C. T. 1964. Relationship between physical fitness and academic success. *Research Quarterly 35,* 443-445.

Ismail, A. H., and Trachtman, L. E. 1973. Jogging the imagination. *Psychology Today 6,* 78-82.

Kozar, A. J., and Hunsicker, P. 1963. A study of telemetered heart rate during sports participation of young adult men. *Journal of Sports Medicine and Physical Fitness 3* (1), 1-5.

Locke, L. F., and Jensen, M. 1971. Prepackaged sports skills instruction: a review of selected research. *Journal of Health Physical Education and Recreation 42,* 57-59.

Osborne, M. M., and Gordon, M. E. 1972. An investigation of the accuracy of ratings of a gross motor skill. *Research Quarterly 43* (1), 55-61.

Robb, M. 1966. Feedback. *Quest 6,* 38-43.

Rushall, B. S., and Siedentop, D. 1972. *The development and control of behavior in sport and physical education.* Philadelphia: Lea & Febiger.

Slusher, H. S. 1967. *Man, sport, and existence: a critical analysis.* Philadelphia: Lea & Febiger.

Warren, W. E. 1970. Physical education and happiness. *Physical Educator 27,* 19-21.

Weber, R. J. 1953. Relationships of physical fitness to success in college and to personality. *Research Quarterly 24,* 471-474.

Programmed Materials on Sports Skills

Adler, J. D. 1967. The use of programmed lessons in teaching a complex perceptual-motor skill. Eugene, Ore: Microcard Publications. No. PSY 341. (This study focuses on a five-iron golf shot.)

Bierscheid, R. L. 1969. A study of the effects of utilizing three methods of programmed instruction on selected motor skills in bowling and the knowledge of bowling etiquette and safety. Unpublished master's thesis, Temple University.

Carroll, H. A. 1969. A written program of self-instruction for learning the cartwheel in gymnastics. Unpublished master's thesis, Southern Illinois University at Carbondale.

Farrell, J. E. 1967. An application of programmed instruction to the perceptual-motor skill of tennis. Ann Arbor, Mich.: University Microfilms. No. 67-17756.

Feddeler, Caryle. 1965. Programmed circuit bowling. Unpublished master's thesis, Northern Illinois University.

Holt, V. R. 1970. A comparison of the effectiveness of a traditional instructional method and a programmed instructional method on the achievement of selected elementary golf skills. Unpublished doctoral dissertation, University of Tennessee.

Johnson, M. J. E. 1968. The effectiveness of programmed instruction in teaching basic gymnastics. Ann Arbor, Mich.: University Microfilms. No. 69-12145.

Latherland, B. A. 1969. The development of a written and audio self-instructional program for a selected folk dance. Unpublished master's thesis, Southern Illinois University at Carbondale.

Mell, S. A. 1966. The design, administration and evaluation of auto-instructional modern dance. Unpublished master's thesis, University of Tennessee.

Moore, B. J. 1968. The construction and evaluation of a written self-instruction program for teaching the jump shot. Unpublished master's thesis, Southern Illinois University at Carbondale.

Neuman, B. J. 1965. The effect of a self-instructional program of badminton rules on the knowledge and playing ability of beginning badminton players. Unpublished master's thesis, University of North Carolina at Greensboro.

Neuman, Jr., M. C. 1967. An investigation of two approaches to the learning of tennis skills. Unpublished master's thesis, Illinois State University.

Stutters, D. G. 1968. The influence of programmed instruction on the achievement of specific skills in a selected physical education activity. Ann Arbor, Mich.: University Microfilms. No. 69-04321.

Van Tassel, A. M. 1969. A written, self-instructional program for learning the lay-up shot in basketball. Unpublished master's thesis, Southern Illinois University at Carbondale.

Note: Many dissertations can be obtained from Xerox University Microfilms, Ann Arbor, Michigan 48106. The standard fee for a microfilmed copy of a dissertation is $4.00 for a Xeroxed copy $10.00, plus shipping and handling charges.

. . .Background music during biology lectures leads to higher achievement
in biology.

Some rather important problems are directly or indirectly attributable to lack of study, ineffective study skills, or both. Consider the number of occupational aspirations that go unfulfilled because the aspiring person never learned how to study. Consider the pernicious guilt feelings that accompany academic failure. The prospect of academic failure often undermines student enjoyment of college life. The Saturday afternoon football game (better still, the party afterwards) just cannot be as exhilarating when you are faced with several F's. The problems of study cut a broad swath across our lives. People who are willing to devote themselves to academic pursuits and who develop effective study behavior can avoid many troubles. Aside from avoiding trouble, people who overcome study problems can develop new skills, explore exciting material, manage their time, and best of all, control their own destiny.

Increasing Study Behavior

Some students are amazingly successful at study. They get all their work done on time, earn good grades, and epitomize scholarship. And then there are other students—those who have extreme difficulty in initiating and sustaining study activity. They have the best intentions, but everything seems to interfere with their acting on those intentions. Are such students less conscientious than their studious peers? It is not a question of integrity; their behaviors are merely under the control of different variables. The scholarly students have accidentally or purposely established conditions that facilitate study, while many of their peers have allowed other conditions to produce nonstudy behavior. If one is concerned enough to try, one can increase study behavior by rearranging those environmental conditions. The self-management model described in Chapter Two again provides a convenient format for identifying what environmental conditions should be altered.

Selecting a Goal

If studying is presently a miniscule or nonexistent portion of your life, your initial goal should be simply to increase the amount of time devoted to study. Although quantity of time is perhaps less important than the quality of study, a minimal amount of time is obviously essential. If you are presently spending zero minutes per day studying, you will want to be exceedingly cautious in defining your initial goal. Perhaps studying ten minutes per day would be a good starting point. To expect more than gradual change is to set yourself up for failure and disappointment. Many students fail to actualize their commitment to study more because they expect too much too soon. You have probably known students who made a firm resolution to start studying a specified number of hours per day only to discard the whole idea because it called for a dramatic change in their present behaviors. "To hell with it" sounds strangely familiar and is often the conclusive ending of grandiose expectations.

Recording Quantity and Circumstances of Behavior

Record-keeping is an especially significant step in altering the conditions affecting your study time. Those records should provide valuable information as to why you are having difficulty. Your records may indicate that you have difficulty trying to study at one time but not at another, or that certain locations facilitate study while others offer hindrances. Once you are more aware of the conditions that facilitate or hinder study, you should be in a better position to implement a program of change. Your records may also reveal that you are spending less, or perhaps more, time studying than you had realized. One of our students estimated that she was spending about fifteen hours a week studying. Her recording, however, showed that only four hours weekly were actually devoted to studying outside of class. She was really spending far more time thinking about studying than she was engaging in it. On the other hand, your records could indicate that many hours are being devoted to study with only poor grades to show for your efforts. This would suggest that a change in method of study is in order. A later section in this chapter will be devoted to developing effective study methods.

To obtain relevant data on your study behavior, you should keep a record of every instance that you initiate study, the time, place, and exactly how long you remain at the task. You might also record your emotional state when you begin. For example if a great deal of anxiety is associated with study, some type of covert control would be indicated. Finally, you should keep a continous record of your test scores and grades. One week of baseline data should give you an adequate fix on your present study habits. After collecting baseline data, you should be ready to implement a self-management strategy. Of course, you will continue keeping records throughout your treatment program. Your records during treatment should help you determine if you are spending more time studying, if you are less anxious, if you are improving your test scores, and so on. The length of treatment will depend upon the kind of results you obtain and how long it takes for study to become a habitual part of your daily routine.

Changing Setting Events

Once you have established your record-keeping system and have pinpointed the present level of your behavior, you are ready to begin a treatment program. The first thing to consider is ways of changing environmental events to increase the probability that you will indeed spend more time studying. Merely wanting to study may be insufficient; other events may negate your wants. It is highly unlikely that you can transcend events in the environment that control behavior. There are ways, however, that you can control these events so as to increase the probability of study.

All of your behavior, both study and nonstudy, occur in the presence of certain stimuli. Any of these stimuli can convey messages about what behaviors are likely to be or not to be immediately reinforced. For example, you might attempt to get in a few minutes of study at the student center. Before long a friend engages you in conversation, or an attractive person catches your eye. These stimuli trigger socializing, not study. For the nonstudier, socializing is almost always more immediately reinforcing than studying. If you try to study at a time usually allotted to tennis, you may find that you cannot get tennis off your mind. You relent and go to the court. If you try lying down to study, you may find that sleep or other more pleasant behavior occurs. You may unwittingly try to study while watching football on TV. Math probably cannot compete with professional sports. What happens is that the setting events (times and places) under which you attempt to study are associated with conflicting interests. You want to study but cannot. So you end up doing something else. To remedy this situation, you first can control the time and place of your study behavior. This could very well be the most potent strategy you use. It certainly represents the principal way of changing setting events to facilitate study behavior.

A time for all things   Part of the problem of achieving control over study behavior is in developing a definite time for study so that study behavior will eventually be triggered during that time span. Behaviors become closely associated with the time when they occur. You might say that we are creatures of habit. More precisely, you could say that certain stimuli exert strong influences over behavior. That is why you get irresistible urges to do things at particular times. We are suggesting, therefore, that you designate times especially for study. Once you have decided to study at a particular time, you are in a position to resist extraneous temptations. It would be great to be able to say, "I'm sorry, but I have to study at three. Could we make it four-thirty?"

You may not be excited about the possibility of scheduling your study time. Many people are not. People tend to question any type of regimentation to which they are not accustomed. If you have never kept a time schedule, you may fear that it would take the fun out of living or transform you into a robot. Let us discuss these reservations before getting into the details of time management.

Will a time schedule take the fun out of living? While some unplanned events turn out to be highly reinforcing, much unplanned time passes quite uneventfully. Have you ever caught yourself engaging in a terribly dull conversation? What about the time you spend just sitting around waiting for something to happen? Scheduling your time would probably uncover many neutral moments that could be put to better use. Students who schedule their study time report no lack of fun activities. The last thing we would suggest is that you divest your life of peak experiences.

Setting up a time schedule does not mean that you will be transformed into an automaton. *You* are the one who arranges the schedule. Consequently, you have the option of altering the schedule at your discretion. In essence, you are managing time to acquire more, not less, control. Who is master and who is servant when you have no plan of action?

If you have decided to schedule your study time, we have some suggestions to make. C. G. Wrenn was making similar suggestions as long ago as 1933. Then, as now, human behavior was subject to environmental controls; whether the suggestions worked for your progenitors and whether they will work for you depends on their use.

Begin by constructing a schedule covering your planned weekly activities. You could use a form similar to Figure 5-1. Your schedule first should include provisions for those fixed time intervals that cannot be changed. Sleeping, grooming, eating, class and laboratory

Figure 5-1   Activity Schedule

Time	Monday	Tuesday	Wednesday	Thursday	Friday	Saturday	Sunday
7:00							
8:00							
9:00							
10:00							
11:00							
12:00							
1:00							
2:00							
3:00							
4:00							
5:00							
6:00							
7:00							
8:00							
9:00							
10:00							
11:00							

time, and part-time jobs fall into this category. Be liberal when you allot time for essential behaviors. You may be surprised with the amount of time left for nonessentials. Next, allocate time for study. There is no hard rule as to how much time you should devote to study. That depends on how long you take to do assignments, the number of courses you are taking, length of assignments, and a host of other variables. Many college teachers feel that students should spend two hours in study for every hour of class time. We doubt that we have many students who consistently devote that much time to study. Our students report studying an average of only fifteen hours weekly. Other professors report even less study time for their students— about fifteen to thirty minutes a day. As a conservative rule of thumb, we recommend that you think in terms of devoting thirty to thirty-five hours weekly to academic pursuits (assuming you are taking a full load of courses). If you are in class for fifteen hours, allocate fifteen to twenty hours for study. (We cannot resist asking for a little more than we are getting.) Such a schedule would be similar to holding a full-time job. You would still have ample time for recreation.

We do not mean that you should go from zero to fifteen hours of study per week. Simply identify fifteen hours that could be devoted to study. You might schedule for an hour of study after each class, but begin by putting in only ten minutes. The logic of this strategy will be clarified under the next heading. For the time being, allot sufficient time for study without expecting an overnight transformation in your behavior. Finally, in planning your study time, consider when you study most efficiently. Some people prefer to study difficult material early in the day when they are freshest, saving routine tasks for last. Some prefer to study late when it is quiet—and then sleep late or take naps. Take your pick.

After you have allowed for study time, fill in the rest of your schedule with fun activities. If you finish your study early in the day, you can have your evenings free for recreation, exercise, transcendental meditation, or what have you. We also recommend that you allot most of your weekends to nonstudy activities. After all that conscientious study, you have earned it.

Scheduling really helps. Benjamin Franklin, Ralph Waldo Emerson, Plato, and William Shakespeare, to name a few, endorsed time management. Bill, Debra, Chuck, Jane, and Joyce (a few of our students) are also sold on the idea. Some of them discovered quite accidentally how beneficial a schedule can be. They undertook reading assignments for a blind student. He required that the reading be done on a regularly scheduled basis. The results: their highest grades were obtained in the classes where they were reading to the student on a time schedule. That attests to the efficacy of either time scheduling or oral reading—or maybe both.

A place for all things   The second way to use setting events in controlling your study behavior is to restrict the number of places where you study. Suppose you ordinarily attempt to study in a room where all sorts of other behaviors occur. You may find yourself sitting down to study but then tuning in to other possibilities. The stimuli of that room (e.g., lighting, sounds) may be more strongly associated with watching TV, drinking beer, or socializing than with studying. Those stimuli do not *cause* you not to study. They merely increase the probability that other behaviors will occur. You have the option to behave differently, but who is strong enough to overcome all kinds of temptations? It seems more logical for you to arrange the place where you study so that it is supportive of study behavior.

By associating a particular setting exclusively with study behavior, you can dramatically increase the probability of study when you are in that setting. A number of researchers (Beneke and Harris, 1972; Briggs et al., 1971; Fox, 1962) have demonstrated the utility of this approach. The typical procedure is for the student to leave his place of study whenever he begins to think of anything inconsistent with study; but before he leaves, he works one problem, reads one page, or completes a small portion of his assignment. The next time the student sits down to study, he might work two problems, read two pages, or complete a larger segment of his assignment after getting the impulse to stop studying. The strategy is to increase gradually the amount of studying by following *some* study with reinforcement (leaving the area to engage in another activity). Figure 5-2 shows the results of this approach for one group of students.

If you are going to use this tactic, you should keep your desk free of distracting materials (e.g., pictures of a girl friend or boy friend, *Playboy, Playgirl*); you should keep the room free of extraneous sights and sounds. Such stimuli frequently elicit behaviors that are incompatible with study activity. Fantasizing about your boy friend or girl friend, as pleasant as that may be, is incompatible with studying. Save those thoughts for your study breaks. What produces incompatible behavior varies somewhat from student to student. For example, some students say they can study better with background music

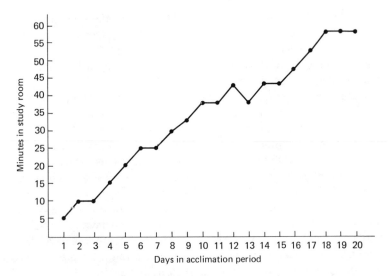

Figure 5-2 An experimental group's mean average of time spent in a study room per class per day for a twenty-day acclimation period. (Briggs, Tosi, and Morley, 1971.)

playing. The research evidence is divided on this point. Konz (1962) found that background music facilitates the performance of manual assembly tasks. Schlichting and Brown (1970) have shown that background music during biology lectures leads to higher achievement in biology. In contrast, Freeburne and Fleischer (1952) reported that music had no effect on students' comprehension of Russian history. Kirkpatrick (1943) has shown that music interferes with work that requires a high level of concentration (e.g., problem-solving activity). Apparently, the effect of music varies not only from person to person but also from task to task. If music makes your study environment more reinforcing and enhances your productivity, flood yourself with it. But be sure you are not fooling yourself. Empirically appraising the effects of background music on different types of study behavior might make an excellent addition to your self-management project.

Establishing Effective Consequences

Altering setting events is a good starting place for changing study behavior. You must not stop there, however. To encourage your efforts and to maintain any behavior changes, you need to establish effective consequences for your actions. You are unlikely to continue engaging in a behavior without a good reason for doing so. You may be thinking that getting a passing grade or remaining in college are awfully good reasons for studying; they are. The trouble is that many people do not consider these ultimate consequences until it is too late. But if the thoughts of passing grades and remaining in school are meaningful enough to get you to study today, not just at the last minute, then perhaps you will want to develop a plan for systematically evoking such thoughts. You could include such a plan under covert processes.

Perhaps the most effective way to reinforce studying is to follow it with an immediate positive consequence. You may previously have engaged in little study behavior because you never derived any immediate reinforcement from it. The events that have competed so successfully with study have probably had reinforcement naturally associated with them. What you will have to do is deliberately associate reinforcement with study. If an activity is associated with something pleasant, you are more likely to engage in that activity. This is undoubtedly a major way to develop an affinity for study. Enjoyment of study does not emerge magically. It is based on the number and types of reinforcers one receives from studying.

While study activities may never become the *most* reinforcing activities in your life, there are a number of ways you can increase the probability of study. When you read one page and then leave a study area to engage in a more preferred activity, you have applied reinforcement for study. This sequence of events demonstrates the Premack principle* (Premack, 1959). Simply stated, the principle suggests that a high probability behavior* (e.g., socializing) can be used to reinforce a less probable behavior (e.g., studying). The principle helps you to arrange the sequence of activities to obtain desired changes in behavior. In short, first work, then play. Part of your study problems in the past may have been due to the wrong sequence of events. You may have had fun first and then tried to study, which can be a letdown. By studying first you have something to look forward to. One of our groggy-eyed students found this principle particularly helpful. He reported that drinking wine and beer was interfering with his study. His solution was to reward study with drink. As a result of

*Defined in Glossary

his project, he halved the time it usually took him to complete reading assignments. (Our next project is to cut his drinking in half.)

Do not assume that the Premack principle is the only way to reinforce studying. Once you have firmly established your study behavior, you may wish to delay reinforcement for longer periods of time. You need not jump up immediately and engage in a more preferred activity. You could establish a point system to be used in bridging the gap between study and subsequent reinforcement. If there are items you have been wanting to purchase but have not felt that you quite deserved them, why not make those items contingent on a certain amount of study time? With a precise record-keeping system, you could reward yourself with a specified number of points for a specified amount of studying. Be sure to identify in advance how many points will be required to make your purchases.

One last word about reinforcing study behaviors. Study behavior is not a one-dimensional concept. A later section will describe several different facets of effective study behaviors. A point system for reinforcing study behavior should entail credit for each of these components of effective study. There are also some prerequisite behaviors without which studying will not occur. These include getting into the appropriate setting (such as going to the library), taking the necessary materials, and getting out the necessary materials once you are in the appropriate setting. Each of these prerequisite behaviors should carry token credit toward the final payoff that makes the whole system functional. (One student at the University of Tennessee was thrown out of the library for bouncing his basketball. We thought he should have been given at least one token, since that was the first time he had ever been to the library.)

Focusing on Contingencies

Now that you have established specific consequences for your behaviors, you need to consider ways of becoming more aware of those behaviors and their consequences. To begin with, you might record your assignments in a notebook and post these assignments in conspicuous places. How many times have you forgotten an assignment or failed to include everything in the assignment that your professor requested? Besides recording and posting your assignments, you might wish to post your time schedule and other record sheets in places where you are bound to notice them. You might even attach them to the TV screen or place them on the cover of your most frequently used notebook. What you are after is anything to remind you of your commitment to study.

Another strategy for sensitizing yourself to study behavior is to spend some time discussing your courses with others. For example, you could schedule time to talk with your professors about course-related matters. That should certainly help to keep studying on your mind. You might also try participating in class discussions. This behavior usually causes people to do more thinking about a course before and after class sessions. In addition, you might consider associating with a few students who devote considerable time to study. Maybe you could work with such people on projects or even associate with them on a social basis. Interacting socially with studious peers should make you more conscious of your own needs to study.

Achieving Covert Control

Probably no area of human behavior is more susceptible to mood swings than is study behavior. You may find that you can use positive thoughts and feelings to enhance study activities, but you may also find that anxiety—over exams, your future in academe, or study in general—will have to be lessened in order for you to engage effectively in academic pursuits. Consequently, you may want to consider including covert processes in your study program.

Covert positive reinforcement might prove an extremely effective way of increasing study behavior. Several of our students have devised self-management projects in which they used this strategy. They reported that just thinking about such events as receiving a good grade or an approving comment from a friend or professor made them feel more positive about study. You may find that positive thoughts can be used to reinforce actual study activity. You could put in a few minutes of study and then reinforce yourself by thinking of that certain person.

Another covert strategy that might increase study behavior is Homme's coverant pairs. You could use negative-positive pairs and then engage in high probability behavior to increase study. One of our students tried emitting a study-related coverant pair every time he went to sleep (a high probability behavior). He avows that he is now spending a considerable amount of time studying on the bed because lying down evokes thoughts of study. (He may never sleep again!) You might think of a situation in which you could use a coverant pair to increase your studying.

If you face anxiety whenever you think about study, or if high anxiety is a problem during exams, you may want to include some relaxation exercises in your self-management plans. Not that you should remove every trace of anxiety; mild tension may provide an impetus to study. But you probably know from first-hand experience that high anxiety can be very detrimental to study behavior. Some students occasionally become so anxious about a course that they avoid all association with the course, the course assignments, and the professor. Muscular relaxation exercises may allow you to engage in study behavior and improve your test performances. Jones (1969) has described in detail a system of relaxation and desensitization that can be used to reduce anxiety toward academics. Essentially, his program involves training in relaxation and movement through an anxiety hierarchy. (These concepts will be presented in Chapter Seven.) Muscular relaxation will not replace test preparation, but it will help you to make good use of that preparation.

A Self-Management Survey

If you are still undecided about the need for establishing control over your study behavior, the following survey may help you reach a decision. The more statements you agree with, the greater the likelihood that a self-management project is in order.

_____ I seldom set definite goals as to how much study I should do.

_____ I have never tried to keep a time schedule for the purpose of regulating study.

_____ I frequently put off studying until it is too late to get my assignments completed on time.

_____ When I do try to study on a regular basis, something usually comes up to interfere with study.

_____ I probably devote less than ten hours per week to study.

_____ Ten or fifteen minutes is about as long as I can concentrate without getting restless.

_____ My place of study sometimes gets cluttered with popular magazines and other material that could distract from study.

_____ Bull sessions frequently occur in the locale where I study.

_____ Daydreams keep interfering with my studies.

_____ I have never consciously tried to reinforce any of my study behaviors.

_____ Although I have good intentions, I periodically forget to do assignments.

_____ I frequently feel anxious about a class, study, or an exam.

_____ I almost have to force myself to study.

Increasing Reading Comprehension

Some students' problems end once they develop procedures for increasing study time. They know how to study once they actually begin. If you are such a student, perhaps you need read no further. For others the problem is not simply one of study time but rather how to study properly. Students who read for hours and cannot tell you what they have read, who memorize meaningless trivia, who cannot understand their notes, who end up underlining every other word in their books—these people are the victims of inefficient study habits. Efficient study means that you are utilizing the quickest and easiest methods of learning. Anything else is a waste of time.

To a great extent, success in any venture is a matter of determining what works for you and then systematically applying that procedure. To assist you, we offer *one* systematic approach for reading and studying books that follow an outlined, organized sequence. Since reading assignments constitute a major portion of your college work, becoming an effective reader is fundamental to success in college. Compare your present strategies with those on the following pages. Perhaps you will pinpoint a weakness in those strategies or confirm their strengths.

The best known and probably the most widely tested strategy for improving reading study skills is Robinson's (1970) SQ3R method. Survey, question, read, recite, and review are abbreviated in the SQ3R title to make it easier to remember. Each step is briefly described below.[1]

[1]"The SQ3R Method of Studying" in *Effective Study*, Fourth Edition by Francis P. Robinson. Copyright © 1970 by Francis P. Robinson. By permission of Harper & Row, Publishers, Inc.

S (Survey)

The first step in the SQ3R method is the survey. This step involves an examination of a chapter's headings and subheadings in order to get a general outline of the material to be studied. In this text, primary headings, in boldface, represent the major ideas we wish to cover. The secondary headings, in text type, represent subordinate parts of the major idea. For example, our primary heading, *Increasing Study Behavior*, is a major idea. The secondary headings, *Selecting a Goal*, *Recording Quantity and Circumstances of Behavior*, *Changing Setting Events*, *Establishing Effective Consequences*, *Focusing on Contingencies*, and *Achieving Covert Control*, constitute subordinate parts. From the secondary headings, you immediately get a rough idea of what is involved in controlling study time. If you further examine the subheadings of *Changing Setting Events*, you will determine that that concept involves the time and place of study. Surveying can also be enhanced by reading an occasional topic sentence. Topic sentences, as you know, contain major ideas and are usually found at the beginning or end of paragraphs. In addition, summary statements at the end of sections should be examined in your initial survey of material.

The primary value of the survey appears to lie in increased comprehension. By knowing in advance what you are to study, you can attend directly to the task of learning the material. You do not waste unnecessary time trying to figure out how material fits together. Surveying may also eliminate some of your reading. By looking at the headings, you may determine that you already know what is in a section. You do not have to read three or four paragraphs to determine that you need not study that section. Perhaps you already take note of headings. Quick check: what is the subheading of this section?

Q (Question)

The second step calls for the creation of questions from section headings. You can begin the questioning process by turning the first heading into a question. In formulating questions you can use the familiar who, what, when, where, why, and how strategy of newspaper reporters. You might also check the end of the chapter to see if the author has provided questions for you. You might decide to use the author's questions as a guide for structuring your own questions. You could also try posing the kind of questions that your professor typically asks in class.

Raising questions can provide you with an immediate purpose for your reading, can assist you in preparing for class discussions and exams, and might provide enough personal challenge to make study more interesting. When you raise questions to yourself, you become an active participant in the learning process; no longer are you a passive reader who trudges through an assignment. What are some questions you might pose regarding the next section on reading? One possible question would be, "How does one read for comprehension?"

R_1 (Read)

Having formulated a question on a section, you are prepared to begin your quest for an answer. Some students feel that they have actually studied when they passively read every word in an assignment. However, everyone has had the experience of reading page after page without the slightest idea of what was just read. Words acquire meaning when you read them with a purpose, when you are no longer a caller of words or a reader of lines. Your purpose is to get an answer. In fulfilling that purpose, you need not get bogged down with every *a, an,* and *the* on the page. Effective reading means that you are listening for an answer. When you hear that answer, you are prepared for the next step. This is what we mean by reading for comprehension. Robinson's strategy is obviously a much more active approach to reading than students typically take.

R_2 (Recite)

After you have read the first section, pause for a moment to recite the answer to your question. (What was the answer to our question on the preceding section?) You should close your book or at least look away from it while you formulate your answer. Being able to make your own response will insure that you comprehend the material. One useful means of conducting the recitation is to write down your answer from memory in very brief note form. Do not try to reproduce the text. That would undoubtedly make the process aversive. If you dislike note taking, you could incorporate underlining into the process. To accomplish recitation through underlining, you would first think of your response and then look for key phrases that correspond to your recitation. Do not underline until you have read the entire section and actually know what are important answers to your questions. Even then, Robinson suggests that you use a coding system to indicate the order of importance of various points. For example, in our underlining system we divide material into three categories. Material of some importance merits an underline, that of greater importance brackets, and that of greatest importance brackets plus an asterisk in the margin. Just considering how to code a point will probably help you remember it.

Having completed your recitation for the first section, you are prepared to continue with additional sections. Move to the next heading: question, read, and recite. Continue this procedure until you have completed the entire assignment. Although recitation may take as much time as reading, you will not regret the expenditure of that time. Spending time in recitation will probably make a far greater difference in your examination scores than spending the same amount of time in reading alone.

Self-recitation offers several important benefits, among them increased retention of material. Recitation can also enhance the clarity of your expressions. Have you ever thought that you had an idea clearly in mind until you started to express yourself and wound up saying, "Oh, you know what I mean"? In casual conversation others may smile and nod understandingly to your "you see" and "you know" statements. Professors are a different breed, however. They neither see nor know, especially when it comes to exam answers. You must make yourself clear. Recitation will help. Students who do not use this method sometimes wear themselves out reading and rereading and still experience difficulty on exams when they are reciting for the first time.

R₃ (Review)

When you complete your assignment, conduct a brief review of all the material. A review of most chapters should not take more than a few minutes. You do not have to reread. You have your notes or your underlinings to go by. If you have made brief notes, look over them and then try to recall as many of the major points as possible. This will help you establish the relationship between the parts of a chapter. Next, recite the details under each major point. If you used the underlining approach, begin your review by looking over your underlinings and then proceed to recite answers to your questions.

Very good reasons exist for this early review. A rapid decline in retention of material occurs immediately following study. An immediate review can substantially reduce this information loss. Retention can further be aided by periodic follow-up reviews. You can determine the necessity for a review by judging how well you recite answers. A fifteen-minute review for three consecutive days might be all that is required for you to remember large blocks of information for an entire term. In general, it is far better to have several short review sessions than a few lengthy sessions. A well-known fact of psychology is that distributed practice facilitates retention more than massed (lengthy) practice.

Summary

Robinson's SQ3R is a well-established method for increasing reading and study skills. It can be adapted for all your reading, but the method described here is most applicable to texts that utilize an outlined, organized sequence. Texts in the social sciences, business, and applied arts, for example, usually follow such a pattern. Novels, poetry, and some of your other reading assignments may not. If you have a particular interest in adapting the SQ3R strategy for any or all of your reading, you are directed to Robinson's definitive text, *Effective Study* (1970). Before you decide on a method for your reading assignments, you may have to analyze the purpose for your reading (e.g., whether you are reading for a major idea, details, style), how the material differs from traditional assignments, and how you will be held accountable. In using a systematic approach such as SQ3R, be sure to reinforce your application of the various components of the approach. If you are using a point system, for example, allocate points (reinforce yourself) for "recitation" and "review" as well as "time" and "pages read."

A Self-Management Project

Now that you have explored procedures for controlling study time and have analyzed a systematic approach to reading, you might combine the two into a self-management project. Such a project would be appropriate if you have experienced difficulty in getting yourself to study and have had poor results (e.g., grades) when you did study. While putting in some time is essential, how you use that time is also important. Let us run through the Williams-Long self-management model, reviewing briefly the procedures for increasing study time and examining how Robinson's SQ3R method might be used to enhance study efficiency. You might be interested in knowing that several researchers (e.g., Fox, 1962; Beneke and Harris, 1972; Briggs et al., 1971) have successfully combined efforts to increase study time with the SQ3R method.

1. *Selecting your goal:* How much time are you now spending on your studying? What would be a reasonable increase over your present level? Can you visualize how to utilize the SQ3R method while gradually increasing your study time? *Hint:* If you get the urge to stop studying after only ten minutes, try completing the SQ3R for one section. You already would have surveyed the material, so you would only need to question, read, recite, and review before leaving the study area.

2. *Recording the quantity and circumstances of behavior:* Are you recording the time, place, and mood of your study efforts? Could you also record how frequently you have used the SQ3R method? Are you actually surveying before you begin an assignment? Are you using the questioning technique? Are you using the SQ3R method to periodically review materials before exams? Do you plan to maintain graphs of your progress?

3. *Changing setting events:* Do you see the need for changing your present time or place of study? Is changing your method of study (e.g., adopting the SQ3R method) essentially a change in setting events? For example, is your present system of underlining effective? If you have every other word underlined, it surely is not.

4. *Establishing effective consequences:* Do you plan to use the Premack principle or a point system for reinforcing study behaviors? Remember that each component of study (e.g., preparing to study, getting out materials, keeping records, changing setting events, applying the steps in the SQ3R method) needs to be reinforced if you are to establish a smooth and enjoyable process. What eventually looks like one behavior (i.e., studying) is really a chain of many behaviors established through the controls you provide.

5. *Focusing on contingencies:* Have you thought about recording assignments, posting assignments and record sheets, talking with professors, participating in class, and interacting with studious peers? Anything to remind you of what you want to do (study) could be included under this section.

6. *Achieving covert control:* Do you plan to use covert positive reinforcement, coverant pairs, desensitization, or other covert

strategies to help you get down to the business of study and to help you function more effectively when you devote yourself to study?

Completing Major Projects

Some students have no problem with reading assignments or other work assigned on a regularly scheduled basis; they experience difficulty only when confronted with a major task, such as completing a term paper. They delay until the time is past for doing an adequate job. This problem gets to the heart of self-management. Students who can complete day-to-day assignments may be able to do so only because other people have laid out their work and are providing immediate consequences (class discussion, tests) to help control the study behavior. On the other hand, the student who is given an assignment to be completed by the end of a term does not have those immediate, externally imposed consequences. There is no sphere of academia that makes greater demands on your self-management capabilities than the infamous term project. If you procrastinate over term projects, that could be the area of study where a self-management approach might prove most helpful.

Pigeons Show the Way

B. F. Skinner's early work with pigeons illustrates how organisms learn to tackle major tasks. Skinner found that pigeons can be trained to peck a disc as many as 10,000 times for a food reinforcer. (That sounds almost as formidable as writing a term paper.) This feat was accomplished by breaking the task into component parts and then gradually increasing the requirement for reinforcement. For example, a pigeon would initially be rewarded for moving slightly in the direction of the disc, then for closer proximity to the disc, and finally for pecking the disc. Eventually, the number of pecks required for reward would be increased. Without such training, any pigeon would surely starve to death before emitting the desired number of behaviors.

Surprisingly enough, humans respond to work in much the same way as pigeons. Students may be overwhelmed by term papers unless their behavior is also properly programmed. Unlike the pigeon, however, students can break their tasks down and can provide their own consequences. Eventually, by requiring more of themselves, students can face major tasks with a minimum of discomfort. Students thus do for themselves on long-term tasks what their professors may have been arranging on short-term assignments—small parts and immediate consequences.

Breaking Down the Task

The instructor announces that a thirty-page term paper is due in one month. You barely avert an anxiety attack, your hands get clammy, and finally you shake your head in self-pity. How can you possibly write a thirty-page term paper with the plethora of other tasks you have pending? As long as you think in terms of the *total* project, you probably will be immobilized. Only the severest of anxiety attacks (a day or two before the paper is due) will get you to the library. In absolute agony, foregoing sleep for forty-eight hours, you will frantically piece something together. Can there be any question that this is *not* the most reinforcing way to do a term project?

A first step in doing a term project is to break the task down into smaller parts. For example, writing a term paper might involve (1) selecting a topic, (2) finding related materials, (3) taking notes on relevant materials, (4) formulating questions to be answered in the paper, (5) producing a tentative outline of the paper, (6) writing a rough draft for each section of the paper, (7) reorganizing the paper, and (8) preparing the finished draft for each section of the paper. Obviously, each of the subunits can be divided into smaller segments of work. Keep subdividing until you reach an amount that does not intimidate you. Some might think in terms of what could be accomplished in a week, others may be discouraged by the prospect of any task that requires more than thirty minutes. Once you have divided your work into subunits, give your undivided attention to subunit one. You will find this approach far more palatable than constantly reflecting on the total magnitude of the project. The latter would probably produce more brooding than working.

Formulating a Time Schedule

You know that the paper must be turned in by October 30, but what about those subunits of work? Formulate a tentative schedule as to when each subunit is to be completed. The schedule should require early completion of the first subunit (that gets you started on the project) and should specify a final completion date slightly before October 30 (this will give you some breathing room at the end and allow time for resolving unexpected problems). After defining your schedule, focus on one deadline at a time. Instead of saying, "I have a term paper due October 30," you now say, "I need to identify a topic by October 3."

In fact, most people do not work in such a highly organized fashion. Many students write term papers in the fashion we described initially. We have done a few like that ourselves. But we have found that a more reinforcing and productive way to complete long-term projects is to define subunits of work, make out an overall time schedule, and then tackle one task at a time. In writing this text, for example, we thought first about the theme of the book, next about the kind of chapters we wanted to include, and then about the overall organization of the book. Then we made a commitment to our publisher as to when each chapter of the book would be submitted. Consequently, we were not faced with writing an entire book—we were faced with one chapter at a time. This strategy resulted in our writing the book during a six-month period, as we had originally planned. Nothing is more paralyzing than being bombarded by eighty-eight different tasks simultaneously. Manage task one first, and the remaining eighty-seven will be just as manageable.

Reinforcing Productive Behavior

The impetus for attacking subsequent parts of a project is partially a function of completing earlier parts. Completing that first bit of work is especially reinforcing; it makes part two appear considerably less foreboding. The reinforcing effects that accrue from completing different segments of a project are probably cumulative in nature; that is, each subsequent part becomes easier to work on. You can see why it is important to divide a project into many subunits. That arrangement not only increases your frequency of positive reinforcement but also makes it easier to initiate and sustain work on a project.

Because of your reinforcement history, you may not find completing units of work intrinsically reinforcing. In that case you may wish to devise a system of external payoffs for productive behavior. Such events as getting a drink of water, reading the newspaper, and even changing work settings can serve as short-term reinforcers for completing a specified amount of work. We have found that simply moving to the other side of the library reinforces completion of work as well as providing a refreshing setting for additional work.

Beyond the natural reinforcers mentioned in the previous paragraph, you may want to establish a point system in which each of the subunits is worth a certain amount of credit toward tangible items or weekend privileges. A privilege or item that has been earned becomes doubly reinforcing. When we make purchases or partake of privileges without earning them, we sometimes experience ambivalence; "Should I have spent that much money on that item?" "Do I really need that?" "Can I spare the time?" But when we have established our reinforcement contingencies, we seldom experience that ambivalence. In fact, we feel obligated to make good on our reinforcement commitments.

In case you distrust your ability to administer self-imposed reinforcement contingencies, you might consider a strategy proposed by Nurnberger and Zimmerman (1970). They reported on a Ph.D. candidate who completed his doctoral thesis by committing himself to a series of small, attainable goals. He had successfully finished all his degree requirements except for a thesis. He took a teaching position and for two years did not write a single page of the thesis. He reported feelings of inadequacy, extreme sensitivity towards his colleagues, irritability, and insomnia. After undergoing fourteen, ninety-minute sessions of psychotherapy to help him gain insight into his problem, he showed little behavior change with his multiple problems. He wrote nothing on his thesis. Finally, he and a therapist worked out a writing program with consequences to control the writing. The initial plan required that he submit three pages at the end of the first week. After completing a previously planned two-week vacation (not part of the program), he was to submit four additional pages after the fourth week. After the eighth, thirteenth, and seventeenth weeks, he was to submit twenty-six, fifty-five, and fifty-three pages, respectively. He had given his therapist five $100 postdated checks, one to be forfeited for each failure to meet a deadline.

He met the first three deadlines, but asked for a revised program before the fifty-five-page deadline was due. His writing had stopped. Consequently, the initial program was revised on the eleventh week to provide for daily and weekly deadlines. He wrote three $25 postdated checks to be forfeited one at a time for failure to meet deadlines. On the fourteenth week of the program, he moved back to a weekly program and this time made forfeitable checks payable to organizations that were highly aversive to him. The organizations were the Ku Klux Klan, the American Nazi Party, and the John Birch Society. He wanted to be certain that forfeiting the checks was avoided.

Figure 5-3 shows the individual's writing progress. A follow-up showed that he received his Ph.D. He accepted a highly responsible administrative position, relationships with his family improved, and his other problems subsided. To our knowledge he never had to give up a penalty check. You could utilize the strategies employed by Nurnberger and Zimmerman by enlisting the services of a friend who has the same problem you have. Why not agree to administer the contingencies to each other?

Choosing a Topic

Because choosing a topic represents the first hurdle in doing a term project, we will devote special attention to that task. Actually, selecting a topic may be the most confusing part of a term project. One of our students experienced near-panic in the library one day. He was in the process of trying to identify a topic for a term project when the realization that he was making absolutely no progress seemed almost overwhelming. We doubt that his experience is unique. Student anxiety is often exceedingly high during this period. You know you should be doing something, but you are not sure what. You go to the library, walk through the stacks, thumb through a few randomly selected

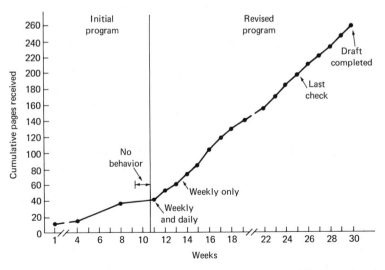

Figure 5-3 Cumulative pages of thesis copy successfully completed. (Nurnberger and Zimmerman, 1970.)

books, and gain nothing for your efforts but bad feelings and a throbbing headache.

Trouble begins when students try to identify the most profound, far-reaching theme ever contemplated. Students often begin with aspirations of writing papers that will provide the ultimate cure for mental illness, revolutionize education, or whatever. As yet, no student has identified such a theme. The most profound human creations usually result from several years of relatively mundane and inauspicious work. You will save yourself a great deal of time and frustration by *not* looking for a topic that no other mortal has dared to think about.

While you will not be able to generate the totally unique, infinitely erudite topic, you should search for a theme that interests you. That will make doing the project more reinforcing, and it will give you a place to begin searching for a topic. Here are starting points we have suggested to students attempting to identify topics in the field of psychology: (1) Population: Is there a particular group of persons, e.g., retarded, brain-damaged, gifted, infants, that you are especially interested in? (2) Behavior: Is there a specific kind of behavior, e.g., disruptive activity in the classroom, autistic responses, isolate behavior, covert activity, that you want to study? (3) Model: Is there a certain orientation, such as behavior therapy, psychoanalysis, nondirective therapy, or gestalt therapy, that has excited you? (4) Technique or concept: Within your favorite system, is there a technique or concept that offers special intrigue? A student turned on to self-management (like you, for example) may find Cautela's concept of covert reinforcement unusually stimulating. (5) Theoretical proposition: Is there some aspect of a given theoretical orientation that you think needs testing? If no aspect of your favorite theory can be reduced to a testable hypothesis, perhaps you should consider another theory. You can probably think of additional reference points for getting an initial focus on a topic. (If so, drop us a note and we will include them in the next edition of this text, giving you proper credit, of course.)

If you can respond to only one of these considerations, at least you have a place to begin. If you can respond to a number of them, your topic will practically identify itself. For example, you may determine that your special population is the retarded, that you are particularly concerned about cooperative behavior, that you are interested in behavior modification, and that you are especially intrigued with the concept of token reinforcement. How does "The Effect of Token Reinforcement on the Cooperative Behavior of Mentally Retarded Children" sound to you? If you go to the library with this general topic in mind, you will undoubtedly accomplish far more than if you go expecting a topic to jump out of the stacks and seize you. Actually, this topic is probably too broad for most term projects. What age retarded children do you want to study? What type of cooperative behavior do you plan to focus upon? What kind of token reinforcement do you have in mind? Answering these specific kinds of questions can sharpen dramatically the task of doing a literature review and/or defining an experimental design.

Self-Management Project

If you presently accomplish your work with impeccable efficiency, skip to the next section. However, if you are one of those last minute students, consider the following suggestion. If this is a typical quarter or semester, you probably have more than one long-term project to do. Identify two projects that appear to be of equal magnitude and palatability. Do one project in the usual way. (Just stock up on your supply of coffee, ice water, and cigarettes for the last minute rush.) Do the other project according to the Williams-Long format. See which project proves to be more reinforcing and/or yields the better grade.

Becoming More Creative

Creativity is a concept that is extremely difficult to explain from a self-management perspective. The difficulty begins with our inability to define exactly what creativity is. The principal criterion appears to be novelty or originality. Therefore, one cannot define in advance what a creative accomplishment will look like. So it is very difficult to know what behaviors to monitor and how to arrange setting events and reinforcement contingencies to produce the unknown behaviors.

Another difficulty relates to the matter of external contingencies. Our social environment often supports the behaviors we attempt to produce by means of self-management. Turning in our work on time, losing twenty pounds of weight, and eliminating nervous tics would usually be reinforced by others. This pattern does not hold true for creative responses. Instead, society usually reinforces conforming behaviors. This is unfortunate because external contingencies can be be very facilitative of novel behavior (Goetz and Baer, 1971; Goetz and Salmonson, 1972). However, since external contingencies generally do not support creative responses, it is exceedingly difficult to achieve that mode of behavior through self-management.

In discussing the relationship between self-management and creativity, we must also accept the relative nature of creativity. You may consider an accomplishment to be creative (and it truly may be for you), but someone else may see it as commonplace (and it truly may be for that person). Since we are examining creativity primarily in an academic context, we must consider your instructor's perception of originality. And that is a domain where we cannot offer too many assurances. But if you can produce a piece of work that you consider creative, it seems more likely that your instructor will also perceive some originality in that work.

Responses Associated with Creative Accomplishments

It was previously recommended that students formulate questions about material that they are about to read. A similar strategy is suggested for writing. The originality of your work is related to the kinds of questions you are attempting to answer. A question that requires a direct factual response allows for a minimum of creativity, while a question that calls for a statement of opinion permits a high degree of originality. How original can you be in answering a question such as, "What is the present population of the United States?" But if you ask, "What effect will population control have on race relations in this society?" you have far greater potential for originality. Asking questions that do not have one correct answer or that require you to relate seemingly incongruous concepts (e.g., how can external incentives be used to foster self-direction?) will allow you to actualize more of your creative potential.

In formulating responses to your provocative questions, you may be inclined to go to the "authorities" for an answer. That could be a mistake. If you initially depend on what others have to say, you may have difficulty transcending their thinking. The better strategy is to formulate your own responses to a question and then appeal to the authorities. This prevents their enlightenment from blinding you to your own ideas.

In jotting down our initial responses to a question, we find it most helpful to do some brainstorming. We put down all ideas that come to mind and defer evaluating them until later. Nothing is more paralyzing than trying to formulate only *good* ideas. That is the kind of strategy that will keep you staring at a piece of paper for thirty minutes without recording a single word. Go the brainstorming route. Research (Meadow and Parnes, 1959) supports its value in generating more ideas and higher-quality ideas.

Setting Events for Creativity

While it is rather difficult to make creative responding occur on cue, certain times and settings may be correlated with original activity. This is a domain in which self-management is very idiosyncratic. No one can say what those times and settings should be for you, but you can keep a log as to when and where you do your most original work. We find a quiet setting early in the morning most conducive to new ideas. Your most auspicious setting events may be entirely different. In any case, you should monitor your behavior closely enough to be aware of relationships between times, places, and your creative accomplishments.

There may be instructional input that can enhance one's ability to think creatively. Parnes (1967) has developed a set of programmed materials that present problem situations to which a number of different responses could be made. A key element in his approach is teaching people to define problem situations in more accurate terms. We are frequently unable to resolve problem situations because we misdefine the problem. In contrast to more conventional programmed materials, Parnes' program allows for a number of different responses to the same frame. The student is given feedback in terms of possible responses to that frame but is informed that his response may be superior to any of the suggested responses.

Reinforcing Creative Behavior

Since others are frequently threatened by unusual responses (and therefore will not reinforce them), much of the reinforcement for these behaviors must come from you. Learning to respect your own ideas is a fundamental requisite to creativity. We take the view that every person's ideas are worthy of consideration. It is legitimate to pat yourself on the back any time you express your ideas. If those pats on the back are not sufficiently potent, you will need to reward expression of ideas in a more systematic, tangible fashion. You might allow yourself to partake of an attractive privilege only after you have expressed a specified number of ideas.

Despite the pessimism expressed earlier, support from others for creative accomplishments is not entirely out of the question. Chapter

Eight suggests a correlation between approval given and approval received. If you approve others for expressing unusual ideas, they will be more inclined to support your unique responses. In other words, external support for novel behavior is to some degree a matter of reciprocal reinforcement.

Self-Management Projects

Why not put to a test some of the ideas presented in our discussion of creativity? On the other hand, you may have more original propositions to pursue.

1. In defining a list of questions to be considered in a specified term project, make sure that at least 75 percent of those questions call for an opinion response. Formulate a procedure for evaluating the impact of this strategy, e.g., grade on this project as opposed to grades on other projects, completion time for this project compared to completion time for other projects.
2. Each time you have what you consider to be a highly original thought, note the time and place. See if you can establish some kind of pattern in setting events for your creative behavior.
3. Identify a friend who tends to think very conventionally. Every time your friend expresses an idea that deviates even slightly from the norm, comment on the uniqueness of that idea and indicate that it is an idea worthy of much consideration. Systematically evaluate (you remember the baseline and treatment procedure) the effect of your strategy on the number of nonnormative ideas your friend expresses and the number of times he/she approves your expressions of unusual ideas.

Concluding Comments

The recommendations of this chapter can have an impact on your studying behavior and academic accomplishments. Of course, strategies to help you put in study time and enhance your study efficiency are effective only to the extent that you use them. Some students have told us that our tactics do not work. On closer questioning we found that they were not really using our suggestions. However, we assume that you are still reading what we have to say because you care about your study behavior and are willing to try some new strategies for improving that behavior. On that optimistic note, we conclude our remarks on the topic and wish you well in your pursuit of scholarship. Remember—none of that last minute stuff. There are better ways to spend the night before.

References

Beneke, W. M., and Harris, M. B. 1972. Teaching self-control of study behavior. *Behaviour Research and Therapy 10,* 35-41.

Briggs, R. D., Tosi, D. J., and Morley, R. M. 1971. Study habit modification and its effect on academic performance: a behavioral approach. *Journal of Educational Research 64,* 347-350.

Fox, L. Effecting the use of efficient study habits. 1972. *Journal of Mathetics 1* (1), 75-86.

Freeburne, C. M., and Fleischer, M. S. 1952. The effect of music distraction upon reading rate and comprehension. *Journal of Educational Psychology 43,* 101-109.

Goetz, E. M., and Baer, D. M. 1971. Descriptive social reinforcement of "creative" block building for young children. In *A new direction for education: behavior analysis,* ed. E. A. Ramp and B. L. Hopkins, pp. 72-79. Lawrence: University of Kansas, Support and Development Center for Follow Through.

Goetz, E. M., and Salmonson, M. M. 1972. The effect of general and descriptive reinforcement on "creativity" in easel painting. Paper presented at the 3d Annual Kansas Conference on Behavior Analysis in Education, Lawrence, May.

Jones, G. B. 1969. Improving study behaviors. In *Behavioral counseling: cases and techniques,* ed. J. D. Krumboltz and C. E. Thoresen. New York: Holt, Rinehart and Winston.

Kirkpatrick, F. H. 1943. Music in industry. *Journal of Applied Psychology 27,* 268-274.

Meadow, A., and Parnes, S. J. 1959. Evaluation of training in creative problem-solving. *Journal of Applied Psychology 43,* 189-194.

Nurnberger, J. I., and Zimmerman, J. 1970. Applied analysis of human behaviors: an alternative to conventional motivational inferences and unconscious determination in therapeutic programming. *Behavior Therapy 1,* 59-69.

Parnes, S. J. 1967. *Creative behavior guidebook.* New York: Charles Scribner's Sons.

Premack, D. 1959. Toward empirical behavioral laws: positive reinforcement. *Psychological Review 66,* 219-233.

Robinson, F. P. 1970. *Effective study,* 4th ed. New York: Harper & Row.

Schlichting, H. E., Jr., and Brown, R. V. 1970. Effect of background music on student performance. *American Biology Teacher 32,* 427-429.

Wrenn, C. G. 1933. *Practical study aids.* Stanford: Stanford University Press.

six

"Life's Inmost Secret": Career Planning

One of your major problems may be finding sources of approval that will counteract parental pressure.

And in keeping yourself with labour you
are in truth loving life,
And to love life through labour is to be
intimate with life's inmost secret.

— From Gibran's *The Prophet*

To Gibran, work is more than a means of survival or a route to affluence; it is truly a way of loving life. As we look about us, we see few people who derive that degree of fulfillment from their work. Certainly, there are those who invest long hours in their labors; but if you look closely, you may discover that it is the economic payoff, not the work itself, to which they are attracted. Others literally detest their work and stay on the job only to avoid financial trouble. Both these circumstances are an affront to the dignity of work and the dignity of human beings. Some developmental theorists, such as Erik Erikson (1959), proclaim that a sound vocational identity is crucial to psychological adjustment. We believe that work should satisfy three kinds of goals: economic comfort, contribution to humanity, and self-fulfillment. Whether your labors will lead to these goals is intimately related to the career planning you do in your college years.

Educational-vocational decisions confront every college student. You must decide on a major, courses to be taken within that major, and, most importantly, where your college work should lead. Eventually, you will have to decide whether you will take a particular job, keep that job, accept a promotion, transfer to another locale, and so on. Educational-vocational choice is an ongoing process. Seldom does one make *the* decision for life. Choices that concern you today, such as selecting a major or minor, are only steps in a lifelong process. But do not demean the importance of today's decisions—few things have as much impact on your total life as career choices. While some people seem to drift almost by chance into exciting professions, the probability of your finding excitement and fulfillment in your work is greatly enhanced by some systematic planning.

In this chapter we will explore some of the factors to consider in selecting a college major. Ordinarily, a college major should be chosen with a vocational goal in mind. As you work through the chapter, consider career options and the preparation needed to pursue those options. If you have already chosen a college major, perhaps you will want to confirm the wisdom of that choice. Specifically, we will ask you to conduct a self-study, a study of occupational options, and then to relate your self-study to vocational alternatives. This approach was suggested more than sixty years ago by Frank Parsons, but it is still relevant today. We will conclude the chapter by considering how to use self-management to achieve behaviors required in career planning. In a word, our goal is to help you select a career that is consistent with your interests and abilities.

Self-Study

You cannot decide wisely on a career without taking an honest look at yourself. First of all you need an accurate appraisal of your interests and abilities. You undoubtedly already know a great deal about yourself—more than anyone else—but you probably can learn even more. Perhaps you have been reluctant in the past to confront your abilities and interests. A multitude of social pressures and expectations can keep us from evaluating ourselves candidly. Our first aim here is to determine what an objective self-examination involves.

Interests

In making academic and career decisions, you should first think in terms of what is reinforcing to you. Do you most enjoy working with people, things, or ideas? Some people reject their own interests in favor of the interests of others. They let the interests of their friends or parents lead them into fields that would best be suited for their friends and parents. However, it will not be mom or dad who will be pursuing that vocation to which you are making a long-term commitment.

Course work   Determining which college courses you enjoy is indispensable to career decisions. It is also vitally important to determine why you enjoy a course before launching a major in that area. Was it the teacher's charisma, the grading system, the attractive student who sat next to you, or the subject matter? Enjoyment of the subject matter obviously provides a much stronger foundation for long-term decisions than the other characteristics. On the other hand, if you dislike a course, do not forever shut yourself off from that area. Self-examination may reveal that it was something other than the subject matter that turned you off. The fact that the class met at 6:55 A.M. probably did not help your morale.

Extracurricular activities   When you have finished examining your courses, take a look at your extracurricular involvements. These activities undoubtedly indicate strong interests and should be considered when exploring possible majors. Maybe you work as a writer or photographer on the college newspaper, perform in plays, participate in athletic activities, broadcast on the college radio station, or are a member of the debating team. What is it about these activities that attracts you? Is it coordinating, supervising, or working as part of a team? These dimensions suggest academic and career possibilities. And just think of earning a living by doing what you enjoy. We were lucky enough to find such a profession. In fact, we have often said that if we were independently wealthy, we would work as college professors without pay.

Work experiences   Your previous work experiences may provide many useful clues for making educational-vocational decisions. Any work, whether volunteer or for pay, can tell you something about what is and what is not reinforcing to you. A job in a hospital, even as an attendant, could give you an idea of what it is like to work in a hospital setting. Work as a counselor in a summer camp could indicate whether you would enjoy supervising young people. Similarly, sales work, production work, or work in a social agency might reveal that one of those activities holds reinforcement potential for you. As with courses you should attempt to determine why an occupational experience proved reinforcing. Perhaps the earnings, place of employment, freedom to be creative, opportunity for advancement, social status of the profession, or opportunity for public service were attractive to you. If you have had an unsatisfactory work experience, do not automatically rule out that vocation without considering why the experience was distasteful. Even if you disliked the work, do not give up. The work you did as a part-time or summer employee may be vastly different from what you could do as a full-time employee.

Interest tests   Taking a test to find out where your interests lie might seem silly, but standardized interest tests often reveal vocational possibilities that simply do not emerge from your previous courses and work experiences. Such tests are categorized as interest inventories,* since there are no right or wrong answers, no good or bad scores. The inventories require only that you express your preferences among a wide variety of activities. Your preferences may be compared to those of individuals engaged in different occupations or career programs. The basic assumption underlying this approach is

*Defined in Glossary.

that if your interests are similar to those of people successfully engaged in a given occupation, you are likely to find satisfaction in that occupation.

Two of the most widely used interest inventories are the *Strong-Campbell Interest Inventory* (1974) (SCII) and the *Kuder Occupational Interest Survey* (1966) (OIS). The SCII is a current revision of the *Strong Vocational Interest Blank.* The new SCII merges the separate men's and women's forms of the older *Strong Vocational Interest Blank* into a single inventory. This permits both sexes to respond to items and receive scores on occupations previously unavailable on separate forms for males and females. However, your scores are still compared with scores derived from male *or* female groups. On the SCII, you are asked to express preferences for different kinds of occupations, school subjects, various activities (such as taking responsibility, repairing electrical wiring, watching an open-heart operation, living in a city), amusements, and types of people. You are also asked to indicate a preference between pairs of activities and to evaluate such characteristics as abilities and social behaviors.

After taking the SCII, you receive a number of scores in three different categories. First, you receive scores on six General Occupational Themes (realistic, conventional, enterprising, investigative, artistic, and social) based on J. L. Holland's work. These scores may help you identify overall occupational themes to pursue. For example, if you find that your answers fall principally into the artistic and social themes, you might want to study occupations that are classified under these themes. Second, you receive scores on Basic Interest Scales. These scores reflect the strength of your likes and dislikes in twenty-three specific interest areas. Finally, you receive scores on 124 Occupational Scales. Your scores on the Occupational Scales reveal the extent to which your likes and dislikes agree with those of men and women who are satisfied with their work in each of a wide range of occupations, while your scores on the six Occupational Themes and the twenty-three Basic Interest Scales are compared with those of people in general.

The Kuder OIS is another interest inventory you might consider. Your scores on the OIS represent the degree of agreement between your interests and those of satisfied men and women in each of approximately 110 occupations. In addition, the OIS compares your interests with those of satisfied graduating seniors in over thirty college majors. Men and women take the same form, but men receive scores for occupations and college majors developed using male groups, and women receive scores developed using female groups. However, women also receive scores in selected occupations and college majors listed in the men's group where opportunities for women are increasing.

You should remember that interest inventories are not measures of ability. While interests may influence strongly whether you enter a certain field and persist in it, you must also have ability in the field if you are to succeed. However, even when certain abilities are lacking, a knowledge of your interests can prove exceedingly useful. You may lack the grades in theoretical engineering, but decide on a technical field that is part of the engineering family. Similarly, although you may have interests in becoming a physician, the requirements for that occupation may transcend your past achievement. You could nevertheless enter a related health field. You surely enhance your chances for success and overall happiness in life when you identify areas in which your abilities and your interests correspond. Incidentally, if you took an interest test in high school, you probably should take another one now. Research has shown that interest patterns differ considerably between ages fifteen and twenty-five.

Stated interests   For quite some time, you may have been saying that you are going to enter a certain field. What do the interest tests say regarding your suitability for that vocation? Stated interests and measured interests can be drastically different. Stated interests are sometimes based on misconceptions, lack of information, or both. On the other hand, measured interests do not account for the atypical individual who succeeds in a field although his expressed preferences may be different from others in that field. Where your stated and measured interests are dissimilar, you have the option of further exploration. You can attempt to identify more precisely what factors led to your stated interests, or you can examine more fully what is involved in the vocation you have chosen.

Abilities and Potential

Before making a career choice, you should assess both your current abilities and your potential abilities. This is where self-study really demands a high degree of honesty. Your past performance may suggest certain alternatives, but it may also indicate weaknesses that must be remedied before other alternatives can be considered. Knowing your limitations can be just as helpful as knowing your strengths. Your past accomplishments may have fallen short of your potential; you therefore should appraise your potential to perform better in the future.

Course grades   The first area to examine is your course grades. Although grades are not precise indices of ability, they may suggest potential abilities and limitations. For example, a person majoring in psychology who has good grades in science courses might well consider a minor in the sciences. It would probably enhance his/her study of psychology. In addition, many graduate schools in psychology prefer students with a good background in the biological and physical sciences. We are not suggesting that you select a major or minor only in those fields where you earn the highest marks; average grades in some fields might open more occupational doors than superior grades in an overcrowded field. But when all other things are equal, high grades certainly constitute one criterion for selecting a course of study.

In addition to considering areas where you get good grades, do not overlook the impact that poor performances have on your career choices. You cannot realistically expect to select a program in drafting, accounting, math, or forestry if you are failing courses required for entering that field—not unless you can make considerable improvement. Current poor performance does not automatically mean that you can never do well. It does mean, however, that you must analyze the reasons for your poor performance and take steps to correct them. Your difficulty might be due to your study habits or your lack of prerequisite skills. Maybe you did not take certain subjects in high school, or perhaps your instruction was less than adequate. You may have been sidetracked by emotional involvements when you took the prerequisite courses. It may be helpful to withdraw from a course, get tutoring, take an incomplete, or begin a remedial or developmental program to correct your deficiencies. These behaviors could lead to career options that otherwise would be unattainable.

Perhaps you are not doing poorly in any of your present courses but are about to rule out certain career options because you fear one or two courses. For example, people who are interested in nursing sometimes eliminate that career option because it requires some basic courses in chemistry. Other people avoid majors that require physics, statistics, or a foreign language. Frequently, however, there is nothing to fear except one's own imagination. A good student sometimes carefully avoids taking courses that are not likely to result in A's and B's. Ironically, courses with a bad reputation often are not that closely related to activities within a career. You might be willing to tolerate an average grade in a few of these subjects in order to reach a career goal that you really want. A program of self-desensitization aimed at reducing unnecessary anxiety about these courses might prove helpful. The need to always make A's can be a terrible burden—a burden that can preclude some worthwhile career alternatives.

In addition to assessing your individual course grades, you might also consider your overall grade point average (GPA). If you do not know your GPA, your registrar can supply you with that information. By keeping a record of your cumulative GPA and your GPA for each grading period, you can determine whether you are making any improvement. A trend in your GPA can sometimes be as important as your overall GPA. For example, people who are thinking about careers that require graduate training (e.g., psychology) or professional school (e.g., law) might be encouraged by upward trends in GPAs.

Aptitude test scores   In assessing your abilities and potential, you may wish to examine standardized tests you have taken or to arrange for additional testing at your counseling center. A word of caution is in order, however: tests cannot make decisions for you. The test is yet to be devised that can tell you what you should or should not do. But tests can identify areas where you might benefit from remedial or developmental programs; they also can point out abilities that you never knew you had.

In gaining entrance to college, you probably took some tests that purported to reflect your ability or potential to achieve in college. Theoretically, these aptitude tests show what you can achieve rather than what you have achieved. This is accomplished by presenting new situations and evaluating your performance in those situations. Realistically, however, what you can achieve is largely a function of what you have already achieved. If you have not been exposed to learning situations similar to those on the test, you will probably score lower than people who have been so exposed. Aptitude tests do not indicate native ability, but they may suggest areas where you can expect to do well and areas where you will need remedial training.

An aptitude test required for entrance into many colleges is the

Scholastic Aptitude Test (SAT). The SAT yields scores on your verbal and mathematical potential. Another commonly used entrance examination is the American College Test (ACT), which yields scores on English, math, social science, and natural science. If you have taken a standardized test to gain college admission, examine your scores on that test. (Your counseling center may have a copy, or you can probably obtain a copy from the admissions office.) You may have scored particularly high in an area in which you have not explored academic and career possibilities. Women should be especially cautious about overlooking areas of strength. Phyllis Boring, (WEAL, 1973) a leader of Women's Equity Action League, noted that during high school she had scored very high on four tests measuring engineering aptitude. She minimized the importance of these scores after her high school counselor dissuaded her from any interest in engineering. She also gave little thought to the fact that she scored in the 97th percentile on the math aptitude test of the Graduate Record Exam. In retrospect, she realized the significance of these scores. It is noteworthy that 40 percent of the people who show high aptitude on engineering tests are women, but only 1 percent of engineers in this country are women.

Nonacademic abilities We have primarily stressed academic abilities, but you may possess other abilities that could suggest occupational choices. Perhaps you have sports skills, artistic skills, or musical talents. There are many fields of endeavor that captialize on these abilities. For example, being a professional athlete is not the only occupation open to a person with athletic abilities. You might become a recreation director, physical education instructor, coach, or dancer. It has often been said that college athletics provide useful preparation for the responsibilities of adulthood. Something can be said for team effort, rigorous training, and the ability to perform under stress. These experiences also apply to many nonathletic vocations.

Summary of Self-Study

Deciding on a college major and a possible career requires that you know a great deal about yourself. Since you will probably be working four or five days a week for the next thirty years, you should base your career decisions on thorough and honest self-exploration. To determine what academic and career activities would be reinforcing to you and your potential for those activities, you should identify the courses you have found enjoyable, evaluate why those courses were enjoyable and consider the dimensions of extracurricular activities you have found most satisfying. In addition, examine the work experiences you have found fulfilling, your scores on interest tests, and reasons for inconsistencies between stated and measured interests. To appraise your academic and career potentials, consider your grades in various courses, trends in your GPA, your scores on such standardized tests as the ACT, and your nonacademic skills in such areas as music, art, and athletics.

Self-Management Checklist

Before discussing strategies for obtaining occupational information, let us determine where you stand relative to the behaviors recommended in this first section. At the conclusion of the chapter, we will describe how to use self-management to achieve the desired behaviors. Those items that you do not check could become goals of a self-management project.

__I have identified in rank order the five courses I have enjoyed most in college and have isolated the specific factors that account for my enjoyment of each.

__I have identified three facets of my extracurricular involvements that I find especially rewarding.

__I have taken at least one standardized interest inventory and know my score profile on that inventory.

__I have explained the discrepancies between my stated interests and my measured interests.

__I know the kinds of courses in which I do well and have identified the factors responsible for my success in those courses.

__I know my overall GPA and any consistent changes that are occurring in that GPA.

__I know my score profile on at least one standardized aptitude test, such as SAT or ACT.

__I have identified at least three of my nonacademic skills that should be considered in making a career decision.

A Study of Occupations

You cannot divorce wise career planning — be it the selection of an occupation or the selection of a college major — from occupational information. Wise choices can only be made once you know what you are choosing. Too frequently, individuals choose on the basis of stereotypes or such single factors as beginning salary, possible top salary, or imagined prestige. Sometimes people decide to choose a career simply because their friends intend to choose that career. This course of action can lead to some devastating surprises. Choosing a vocation should not be like reaching into a grab bag; you should exercise every option to inspect the wrapping, shake the package, and peek inside.

Facts are available on every conceivable occupation you might choose. You can get ideas about the future of a field; the abilities, skills and other personal traits required; the duties performed; the course work and training needed for entry; lines of promotion; and how your interests and abilities fit into that occupation. While it would be impractical for you to study thousands of specific occupations, you can certainly study the occupational groups toward which your interests and abilities point. At this stage, you may be concerned with selecting a general field, rather than a narrow specialty. Specialization usually comes after extensive exposure to a field. Looking at occupational families or clusters will make that search easier. We will begin our study of vocations by examining the general occupational outlook for the late 1970s; we will then identify some specific sources of information about occupational families and about specific jobs within an occupation.

General Outlook

Occupational growth   You may be apprehensive about the vocational outlook for college graduates. You have probably heard talk about unemployed college graduates pounding the streets looking for work. Perhaps you have even thought, "Why remain in college if I can't get a job when I finish?" The boom period of the 1960s, when employers came to colleges in large numbers looking for graduates, is past. Data from the Bureau of Labor Statistics indicate that a rough balance is taking place in the supply and demand for college-educated workers. The number of new college graduates to enter the labor market from 1970 to 1980 is expected to total over nine million, with estimated needs also approximating that figure. That means your future employer can probably be more selective in his hiring, but that does not mean the outlook is bad. The area of greatest growth will be in the professional and technical fields. All projections indicate that people with the most education will face the brightest job prospects, although some areas will offer more promise than others.

Figure 6-1 shows how professional and technical occupations will grow in comparison to other occupations. It also provides an indication of the growth expected for various professional groups. Notice that engineering is one field that will enjoy substantial growth. Some

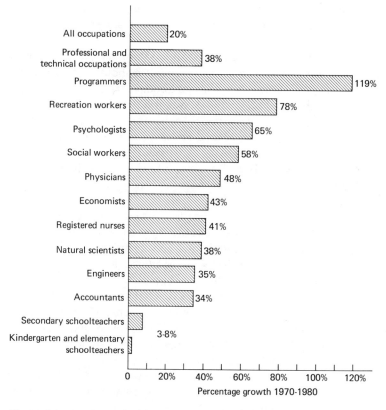

Figure 6-1 Job Outlook for Future Grads (Department of Labor).

people have avoided engineering because of recent unemployment in such industries as aerospace. However, the supply of engineers in the next decade will probably fall short of the demand. That should be good news for engineers and for technicians who support the engineering profession.

Growth, however, is not the only indicator of employment demands in an occupation. Death, retirement, and the movement of workers to other fields create many vacancies each year. Notice that kindergarten, elementary, and secondary teaching will enjoy only minimal growth during the 1970s; however, the fact that over two million people are now employed as kindergarten, elementary, and secondary teachers means that many replacements will be needed each year. Unfortunately, the supply may exceed the demand, thus creating keener competition for employment in teaching. Opportunities for teachers in math, physical sciences, and special education are expected to be very favorable.

At this point in career planning, it is important that you not be shaken by unfounded rumors and skepticism about the future. While no one can predict the future, current trends make the future occupational outlook appear optimistic for well-trained people. Government, education, service agencies, trade, finance, and practically every sector of the economy needs college-educated and highly trained workers. No one is demanding less educated workers. You may have to make more careful career plans and be more thoroughly prepared than your college predecessors of the 1960s, but the overall job market looks promising.

Women   We are not discriminating against men by giving additional information to women, but there are certain facets of the job market to which women should give special attention. Shortages of well-trained workers in selected areas plus legislation barring discrimination in employment should enhance the employment outlook for qualified women. But there are potential problems. Labor statistics show that most professional female workers are concentrated in a limited number of professions. Teaching, for example, employs about 40 percent of all women engaged in professional work. Nursing, library science, and social work also have a high percentage of women. Although these professions can expect growth in the future, they cannot accommodate the vastly increasing numbers of women who are going to college. And women can also expect increasing competition from men in what were once "female" occupations. If most women continue to train for a restricted number of professional occupations, they can expect keen competition for employment.

To enhance their employment prospects, women should consider occupations where shortages are apt to exist. More women are needed as chemists, engineers, physicians, optometrists, dentists, technical writers, lawyers, and business executives. Women should also consider fields where new technology is developing. Computer programming and related work, for example, holds considerable promise. Finally, women who are going into teaching should definitely explore fields where teacher shortages may exist. School administration, math, physical science, and industrial arts are prime examples. New possibilities are emerging every day; occupations are sexist only to the extent that we allow them to be so.

Published Information

An abundance of published material is available to help people learn about the thousands of occupations that exist. Your library will probably house most of this occupational information. Your reference librarian can tell you about government documents, pamphlets, indexes, tapes, and occupational files you never knew existed. You should make a tentative list of the occupations that you would like to explore. You may be interested in training requirements, worker traits, duties, salaries, discrimination practices against women and minorities, or lines of promotion for these occupations. If you have some idea of what you are seeking, your librarian can help you locate the appropriate materials.

Occupational Outlook Handbook   One of the most accurate and useful sources of occupational information is the *Occupational Outlook Handbook*, published biannually by the Bureau of Labor Statistics. The *Handbook* provides occupational monographs on over eight hundred occupations. For each occupation there is a concise and readable description of the nature of the work, training, other qualifications and advancement, employment outlook, earnings and working conditions, and sources of additional information. You will find the information up-to-date since the *Handbook* is revised every two years.

A supplement to the *Occupational Outlook Handbook* is the *Occupational Outlook Quarterly*, which provides current occupational information between editions of the *Handbook*. The *Quarterly* contains timely articles on practically every aspect of career planning. Recent *Quarterly* articles have included: "The College Graduate—1989 Job Prospects," "Why Junior College," "Putting a Bachelor of Arts Degree to Work," "Toward Matching Personnel and Job Characteristics," "Women College Graduates — Will They Find Jobs."

Dictionary of Occupational Titles   This reference work, published by the Department of Labor, would probably not be your first choice for fireside reading, but with careful study it can provide you with valuable occupational information. The third edition of the *Dictionary* includes two volumes and two supplements. Volume One gives definitions and brief descriptions of over twenty-two thousand jobs. Volume Two first groups similar jobs into nine broad categories (e.g., professional, technical and managerial, clerical and sales) and then specifies twenty-two areas of work (e.g., art, business relations, mathematics and science, medicine and health) according to worker traits. Each of the twenty-two worker trait groups also indicates the worker's level of involvement with data (ideas), people, and things. A description of the training time, aptitudes, interests, personal temperaments, and physical demands of the work are given for each group. The two supplementary volumes contain tabular information on the physical activities, working conditions (physical surroundings), and training time for various jobs. Volume One should give you a good idea of what a worker does, how he does it, and why he does it for any job in which you are interested. Volume Two should help you visualize how training for one job is really training for many other related jobs. You will also learn from Volume Two and the supplements what personal traits and abilities are required for the occupational groups in which you are interested.

Other published materials   After you examine the *Handbook,* the *Quarterly*, and the *Dictionary*, you will be prepared to seek additional information. Your librarian can help you locate the materials you need. Women should inquire about materials especially relevant to women. Your library probably has items from the Women's Bureau of the Department of Labor. For example, a series of pamphlets entitled *Why Not Be —* (an Engineer, an Optometrist, a Pharmacist, etc.) should be helpful. Whatever the source, evaluate carefully who has prepared the material and for what purpose. For example, do not take too literally glamorized information disseminated by organizations (e.g., the French Foreign Legion) trying to recruit workers. Finally, be exhaustive in getting all the current facts on the few occupations for which you seek information.

Interviewing Others

One helpful way of securing occupational information is to interview people who hold positions that interest you. These individuals can give you first-hand information about the kind of training they received, how they secured their first position, local supply and demand for their services, and information on the nuances of their work. Of course, one individual cannot possess all the answers, but he/she can help you with some questions you may be unable to answer from published sources.

We advise you to prepare thoroughly for this kind of interview. Read what you can about the occupation and know what information you are seeking. You will probably want to prepare a list of specific questions for which you are seeking answers. This will permit you to get details without taking an undue portion of a person's time. Rather than asking, "Would you tell me about the field of accounting?" you might ask, "What opportunities exist for accountants in this locality?" "What college courses did you find most useful?" "How is your work similar or different from that of other accountants?" You should avoid putting the individual "on the spot." For example, "What do you dislike about your work?" would be more diplomatic than "Do you dislike your work?"

Behavioral Checklist

At first glance a study of occupations may seem like a massive undertaking. To reduce an overwhelming task, we suggest that you use the following checklist. This will tell you the specific things you must do to complete your exploration of occupations. If you are willing to do these things one by one, you will not find the task overwhelming.

___I know where the *Occupational Outlook Handbook* and the *Dictionary of Occupational Titles* are located in my library.

___I have looked through these two documents.

___I have identified at least three vocational areas (consistent with my interests and abilities) for which employment opportunities look good in the late 1970s.

___I have identified the worker traits in these three vocational areas.

___I have interviewed workers in all three of these vocational areas.

Choosing A Career

The purpose of your self-study and study of occupations is to broaden your career alternatives. You began your self-study with an asessment of your likes and dislikes. This consisted of assessing various activities to determine what attracted you to those activities. Suppose your self-study showed that you like to work with people and ideas, that you like to supervise people and coordinate programs, that you prefer working in a large city, that you like high levels of responsibility, that you dislike repetitious work, and that you are energetic and like jobs that require physical stamina. Can you match your interests with worker traits? (You can locate worker traits in the *Dictionary of Occupational Titles*. Or, you can read an excellent article, "Toward Matching Personal and Job Characteristics," by D. Dillion, in the Winter 1971 issue of *Occupational Outlook Quarterly*.) Do other aspects of the job (e.g. working conditions, salary) agree with your stated interests? Perhaps you will find that your interests coincide exactly with what the occupation offers. If not, to what extent are you willing to compromise your interests? If you learn, for example, that a job requires little physical activity, would you lose interest in that occupation for that reason alone? What we are really asking is that you decide what about a job holds greatest reinforcement potential for you. Would you accept a modest salary if you could do what you most enjoyed?

Second, your self-study involved an examination of your achievement and potential to achieve in various areas. How do your abilities compare with those required in the occupations you would find reinforcing? Do the occupations require skill in math, the natural sciences, or the social sciences? Are any special language skills involved, such as technical reading, public speaking, or report writing? Are any special aptitudes required, such as memory for details, physical dexterity, or artistic talents?

After exploring different career possibilities, you must narrow your focus. You cannot major in everything, and you cannot prepare for all careers. After deciding on an occupational area, you must decide what major would best prepare you for that occupation. If no special major is required for that field, you can pursue what comes naturally. But more likely, your selected area will require some specific courses and some specific skills. Examine the list of college majors offered in your college. If possible, talk with several of the professors or the department head in the area that you are considering. Determine if a major in that area would indeed help you enter the field of your choice.

Self-Management

We have been offering suggestions throughout the chapter on how to secure and analyze information about yourself and the world of work. Information, of course, can prove worthwhile only if you find and use it. You may need a self-management plan that would allow you to stop worrying about career planning and start doing something about it. You need not make any quick decisions, but you do need to plan. Too many people leave their future primarily to chance, and chance often deals a bad hand.

Self-management can be applied to career planning, since career planning involves certain specifiable behaviors. Let us examine how self-management can be used to produce the behaviors appropriate to satisfactory career planning.

1. *Selecting a goal:* Let us assume that your overall goal is to conduct a self-study and a study of occupational information. You should identify which of the behaviors on our checklist will be your initial goal.

2. *Recording the quantity and circumstances of behavior:* You should establish a record-keeping system. Your records could include a list of your interests, abilities, and limitations. You could also record data on the abilities and interests that seem essential for each occupation you study. Next, you might keep a record of all the people you have consulted or wish to consult about your career plans (e.g., professors, department heads, counselors, librarians). You might also record the time you spend exploring your interests, your abilities, and designated occupations. In a word, any behavior directed toward any activity on our two checklists should be recorded.

3. *Changing setting events:* You may find that establishing a time schedule for such behaviors as visiting the library, interviewing, and taking interest tests would help to produce those behaviors. Beginning your project in the setting that you find most supportive would also be a good step. Would the counseling center, library, or an industrial site be the best starting place for you?

Remember that you want to arrange conditions (time and place) to facilitate career planning.

4. *Establishing effective consequences:* There are many procedures that could be used to establish consequences for your information-seeking and decision-making behaviors. You might try setting up a token economy and reinforce yourself after each action you take, regardless of how small the action. You might contract with a friend who is also attempting to make career decisions to provide reinforcement for each other. Research has shown that counselor approval for information-seeking (e.g., Thoresen and Krumboltz, 1967) and decision-making (e.g., Ryan and Krumboltz, 1964) increases the frequency of those behaviors. One of your major problems may be finding sources of approval that will counteract parental pressure. Dad may want you to be a physician and be disappointed if you consider other career possibilities. Can you identify some significant other people—fellow students, counselors, teachers—whose approval would soften the impact of parental disdain? If so, how can you marshall that approval for your career choices?

5. *Focusing on contingencies:* You could post cues in conspicuous places, or you could write an essay about your career aspirations, including the steps you are taking to fulfill those ambitions. Writing about your self-study, or need for it, could heighten your awareness of the importance of careful career planning.

6. *Achieving covert control:* Covert processes could be included to facilitate information seeking or to help deal with related problems that occur in your career planning. For example, you might use covert positive reinforcement to facilitate information-seeking behavior. Or, you may find yourself anxious over a course that you must take to meet certain career objectives. In this case, relaxation exercises might be helpful (see Chapter Seven).

Concluding Comments

The purposes of this chapter were (1) to specify what is involved in self-study and a study of occupations, and (2) to identify self-management procedures that can be applied to that self-study and occupational study. If you follow some of our suggestions, you will come into contact with librarians, counselors, teachers, and workers in the field; but do not expect any of these people to make decisions for you. Going to these people with specific requests will increase the chances of their helping you decide judiciously. The career planning you are doing today can fundamentally affect the quality of your tomorrows. Joy, excitement, and fulfillment can be found in many careers. Please accept no less.

References

American college testing program—technical report. 1965. Iowa City, Iowa: American College Testing Program.

Angoff, W. H., ed. 1971. *The college board admissions testing program: a technical report on research and development activities related to the Scholastic Aptitude Test and Achievement Tests.* New York: College Entrance Examination Board.

Dictionary of occupational titles. 1963. Two volumes and supplements. Washington, D.C.: U.S. Government Printing Office.

Erikson, E. H. 1959. Identity and the life cycle. *Psychological Issues 1*(1), Monograph 1.

Holland, J. L. 1973. *Making Vocational Choices: A Theory of Careers.* Englewood Cliffs, N. J.: Prentice Hall.

Kuder, G. F. 1966. *Kuder occupational interest survey, general manual.* Chicago: Science Research Associates.

Parsons. F. 1909. *Choosing a Vocation.* Boston: Houghton Mifflin.

Occupational outlook handbook, 1972-73 ed. Washington, D.C.: U.S. Government Printing Office.

Occupational Outlook Quarterly. Washington, D.C.: Bureau of Labor Statistics.

Ryan, T. A., and Krumboltz, J. D. 1964. Effect of reinforcement counseling on client decision-making behavior. *Journal of Counseling Psychology 11*(4), 315-323.

Strong-Campbell Interest Inventory. 1974. Stanford: Stanford University Press.

Thoresen, C. E., and Krumboltz, J. D. 1967. Relationship of counselor reinforcement of selected responses to external behavior. *Journal of Counseling Psychology 14*(2), 140-144.

WEAL K-12 Education Kit. 1973. Washington, D. C.: Women's Equity Action League.

Why not be —. Washington, D.C.: Women's Bureau, Department of Labor.

seven

"The Inner Sanctum":
Changing Internal Unrest

Many people find that once they can deal with an experience in imagination, they can deal with it in actuality.

One of the most chilling radio melodramas of years gone by was "The Inner Sanctum." Although this chapter differs in focus from that program, the phrase *inner sanctum* aptly describes our present concern. Webster's dictionary defines *sanctum* as "a sacred place; hence, a place of retreat where one is free from intrusion." Nothing is more sacred about the human organism than feelings and thoughts; and nothing is more inaccessible to others. Certainly, some thoughts and feelings are reflected in one's behavior, but many others are known only to oneself.

Our investigation of thoughts and feelings does not mean that we are abdicating a behavioral emphasis. Most self-management attempts, particularly the initial ones, should focus on overt behaviors rather than internal events. In fact, modifying overt behaviors will indirectly alter many internal responses. Perhaps the best way to reduce anxiety is to change the overt behaviors that are related to that anxiety. But we must admit that internal changes do not always follow overt changes. You may condition yourself to speak before groups and still experience pronounced anxiety whenever you speak. You would undoubtedly prefer to emit the appropriate overt behavior without the underlying trauma.

Other types of problem reactions appear to be almost exclusively internal in nature. Troublesome thoughts and depressed moods can occur in practically any situation. For instance, you may be unable to get something off your mind or may feel despondent for no discernible reason. Such internal responses can be exceedingly distressing. They often represent dimensions of our being that we would most like to change.

In the examples cited above, self-management strategies must be directed toward what is happening inside the person. While these internal reactions can affect overt behaviors (for example, anxiety can affect eating, smoking, drinking, sports activity, and study behavior), our present concern is with internal reactions per se. Anxiety, depression, and troublesome thoughts are important in themselves. Even if they did not affect overt behavior, they would still merit our attention.

Anxiety Management

The term *anxiety* refers to internal discomfort that is habitually associated with certain people, events, and situations. The discomfort can be precipitated by the actual stimulus or by thoughts of that stimulus. This internal trauma is known by a number of labels: anxiety, fear, panic. Although these words denote slight differences in emotionality, we suspect that the same treatment procedures are applicable in any case.

Behavioral therapists (most notably Joseph Wolpe) have attempted to allay anxiety by means of a strategy known as systematic desensitization.* This approach has been quite effective in reducing anxiety, but it has not been used on a totally self-directed basis. Individuals may do desensitization exercises on their own, but they typically receive therapeutic assistance in initiating those exercises (see Baker et al., 1973; Evans and Kellam, 1973; Migler and Wolpe, 1967; Phillips et al., 1972). Since it is unlikely that you could apply the desensitization model simply by reading about it, we have chosen not to specify the details of this approach.[1] Instead, we will emphasize those dimensions of anxiety management that you could use without direction from a therapist.

Achieving Muscular Relaxation

The principal objective of anxiety management is to replace anxiety with muscular relaxation. You may experience other manifestations of anxiety, such as nausea, accelerated heartbeat, perspiration, shortness of breath, and headaches, but these responses are usually preceded or accompanied by muscular tension. If you can achieve a high level of muscular relaxation, the other physiological reactions will probably disappear.

The strategy used in desensitization for achieving muscular relaxation is the repeated tensing and relaxing of various muscle groups (e.g., hand and forearm, upper arm, forehead, eyes and nose, cheeks and mouth). The traditional approach is to tense a specific set of muscles for several seconds and then relax those muscles for several seconds. In using this procedure, you should cover all the major muscle groups from the lower to upper extremities and use about two tension-release cycles per muscle group.[2] In our estimation, the sequence in which you relax muscle groups is relatively unimportant.

Since the relaxation procedure just described requires twenty to

---

*Defined in glossary.

[1]The specifics of desensitization are provided in J. N. Marquis, W. G. Morgan, and G. W. Piaget, *A guidebook for systematic desensitization* (Palo Alto, Cal.: Veterans Administration Hospital, 1971).

[2]A relaxation tape following this procedure is available from Instructional Dynamics, Inc., 116 East Superior Street, Chicago, Illinois 60611.

thirty minutes to complete, some researchers (Russell and Sipich, 1973) have suggested a way to shorten this process. The person initially goes through the muscle groups to achieve deep muscle relaxation and then pairs that relaxation with a self-produced cue word (e.g., "calm" or "control"). When totally relaxed, the individual focuses all of his/her attention on breathing and silently repeats the cue word with each exhalation. The obvious objective is to associate relaxation with a specific cue. Henceforth, when the person begins to experience anxiety, he/she begins to breathe deeply and repeat silently the cue word.

An even simpler method for inducing relaxation has been proposed by Bugg (1972). He advocates that a person do three things when confronted with stress: (1) Take a deep breath and let it go suddenly. According to Bugg this procedure forces relaxation at least for a split second. (2) Tell oneself to relax. (3) Focus for a few seconds on something very pleasant. After completing these steps, the individual redirects attention to the problem situation. If the anxiety recurs, the three-step model is repeated. Because of the ease of application, this procedure can be applied hundreds of times to both imagined and actual situations.

Another efficient way to reverse anxiety reactions is self-directed guidance (Meichenbaum and Cameron, 1974). When beginning to get anxious, people probably say a number of things to themselves that accentuate that anxiety (e.g., "I'm going to panic," "I just can't do it," "I'm really going to be embarrassed!"). If an individual would start emitting positive self-utterances (e.g., "I'm well prepared for this speech," "My ideas are as important as anyone's," "All I need to do is just take my time") at the first sign of anxiety, a full-scale anxiety attack can be prevented. If you are going to use this strategy, think of your positive self-statements ahead of time. They do not easily come to mind when you are about to be seized with anxiety.

Imagined vs. Real Situations

Not only do certain situations make you anxious; just thinking about those situations makes you anxious. In desensitization people are first taught to maintain relaxation as they visualize threatening scenes. The assumption is that they will then find it easier to achieve relaxation in the actual situations (in vivo desensitization). Before visualizing anxiety-provoking scenes, you might develop what behavior therapists call an anxiety hierarchy.* Suppose you have an aversion to speaking in groups. You can probably think of many group situations that produce varying degrees of anxiety. In attempting to rank these situations, you might consider such factors as the size of the group, composition of the group, formality of the occasion, and the discussion topic. For example, the discussion topic might involve: (1) your favorite topic—sports, food, politics, the opposite sex; (2) a topic that you know a great deal about, such as a subject you researched for a term paper; (3) a topic about which you have done some casual reading but otherwise know little; (4) a topic with which you are only superficially acquainted; and (5) a topic about which you know absolutely nothing.

After you have ranked your group situations from least to most threatening, you are ready to apply muscular relaxation to those situations. If you are using the conventional desensitization approach, you first tense and relax the various muscle groups. The next step is to visualize the least threatening scene on your hierarchy. The situation should be imagined in a detailed fashion, including sights, sounds, smells, and tactile sensations. It is imperative to imagine the situation as unfolding around you at that moment, rather than imagining yourself as being in that situation. In the first case, you are a participant in the situation (much as you would be in the actual situation) and in the second case an observer of yourself in the situation. When you have visualized the situation for ten to twenty seconds, you will probably begin to feel anxious. At that point, stop visualizing the scene and attempt to regain muscular relaxation. This probably can be achieved by tensing the whole body, letting the whole body go, and breathing deeply for thirty to sixty seconds. Keep repeating this sequence of visualization and relaxation until you can visualize the scene without becoming anxious. Then you move to the second scene.

If you are using Bugg's three-step model or Meichenbaum's self-directed guidance, you first visualize the threatening scene and then apply the respective strategy. For example, you might imagine yourself being called on to make a class presentation, in which case you would then start emitting such self-verbalizations as, "I've extensively researched this topic," "I'm well prepared for this presentation," "All I need to do is take my time." You can easily employ Bugg's and Meichenbaum's approaches in combination. After visualizing the threatening scene, take a deep breath, tell yourself to relax, focus on something pleasant for a few seconds, and then emit the appropriate self-verbalizations.

After dealing with the visualized version of threatening situations, you are ready for the real thing. Many people find that once they can deal with an experience in imagination, they can deal with it in actuality. However, some people still experience considerable anxiety when faced with the actual situation. In that case, the individual can employ a combination of Bugg's and Meichenbaum's strategies. Since both can be applied rapidly, they can be repeated as long as one feels anxious.

Our recommendations for reducing anxiety will not produce an anxiety-free life. Speaking personally, there are many situations (particularly new ones) that still cause us to feel uneasy. However, the strategies described in this section are helpful in keeping anxiety to a manageable level in such situations. We still experience those initial twinges of anxiety, but we can usually avert full-scale panic. (This claim does not apply to sky diving or mountain climbing!) One word of caution: if you are an anxiety-ridden person, you may not find our recommendations powerful enough to deal with your anxiety. In that case, we recommend that you seek the assistance of a behavior therapist who can take you through systematic desensitization.

Thought Management

Some people's inner difficulty is the habitual occurrence of distressing thoughts. These thoughts often focus on what *might* be wrong with them, what others *may* think of them, what they *might* do, and what *might* happen to them. In a word, these thoughts usually do not have their origin in empirical reality. A real problem, such as a physical disability, can also dominate a person's thinking. But whether a problem is real or imagined, continuously thinking about it is very unhealthy. Actually, you may find it impossible to distinguish between real and imagined problems. What appears to be an imagined problem to others may seem a real problem to you. All that is necessary at this point is a bona fide commitment to control your debilitative thinking. If you are deriving a great deal of social attention from thinking that you have contracted an incurable disease, our self-management strategy probably will not work for you.

Aversive Consequences

In one of the reported case studies of repetitive thoughts (Mahoney, 1971), the subject marked off a 3 X 5 card into days of the week and subdivided each day into two-hour periods. The card was small enough for the subject to carry with him at all times. He kept his record of compulsive thinking by marking each time block during which the target thought occurred. To reduce the frequency of his undesired thought patterns, he wore a heavy rubber band around his wrist and snapped it whenever he engaged in the target thinking. According to Mahoney, the subject's compulsive thinking dropped off. Perhaps a better agent of punishment than a rubber band is a portable hand stimulator (Wolpe, 1971). The stimulator is small enough to carry with you unobtrusively and allows you to administer an immediate shock following an unpleasant thought. The intensity of the shock can be altered by turning a knob on the stimulator. However, even the most intense levels of shock from this device are not harmful.

There are major difficulties involved in both these punishment approaches. What is to reinforce the inflicting of pain upon oneself? If the unpleasant thinking begins to diminish, perhaps that change will reinforce the application of punishment. But we feel that in the early stages of a punishment program, you need to provide more immediate reinforcement than would result from improvement in target thinking. Thus, you might use an overt activity to reinforce the successful application of punishment trials. In other words, you would specify in advance that a high-priority activity would follow a particular number of punishment trials.

Thought-Stopping

Another approach that has been applied to compulsive thinking is *thought-stopping*. At this point we do not know how successful this strategy can be on a self-administered basis. Thought-stopping is usually initiated in a therapeutic setting. The patient is first directed to close his eyes and deliberately think the vexing thought. When he/she begins to engage in that thought pattern, a signal is given to the therapist, who shouts, "Stop!" As expected, the shout startles the patient. The therapist then asks the client what happened to the troubling thought. The anticipated response is that it vanished. The therapist uses this occasion to indicate that a person cannot think of two things simultaneously. In other words, the startle reaction at least temporarily eliminates the distressing thought. This process is repeated once or twice during the therapeutic interview.

The next phase of thought-stopping puts the process under the patient's covert control. The individual is asked to close his/her eyes and imagine that he/she is shouting, "Stop!" Next, the patient is directed to close his/her eyes, think the disturbing thought, and immediately yell, "Stop!" As the final phase of the training program, the patient is instructed to use thought-stopping outside the therapeutic setting whenever the negative thought begins to occur. To get some practice at thought-stopping, you might first deliberately think the troublesome thought. After engaging in the undesirable thought pattern for five to ten seconds, shout, "Stop"—really blast it out! (A crowded theater probably would not be the best place to begin your thought-stopping exercises.) This procedure will demonstrate that you have some control over the perplexing thought. This is vital because many individuals view their obsessive thoughts as unchangeable. We suggest that you engage in this exercise several times a day for several days until the sequence of events becomes easy to visualize. Thereafter, any time that you think the distressing thought, *imagine* yelling "Stop!" This will allow you to use the strategy in any setting, even at a formal banquet.

A variation of the thought-stopping procedure has been proposed by Campbell (1973). A twelve-year-old boy experienced repeated and distressing thoughts relative to the violent death of a younger sister. The child was instructed to deliberately think the vexing thought and then interrupt that thought pattern by loudly and quickly counting backwards from ten to zero. At the completion of counting, he immediately focused his thoughts on a pleasant scene. When he was consistently able to eliminate the negative thoughts by counting aloud, he started counting subvocally. A three year follow-up indicated complete control over the distressing thoughts.

Depression

Causes of Depression

Low self-esteem and depressed moods result from focusing on the negative dimensions of life. During periods of depression, the positive aspects of life do not entirely disappear. However, people may be so supersensitized to negative events that they completely tune out positive happenings. Under these circumstances a person may get the subjective feeling that everything is going wrong, and begin to expect bad things to happen. In very few instances does this perception approximate empirical reality (whatever that might be). So the strategy for enhancing mood and self-esteem is to direct one's attention to the positive dimensions of life.

Again, this strategy demands a certain commitment from you. Do you genuinely want to feel better about your life? Probably most of us go through periods when we are down on the world and are not about to let anyone make us feel good. (We are talking about those triple-zero days.) It is paradoxical, but self-pity sometimes seems to be highly reinforcing. If your periods of self-pity are relatively transient, lasting no more than a day or so, and do not occur too frequently, once or twice a month, you are probably a healthy individual for whom time solves most hurts and self-doubts. The person for whom depression and self-doubts become a habitual approach to life is the one who needs self-management.

Positive Self-Verbalization

Mahoney (1971) suggested a strategy that should help the depressed person focus on the positive aspects of life. First you take several 3 X 5 cards and write on all but one some positive features about your life (for example, "I'm proud of being in good physical trim"). You then identify an enjoyable activity that can be engaged in several times a day and make that activity contingent on taking out the card deck, reading the top card, and returning that card to the bottom of the deck. When the blank card comes up, formulate an original positive statement about yourself. You can more easily remember to read from your cards if you attach them to the stimulus that would normally be used in the reinforcing activity. For example, Mahoney had his client attach the cards to a cigarette pack. Any time the individual wanted a cigarette, he automatically came face to face with the stimulus cards.

Another lucid illustration of positive self-verbalization was provided by Johnson (1971). Johnson had a depressed male client write on index cards positive statements regarding his therapeutic progress—increased dating, expanded contacts with people, and improved academic work. The client kept the cards in his pocket and read from one before engaging in a specified reinforcing activity, which in this case was urinating.

The potency of positive self-verbalization in allaying depression has been demonstrated by Todd (1972). The subject initially used only negative terms in describing herself. But with some assistance from the therapist, she was able to generate six positive statements about herself. These statements were printed on a card that was small enough to fit inside the cellophane wrapper of a cigarette package, and she was instructed to read one or two of the items before smoking. According to Todd, her depression decreased considerably within a week, and she increased the number of positive self-references to fourteen. By the end of two weeks, the subject reported feeling better about herself than she had in years; her list had grown to twenty-one positive items. The positive thoughts were being emitted even when she was not smoking or getting ready to smoke.

The primary method we have presented for enhancing mood and self-esteem is to focus systematically on the positive aspects of life. This approach may also provide an effective immunization against the hurts that result from other people's comments and nonverbal behaviors. Ideally, your set of positive statements should directly relate to your principal area of depression or sensitivity. Since most of us have more than one vulnerable area, several sets of positive self-references may be needed. These positive self-references have to be realistic to affect your feelings about yourself. We question the value of beginning each day with the proclamation, "I'm the most brilliant, exciting, and attractive person in the world." Even the new ego machines (you press a button and the machine says something nice about you) are likely to have a minimal impact on your depression.

Happiness

We all characterize certain periods of life as happy and meaningful. However, this introspective assessment cannot ultimately be confirmed by another person. There are numerous behaviors that ostensibly suggest happiness, but in the final analysis one cannot discern what is in another's heart. In some cases a person may claim to be happy when a multitude of behaviors suggest otherwise. But at this point we are dealing solely with *you*. To what extent can you describe your life as happy and meaningful? If the good times outnumber the bad ones, we would give you a plus rating on the happiness dimension. Simply stated, our goal is to increase that positive/negative ratio.

In your pursuit of happiness, we recommend something of a selfish orientation to life. The accepted brand of selfishness requires a commitment to do those things that make you happy, even if other people do not share that happiness. You may want to listen to music, go to a certain restaurant, or see a particular movie. While sharing these experiences could enhance their enjoyment, you have the fundamental right to pursue them alone. Learning to do things by yourself (or at least without that special person) will dramatically increase your chances for happiness. If you are true to yourself (i.e., you do what makes you happy), you will contribute more to others' lives than if you sacrifice happiness experiences for them. Such sacrifices are likely to arouse resentment and undermine your relationships.

Identifying Happiness Experiences

At this point we must become very individualistic in our self-management. What experiences usually precede your declarations of happiness? That may be a question that you cannot answer very precisely. In that case keeping a daily record of the events, behaviors, and thoughts that precede your perceptions of happiness could be indispensable to your subsequent self-management. This procedure will probably alert you to sources of happiness that are presently unknown to you. What those happiness experiences are makes little difference. The point is, if events can be identified which lead to happiness, these events can be made to occur more frequently. If your life is practically devoid of happy times, you will have to turn to others for help. You might select two or three individuals who seem to experience frequent happiness and ask them to record events that they find especially enjoyable. If several people do this for you, you should identify quite an array of experiences that potentially could lead to happiness in your own life.

The contention that one's perception of happiness is related to the frequency of certain events may cause you to feel a bit uneasy. Many events lead to happiness because they occur infrequently. For example, sexual interaction may be a euphoric event in your life, but sexual interaction five times a day might lead to boredom as well as exhaustion. We recommend not that you pursue activity A around the clock, but that you incorporate activities B through Z into your life-style. Any one activity might not increase in frequency, but the variety of happiness experiences would increase. Nevertheless, we feel that many euphoric activities could be increased in frequency without risking satiation.

Finding Time for Happiness Experiences

How does one increase the frequency of his happy moments? Just about everything that we have recommended regarding self-directed behavior changes should indirectly contribute to happiness. But what about strategies that focus directly upon happiness? Suppose you have identified a hierarchy of ten experiences that give you a satisfied feeling. How can you give more emphasis to these experiences, not allowing them to be crowded out by the many mundane activities that infringe on your time each day? In attempting to deal with the commonplace activities, many people never get around to the significant events. The individual may say, "When I get caught up in my work, I'll take time for that special event." That sounds like the old Premack principle, but it is a very unreasonable application of it. For one thing, the contingencies are defined far too nebulously. "Getting caught up" is a subjective state that we seldom attain. Because the contingencies are essentially nonfunctional, the prospect of doing great and noble things will have little effect on our day-to-day activities.

What we suggest is the noncontingent* (unconditional) inclusion of meaningful experiences in your life. In view of our previous emphasis on contingent rewards, our current recommendation may seem inconsistent. We are attempting to insure that you will engage in reinforcing activities that you have been neglecting. These activities can be categorized in five levels: (1) immediate: activities that could occur on a daily basis; (2) short-range: activities that could reasonably occur on a weekly basis; (3) intermediate: activities that would occur no more frequently than once a month; (4) long-range: activities that might occur every year or so; and (5) the distant dream: activities that, if they occur at all, would result from several years of planning and preparation. You should build your life primarily around level one activities. They may be reading, listening to music, having lunch with a friend, playing tennis, or helping someone with a personal problem—if you look closely at truly contented people, you will usually discover that they engage in many happiness-producing activities each day.

Levels two through five often take the form of special events and trips. A weekend movie, picnic, mountain hike, and athletic event might be categorized as level two activities. A special concert, a weekend trip to the lake or mountains, or an all-night orgy might be level three activities. Annual vacation trips, so pervasive in our culture, typify level four activities. Level five activities are ventures that many of us dream about but seldom get around to doing. A summer in Scandanavia or an extended around-the-world tour might fall in this category.

Our contention is that levels two through four are within reach of most people in this society and should be noncontingently scheduled into one's life. If you are not willing to make time for these events, do not blame your unhappiness on fate. You have made the decision to be unhappy. As we have implied, we do not see level five activities as indispensable to human happiness. However, such ventures certainly embellish the quality of life. If you periodically depart from the mainstream and pursue those things that others only dream about, you are to be admired and commended. If not—well, dreaming is not so bad after all.

Undoubtedly, you have some major reservations about the strategy we have just proposed. Will all these noncontingent reinforcing activities erode your capability for changing target behaviors through contingent reinforcement? Keep in mind that we are not recommending that all reinforcement be administered on a noncontingent basis—rather, just enough for you to feel that life is generally worthwhile and enjoyable. This arrangement will leave a multitude of other privileges that can be used conditionally to achieve desired changes in behavior.

The next reservation has a more philosophical tone. In the words of a once-popular song, you may respond to our prescription for happiness with the question, "Is that all there is?" Can human happiness be reduced to a series of reinforcing activities? Is there no underlying, integrative, transcendental theme that gives meaning to the diversity of activities in which we engage? We cannot provide an absolute answer to this question. We can only say that our happiness is very much related to the quality of activities in which we engage. Periods devoid of reinforcing activities are not very meaningful, except as a contrast to other periods. (Unhappy periods sometimes sensitize us to dimensions of life that we would otherwise overlook.) But in the main, increased appreciation for life is more likely to result from good times than from bad ones. Our capacity for relating to others and for perceiving the ecstasy of existence is greatest when we are enjoying life's happy moments.

Concluding Comments

The dictum, "above all, know thyself," still represents the greatest challenge to mortal man. It is probably much easier to know and control one's behavior than to know and control one's inner reactions. The latter is a realm into which behavioral psychologists have only begun to tread. The procedures used by behavior therapists to control internal events have been identified in this chapter. Two of these approaches (full-scale desensitization and thought-stopping) probably can best be initiated by a therapist. One or two sessions with a behavior therapist might make you far more effective in applying these procedures on your own. However, we feel that most of the strategies described in this chapter can be used by any individual genuinely committed to achieving an inner peace.

References

Baker, B. L., Cohen, D. C., and Saunders, J. T. 1973. Self-directed desensitization for acrophobia. *Behaviour Research and Therapy 11,* 79-89.

Bugg, C. A. 1972. Systematic desensitization: a technique worth trying. *Personnel and Guidance Journal, 50*, 823-828.

Campbell, L. M., III. 1973. A variation of thought-stopping in a twelve-year-old boy: a case report. *Behavior Therapy and Experimental Psychiatry 4,* 69-70.

Evans, P. D., and Kellam, A. M. P. 1973. Semi-automated desensitization: a controlled clinical trial. *Behaviour Research and Therapy 11*, 641-646.

Johnson, W. G. 1971. Some applications of Homme's coverant control therapy: two case reports. *Behavior Therapy 2*, 240-248.

Mahoney, M. J. 1971. The self-management of covert behavior: a case study. *Behavior Therapy 2*, 575-578.

Meichenbaum, D. H., and Cameron, R. 1974. The clinical potential of modifying what clients say to themselves. In *Self-control: power to the person,* ed. M. J. Mahoney and C. E. Thoresen. Monterey, Cal.: Brooks/Cole.

Migler, B., and Wolpe, J. 1967. Automated self-desensitization: a case report. *Behaviour Research and Therapy 5,* 133-135.

Phillips. R. E., Johnson, G. D., and Geyer, A. 1972. Self-administered systematic desensitization. *Behaviour Research and Therapy 10*, 93-96.

Russel, R. K., and Sipich, J. F. 1973. Cue-controlled relaxation in the treatment of test anxiety. *Journal of Behavior Therapy and Experimental Psychiatry 4,* 47-49.

Todd, F. J. 1972. Coverant control of self-evaluative responses in the treatment of depression: a new use for an old principle. *Behavior Therapy 3*, 91-94.

Wolpe, J. 1971. Dealing with resistance to thought stopping: a transcript. *Journal of Behavior Therapy and Experimental Psychiatry 2,* 121-125.

Applications
to Self and Others

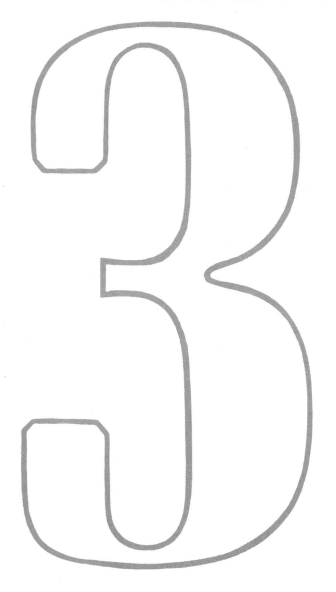

eight

Wealthier than Kings:
Enhancing Interpersonal Relationships

. . . you can practice assertive behavior in front of a mirror.

For thy sweet love rememb'red such wealth brings
That then I scorn to change my state with kings.

—From Shakespeare's Sonnet 29

Shakespeare's analogy graphically portrays the importance of our present topic. Interpersonal relationships contribute fundamentally to the quality of life. A life devoid of friendship and love could hardly be considered fulfilling. In fact, such a life might be described as the ultimate human tragedy. There may be certain facets of your social relationships that you would like to change. You may be experiencing difficulty in some important relationships; you may be unable to establish desired relationships, or have difficulty even interacting with others; or you may feel that you generally rub people the wrong way. Unless you are a very atypical person, some of these concerns will apply to you.

We live in a time when interpersonal relationships have more than just a personal relevance. Inept actions can destroy professional aspirations, friendships, and marriages. Social behaviors also have an impact at the national and international level. The fate of millions is in the hands of a relatively few heads of state, whose social behaviors can start or stop wars. So in some respects, the very existence of the human race is balanced on the relationships between people. Fortunately, we also live at a time when more is known about human behavior than ever before. Increasingly, people are learning that being liked, loved, disliked, or hated are not chance happenings. Indeed, people can regulate how others feel and act toward them.

On Liking and Being Liked

Many psychologists believe that the principle of reciprocal rein-forcement* affects all interpersonal relations. In nontechnical terms this principle asserts that others will like (or value) you to the extent that your behavior is reinforcing to them. In other words, people reciprocate according to what they perceive themselves as receiving. The validity of this principle is well documented in Byrne's (1971) comprehensive study of interpersonal attraction. Our major task is to identify ways in which your behavior can become more reinforcing to others.

*Defined in Glossary.

Listening to Others

The beginning point in being reinforcing to others is to listen to them. Listening implies that you value other people and what they have to say. Unfortunately, many of us become so anxious for our turn to speak that we miss much of what other people are expressing, both verbally and nonverbally. The person who listens well is a rare and usually very reinforcing individual. Three factors possibly account for the added potency that accrues from listening: (1) You clearly demonstrate to others that you care for them; (2) you improve the accuracy of your comments by attending to what others say; and (3) by listening to others, you increase the probability that others will listen to you.

Amount of listening   To improve your listening ability, you might start by simply recording the times when you listen and the times when you speak. One of our students undertook such a project to improve family communications. Family members recorded the occasions they listened and were listened to. Our researcher found that initially she was doing most of the talking. Increased listening, however, produced greater balance in conversation and proved highly reinforcing to the whole family. Rather than recording frequency, you may want to log the time you spend speaking and listening with a stopwatch, especially if your episodes of talking tend to be quite extended. To help increase your listening time in group conversations, you might enlist the support of a friend who could unobtrusively provide you with cues as to when to listen.

Perhaps you are beginning to wonder just how much listening and how much talking you should actually do. We suggest two considerations in making this judgment: (1) Restrict your talking to an equitable portion of the time; that is, if you are talking to one other person, talk no more than 50 percent of the time; if you are talking to two other persons, talk no more than one third of the time, and so on. (2) Avoid long-winded comments. A point usually can be made in a minute or less. People sometimes get so caught up in providing details and parenthetical sidelights that others completely lose track of the intended point. Effective interpersonal relations depend on two-way communication. If the sheer quantity of your verbalizations prevents others from talking, you can be assured that your reinforcement value will not be embellished.

Active listening   Active listening requires more than just allowing the other person to speak. Paraphrasing and commenting directly on what another has just said are basic ways of demonstrating that you are tuning in to what is being said. Paraphrasing has two major benefits. It lets other people know that you are listening to them, and it permits them to correct any error in comprehension on your part. A good way to begin a paraphrase is to comment, "You're saying that . . ." "So you want . . ." "Your feelings are . . ." Counselors have used this technique for years in letting clients know that they are being heard. In paraphrasing or commenting directly on what other people say, you indicate that their comments are worthy of further discussion. What kind of message is conveyed when you abruptly change the topic of conversation following another person's comment?

When you listen actively, you listen for more than another person's words. Hardly anything is more fundamental to a relationship than tuning in to the other person's feelings. We have found that "caring about my feelings" is the principal criterion used by college students in judging the humanistic qualities of another. When people interact with you, try to identify the feelings they express. When you discern that people feel angry, sad, frustrated, elated, or in love, comment to that effect. Nonverbal cues (body posture, facial expression), tone of voice, and rhythm of voice often reveal something quite different from a person's verbal comments. You might ask, "Do you want . . . ?" to which the person replies affirmatively but in a low, hesitant tone of voice. Instead of saying, "Okay, you want to . . ." you should respond, "You feel very ambivalent about . . ." "You're uncertain as to whether . . ."

The following example might help clarify what we mean by active listening. Susan does an equal amount of listening in the following episodes but listens more actively in one than in the other. You be the judge as to which is which.

(Episode One)

Jim: This has not been one of my red-letter days. First thing this morning, the boss . . .

Susan: Oh, do you know who called me today? Steve Turner. I haven't seen Steve in five years. Boy, did he look great!

Jim: As I was saying, the boss came in and blasted me for not having completed the Dobbins Report. He doesn't seem to understand that . . .

Susan: Well, did you get the report finished?

Jim: Yeah, but John and I had a terrible time agreeing on it. Everytime I rejected one of his recommendations, he seemed to take it personally.

Susan: How can grown men act so infantile?

Jim: Well, in trying to appease the boss, I asked him to go to lunch with me. Thought I'd take him to that little place down on the wharf, since he likes seafood so much.

Susan: Steve and I went to Marty's Steakpit for lunch. I never realized that place was so intimate.

Jim: On the way to lunch, I had a flat tire, which wouldn't have been so bad except that the spare was also flat. By the time I had walked to a service station and gotten the tires fixed, we wound up taking an hour and a half just to get to the restaurant.

Susan: How much did it cost to get the tires fixed?

(Episode Two)

Jim: This has not been one of my red-letter days. First thing this morning, the boss came in and chewed me out for not having completed the Dobbins Report. He didn't seem to understand that I had to get some information from John before I could complete it.

Susan: So you feel he was really criticizing you very unfairly.

Jim: Yeah, plus John kept getting upset when I would reject one of his recommendations about what should go in the report.

Susan: That must have been very frustrating to you.

Jim: You bet, but to top it off, I took the boss to lunch—trying to appease his feelings, you know. On the way, I had a flat tire and discovered that my spare was also flat. By the time I had located a service station and gotten the tires fixed, we had spent an hour and a half getting to lunch. Can you believe it—an hour and a half?

Susan: Bet you were feeling almost paranoid by then.

Jim: Right! But that's enough about my glorious day. What happened with yours?

Susan: You remember Steve Turner from college.
         Well, he was passing through on his way to the coast. He called and we got together for lunch. It was great reminiscing and talking about where people are now.

In sum, we suggest that an indispensable step in becoming reinforcing to others is to listen carefully to what they have to say. Putting
aside other activities when someone is speaking to you, looking at
other people when they speak, being careful not to interrupt other
people's comments, and commenting directly on what other people
have just expressed—these behaviors communicate to people that
you care about and understand what they are saying. Incidentally,
you might apply the same criteria in determining whether other
people are interested in what you have to say.

Giving Approval

Verbal approval is unquestionably the most widely used (and abused)
of all would-be reinforcers. Seldom do others accept verbal accolades
without examining closely what is proffered. People are interested in
determining whether you mean what you say or whether you are
acting out of ulterior motivation. If your approval is judged to be
sincere, it can be tremendously reinforcing. But if your approval
appears even slightly artificial, others will be repulsed by it. We reject
the idea that conveying sincerity involves nothing more than being
sincere. Being sincere helps, but it is quite possible for sincere people
to seem artificial. For that reason we shall provide specific guidelines
for giving approval in an authentic and reinforcing way. Specifically,
we shall examine (a) what you approve, (b) how you approve,
(c) redundancy of approval, (d) consistency of approval,
(e) frequency of approval, and (f) pairing approval with other
reinforcers.[1] Overlooking these factors could block your efforts to
improve interpersonal relations.

What you approve   One of the easiest ways to judge the sincerity
of people's approval (praise) is to consider *what* they approve. Most
individuals enjoy being the recipient of praise, but they prefer being
lauded for bona fide accomplishments. Thus, a prerequisite to administering verbal approval is to determine what others consider to
be significant accomplishments. To do this requires careful observation and listening. People usually engage in or talk about activities
that they deem important. You can use these high-priority activities

---

[1]For a discussion of the effects of verbal approval on student-teacher relationships, see R. L. Williams and Kamala Anandam, *Cooperative classroom management* (Columbus, Ohio: Charles E. Merrill, 1973).

and conversations as a basis for legitimate compliments. For example, if a person presented a speech, which he/she has talked about for days, you could congratulate him/her on having completed a difficult assignment. In addition, there may be facets of the speech worthy of commendation. The individual who observes and listens closely will have little difficulty identifying things worth complimenting.

Generally speaking, the more specific you make your approval, the more reinforcing it will be. It does not take much effort or insight to say, "Great job," "I enjoyed your presentation," "Inspiring performance," or "You did beautifully." These statements could be made insincerely after sleeping through a performance. But enumerating the specific features of a performance that were especially impressive requires that you pay attention. The more specific you make your compliments, the more intently you have to listen and/or watch a person's performance. For example, we would be pleased if you wrote us saying that you had given our book to several of your friends because you thought the ideas were worthwhile. But we would be particulary delighted if your letter detailed which suggestions you had found particularly useful.

How you approve   People judge the sincerity of approval not only by what you say but by how you say it. Some people are so lavish in their approbations that others minimize what they have to say. Such people often elicit a host of side glances when they deliver their lofty words of commendation. They may note that your behavior is the "greatest," "the most fantastic," "the best ever," or even "beyond comparison." Since many persons tend to dislike ostentatious, flamboyant approval, we suggest that you reserve superlatives for very special accomplishments. Of course, you must be the judge.

The authenticity of your approval may also be questioned on the basis of your nonverbal behavior. The individual who offers congratulations in a half-hearted tone, the person who says, "That's really a funny story," but fails to laugh, the individual who is "so happy for you" without smiling, and the person who thinks you look "just great," but hardly notices you—these people illustrate our point. In summarizing the research on nonverbal communication, Mehrabian (1969) noted that we turn more toward, stand nearer, and make more frequent eye contact with those we like than those we dislike. Such simple acts as a touch, a smile, or a nod of the head can be profoundly important in conveying the sincerity of your approval.

Redundancy of approval   Another factor that affects the reinforcement value of your approval is its redundancy. An initially rein-forcing phrase, such as "keep up the good work," "very good," or "you look nice," may lose much of its reinforcement value with repeated usage. Most of us assume that the individual who makes the same pronouncement over and over about our behavior really is not paying attention to us. Because of the importance of this issue, you should develop a list of different approval comments and then prac-tice verbalizing them. Otherwise, you run the risk of being perceived as insincere simply because of your limited verbal repertoire.

There are two major ways to word a compliment. First, you can highlight your personal reaction to another's behavior; e.g., "I en-joyed . . ." "I especially liked . . ." or "I was inspired by . . ." Second, you can make blanket statements about the quality of another's be-havior; e.g., "What you said about . . . was inspiring," "Your em-phasis on . . . was great," or "Your analysis of . . . was very creative." To minimize redundancy, you should periodically use both types of compliments. Admittedly, statements of the first type are more con-sistent with reality than those of the second. In complimenting another you ordinarily can speak only for yourself. The first category of statements reflects that limitation, while the second may imply a far more pervasive judgment. However, we suspect that most people who are being approved realize that you are speaking only for your-self when you say, "That was a great job." So that kind of statement generally is considered acceptable. Our point on redundancy is inex-tricably tied to our earlier emphasis on specificity. The more specific your approval, the less the probability of your being redundant—regardless of which category you use.

Consistency of approval   Everyone can attest to the excitement generated by anticipated reinforcement. Recall looking forward to attending a party, going on a date, or participating in an athletic event. We believe your approval can generate similar anticipation; that is, others will look forward to seeing you because of your expected approval. To create such an effect, your approval must be consis-tently given for particular behaviors. Perhaps you have had the ex-perience following a significant accomplishment of actually seeking out particular people who appreciate and compliment your achieve-ment. You sought out those people because past experiences taught you that they approve of such accomplishments. Friendships usually evolve with people who become reliable sources of reinforcement for us. In fact, some psychologists define love as the anticipation of reinforcing events.

People need to know what they can expect when they are with you, but they are equally interested in how you respond to them in their absence. Criticizing others in their absence epitomizes the kind of behavior that erodes relationships. Obviously, people will not relish your approval if you criticize them when their backs are turned.They make that judgment by listening to what you say about others who are not present. For both ethical and practical reasons, it is imperative that you avoid such criticism. Your surreptitious criticism is in no way helpful to the recipient of that criticism and probably undermines your relationship with the confidant of your criticism. At some point people will begin to suspect that you talk about them in their absence in the same way you discuss others in their absence. Because the approval of "two-faced" or "backstabbing" individuals is so open to question, the approval of individuals who are consistent in public and private situations is especially meaningful.

Frequency of approval   We suggest that you increase the frequency of your approval at a very gradual pace. An abrupt increase in the frequency of your approval could make you appear awkward and insincere. "Coming on too strong" is a well-known blunder in interpersonal relations. Therefore, we suggest a practice similar to changing your hair color—change slowly enough to let others adjust to the new you.

Pairing approval with other reinforcers   A final way to add potency to your approval is to pair it with events known to be reinforcing to the other person. Approval that initially lacks value may acquire some of the reinforcing properties of the other event. Praise could be delivered during or after a meal, on a coffee break, while playing tennis, or at any reinforcing time or place. In other words, the pairing and timing of approval are important elements in making your approval maximally reinforcing. There is modest evidence that your mere presence when others are enjoying reinforcing activites will cause you to be better liked (Griffitt, 1968; Lott and Lott, 1960).

Summation of approval   Giving approval is a major means of reinforcing others and, consequently, being reinforced by others. However, not all approval is reinforcing to others. Approval sometimes can seem manipulative and artificial. To increase the reinforcement value of your approval, you should (a) approve specific achievements and behaviors that the other person considers worthwhile; (b) avoid ostentatious approval and make your nonverbal behaviors consistent with your verbal approval; (c) use different ways of expressing approval rather than depending on a few stock phrases;

(d) make your approval consistent in time and in public and private situations; (e) gradually increase the frequency of your approval; and (f) pair your approval with events known to be reinforcing to the other person. There are other factors that can enhance the reinforcement value of your approval. Increasing your self-esteem, being well-organized, keeping your commitments, and developing new skills all fall in this category.

Self-Management Exercises

You might already be aware of much that has been presented in this section, but have not made much headway in improving interpersonal relations. People sometimes equate knowing and doing but the two are quite different. You can be knowledgeable about many matters and not apply what you know. If you are to learn new behaviors, you must practice emitting those behaviors. One can no more become a skillful social reinforcer by merely reading about social reinforcement than a skillful golfer by simply reading about golf. We now offer a few exercises to help you begin implementing what you know about reinforcing others. Be sure to supply reinforcement for your own efforts.

1. If you know someone who is also interested in developing listening skills, take turns listening to each other. You could "earn" your turn to talk by correctly paraphrasing what the other person has said. The other person could then rule on the adequacy of your listening.

2. Identify someone to whom you should listen—a child, an elderly person, a friend, or a spouse. Provide provocative (leading) questions and explore solutions to that person's problems. You have probably noticed that when three or four people start talking, someone always seems to get left out. You may wish to direct questions to that person.

3. Scan the school newspaper or interoffice memo for praiseworthy items about your peers. See if this procedure helps you increase the frequency of compliments passed on to others.

4. Reread the Summation of Approval and identify which dimensions of approval-giving you most need to work on. Formulate a self-management strategy for enhancing your skills in those areas.

Romance

The principles that govern liking generally apply to loving. People learn to like and they also learn to love. Although we hear claims of instantaneous love—love at first sight—we suspect that this phenomenon involves the generalization of learned responses to the new person. You may feel warmly toward the new acquaintance because he/she reminds you of a pleasant old acquaintance. In spite of the learned quality of love, it is always possible to love someone who does not love you, or the reverse. However, the prospect of unrequited love can be minimized by the suggestions in this section.

What can be done to win the affections of another person? At first you might think, "He (or she) will have to take me or leave me as I am." On reflection, however, you should realize that since love is learned, you can do something to affect its course. The concept of reinforcement is the essence of love. The development of reciprocal love is essentially a matter of making yourself more reinforcing to the desired individual.

Becoming a Generalized Reinforcer

The best reinforcer is a stimulus, person or thing, that has been associated with a variety of satisfying events. Such a stimulus is called a generalized reinforcer. Praise and money are examples. Some psychologists have concluded that "when a person becomes a generalized secondary reinforcer for someone, he is loved by that person" (Miller and Siegel, 1972). To achieve this status, you need to provide reinforcement to the other in many different ways and in many different settings. Praise, willingness to listen, thoughtful gifts, outings with mutual friends, movies, parties, and serene settings offer broad opportunities for reinforcement. In other words, love must have a chance to grow through a wide range of pleasant interactions. Limited reinforcement in one setting or of one kind can lead to the declaration, "I'm very fond of you, but we can never be more than friends."

Playing hard to get When that special person begins to tune in to your generalized reinforcement potential, should you, in turn, play hard to get? Yes and no. Researchers (Walster et al., 1973) who have extensively investigated this phenomenon among females say that playing hard to get increases one's desirability, but may also scare away would-be pursuers. Walster and his colleagues conclude that a woman can intensify her desirability by developing a reputation for being hard to get and then conveying her attraction to the target person. However, playing hard to get for everyone, including the desired person, is a highly efficient way of deactivating one's love life.

We do have certain misgivings about the findings of Walster et al. They seem to imply that relationships are most valuable when they are difficult to achieve and are exclusive in nature. Playing hard to get probably evolves as a reaction to adolescent exploitation. The adolescent tendency to pursue relationships only long enough to achieve the other person's attraction is clearly directed toward self-aggrandizement. Other people are hurt by this behavior. As a defense against this potential hurt, people play hard to get and thereby preserve attractions that otherwise might quickly fade. We hate to think that adults would still engage in self-aggrandizing exploitation, but undoubtedly many do. You have to decide whether you want to pursue relationships that have a high exploitative risk. Furthermore, we see no reason why exclusiveness should enhance the value of a relationship. A person can care for two individuals in totally unique ways without having affection for one detract from affinity for the other. However, very few people in our culture feel as we do. The majority of people apparently feel that exclusive relationships are the most valuable relationships.

Sex-Role Behaviors

You may wonder what a discussion of sex roles is doing in a section on romance. Sex-role stereotyping relates to such issues as job discrimination, domestic roles, and the social status of men and women, but it also affects the more intense aspects of human interactions. Rigid sex roles certainly prevent many male-female romances from reaching their maximum potential. We feel that the elimination of sex-role behaviors can make one a more loving and lovable person. So our major concern is how to use self-management procedures in changing sex-role behaviors.

Commitment to change   There is probably no area where commitment to change is more indispensable than in the realm of sex-role behaviors. You may have received enough negative input already to make you anxious to change. If not, consider in concrete terms how sex-role stereotypes can adversely affect male-female relationships.

Take the common example of the husband and wife who both work outside the home, while the wife still assumes most of the domestic duties in the home. Even if the husband is not chastized for this arrangement, he pays a price for it. Such an arrangement often causes the wife to be covertly and/or overtly negative in her responses to her husband. This in turn may adversely affect many dimensions of their relationship, including the sexual dimension. By assuming an equitable share of the domestic responsibilities, the husband not only develops a respect for domestic work but is also likely to evoke far more positive reactions from his wife.

In spite of our intellectual commitment to change, it is frequently easier not to change. Taking a nap, reading the evening newspaper, and watching television probably have higher intrinsic reinforcement value than washing dishes, vacuuming the house, and doing the laundry. If the other person tolerates our present behavior, we may make no effort to change. From a woman's point of view, asking for dates, initiating sexual play, and behaving assertively during sexual play may represent behaviors to which a woman is intellectually committed but still finds difficult to accomplish. For both males and females, setting events and reinforcement contingencies often favor stereotypic behaviors.

Behaviors to change   As we have repeatedly recommended, begin modestly in defining your goals. For example, inviting a man to have lunch with you or suggesting an afternoon coffee break with a man might be a starting point for a woman. A behavior that many men should consider is the open expression of emotions. Perhaps one can learn to express emotions directly by first talking about emotions. To be able to say, "I feel like crying," may be a prerequisite to actual crying. So an appropriate first goal for a man might be to increase the number of instances in which he verbalizes his feelings.

Another behavior with which many men have difficulty is the admission of fault. Such expressions as, "I was wrong in saying that," "I made a terrible mistake," "You're right about that," and "I'm sorry for what I did," are foreign to most men. To back down, to admit errors, or to walk away from the bully are commonly considered unmasculine. Men think that standing firm increases their attractiveness to women. What they actually do is appear nervous, insecure, and insensitive. There are few things that would be more therapeutic for male-female relationships (or male-male relationships, for that matter) than for men to be able to admit fault. The simple admission of error often can avert days of resentment and conflict. The Williams-Long dictum is that it is better to switch than fight.

Strategies for change   We have found two procedures especially useful in altering stereotypic responses. Both depend on assistance from others who share your commitment. The first of these, role reversal, can best be achieved in a relaxed, small group setting. The , objective is for individuals to emit behaviors normally exhibited by members of the opposite sex. We have found that these role reversals not only produce a good deal of hilarity, but they also sensitize individuals to problems created by the conventional sex-role behaviors. Furthermore, they give people a chance to exhibit behaviors (notwithstanding their initial awkwardness) that they eventually want to emit naturally and comfortably.

The more long-range strategy for changing sex-role behaviors is to seek out the company of those whom you can count on to reinforce nonconventional behaviors. You will find that their very presence provides some potent cues for nonstereotypic responses. Since you have nothing to lose by exhibiting nontraditional behaviors around these people, you will have an opportunity to learn new behaviors without jeopardizing previous sources of reinforcement. For example, the male who wants to be able to express his emotions openly should initially work on that behavior among individuals who are sympathetic to human liberation.

Sexual Interaction

Although we strongly favor the elimination of sex-role behaviors that produce difficulties for one sex or the other, we do not favor de-emphasizing human sexuality. When sexual interaction involves exploitation, it is destructive. But when sexual interaction produces mutual pleasure and fulfillment, it is fantastic. Your sexual interaction can be analyzed in terms of the who, how, and when of tactile, visual, and auditory reinforcement. Although some phases of that interaction may defy behavioral explanation, the principles we have previously discussed for improving interpersonal relations do have something to contribute. You cannot separate your impact as a lover from your general reinforcement value as a person. Some people who are physically quite attractive behave in such a nonreinforcing or aversive fashion that their sex life is nil.

Other people have difficulty when they get to the actual sexual activity. We are sure that you are familiar with all the how-to-do-it books on this subject, so we will not attempt to delineate methodology. However, if reinforcing the other person is your paramount consideration, it is likely that you will become much more stimulated yourself. Identifying the facets of sexual activity that are most reinforcing to your partner and then using these to reinforce him/her contingently for stimulating you is a good way to heighten the reinforcement for both persons. There are some basically nonsexual modes of tactile stimulation (e.g., rubbing one's back, running your fingers through one's hair) that can also be used to enhance the reinforcement value of the sexual experience.

Meaningful sexual interaction obviously involves a great deal more than physical stimulation. The quality of sexual interaction cannot be divorced from the quality of other interactions. If other interactions with that special person are reinforcing, it is probable that sexual interaction will also be reinforcing. Similarly, many abrasive conflicts during the day rarely can be negated by sexual interaction in the evening.

A Self-Management Project

We would like to think that our limited information on romantic relationships can improve your chances of having "a luve like a melodie, that sweetly play'd in tune." Let us reaffirm that our suggestions do not insure such mutual love. You may follow our recommendations to the letter and still find that that certain person just does not fall in love with you. An even more painful possibility is that a person who was once irresistibly attracted to you may cease to be attracted. We propose, therefore, that you devise a plan for dealing with such disappointments. How do you get an old love off your mind? If love is learned, how can it be unlearned?

1. *Selecting your goal:* In this case, your goal might be twofold. You may want to reduce the amount of time you spend brooding over the lost romance and at the same time increase your contacts with members of the opposite sex.
2. *Recording the quantity and circumstances of behavior:* You might try recording the names of the people and places that trigger the unwanted memories.
3. *Changing setting events:* Use the information gained by recording to alter (or avoid) setting events that produce brooding. Identify

other setting events that will lead to added exposure to members of the opposite sex.

4. *Establishing effective consequences:* You know your reinforcement priorities better than we do.
5. *Focusing on contingencies:* What would make you more consistently aware of the payoff for pursuing new relationships?
6. *Achieving covert control*: Try thought-stopping for the old memories and covert reinforcement for visualizing new kinds of interaction.

Managing Interpersonal Conflicts

Sometimes our interests are not well served by the actions of others. We know of no one who has freed his life of conflict and we are not certain that a total lack of conflict would be advantageous. Conflicts can sometimes provide tremendous opportunities for personal growth. Negative input, for example, can provide an impetus for changing behavior. However, habitual conflict with another human being in no way enhances the quality of life. Although some people seem to thrive on conflict, it is probably because they have not discovered a better mode of existence.

Sources of Conflict

The first step in resolving an interpersonal conflict is to examine the sources of that conflict. To this end we have identified what we think are the major contributors to interpersonal discord. First, use our suggestions to evaluate your own actions. You may determine that *your* behavior is a major cause of the conflict. Do not attempt to change another person's conduct until you have considered your own behavior.

Defensive reactions   There is probably no greater contributor to interpersonal conflicts than defensive behaviors. Defensive reactions usually involve a quick defense of your own behavior and a counterattack on another person's behavior. This kind of reaction from you undoubtedly causes the other person to respond more defensively. Such reciprocal defensiveness can only serve to accentuate the conflict.

People respond defensively in order to present themselves in a positive light. However, the exact opposite is often accomplished. The other person goes away saying, "He was really sensitive about that issue," "She got very uptight," or "Wow, was he ever defensive!" The individual who responds nondefensively—listens carefully and completely to the other person's views, admits mistakes, identifies valid points in what the other person is saying, and calmly clarifies his/her own ideas or actions—is the unique individual, the one who appears to be secure and tolerant. We believe that nondefensiveness leads to resolution of many conflicts and markedly upgrades your esteem in the eyes of others.

You can become less defensive through planned interactions with people from different backgrounds. People generally seek and associate with individuals who behave and believe as they do. If you associate only with persons whose beliefs are similar to your own, you run the risk of becoming intolerant of other positions. Defensiveness then becomes a synonym for intolerance. Interact with a variety of people, find out what they think and why, and share your ideas with them. You may be encouraged by what you can offer one another. In any event, if you deliberately expose yourself to ideas that are different from yours, you will not be so shocked when your views are unexpectedly challenged.

Needless competition   Many conflicts are generated by unnecessary competitiveness. We have noticed that conflicts among colleagues are often characterized by a high degree of competitiveness; people evaluate their accomplishments primarily in terms of others' accomplishments. These individuals tend to create rivalry out of any situation. They may strive to get a job done first, make a point of never being late, try desperately to win at sports—even against closest friends—and even beat you at showing courtesy to others. This kind of chronic competition engenders dislike from those who must be the losers. Do you occasionally let others know that they are superior to you in some respects? If you always have to outdo others, you are probably eliciting their wrath rather than their admiration.

Misinterpretations   Imagine how many conflicts arise simply because people fail to listen to or to understand what others are saying. People often interpret a comment or glance as meaning far more than was intended. Misinterpretations occur between lovers, on the job, at home, and in the classroom. If you perceive a conflict brewing over what someone has done or said, check to be sure that you clearly understand that person's intentions. One way to do this is to restate or paraphrase what has been said, or to ask what was meant.

Imputing motives   Once a conflict is underway, the participants may ascribe all sorts of motives to each other. You accuse the other person of being dishonest, of deliberately ignoring you, and of not caring about your feelings. Imputing motives can cause minor disagreements to evolve into unnecessary major conflicts. The truth is that no one can see into another's mind, and there is thus no way of telling what a person's motives are. So when we assign sinister motives to people's actions, we are not only aggravating the conflict, we are speaking of that which we know not.

Name-calling   Name-calling or labeling has about the same impact on a conflict as imputing motives. Name-calling tends to dehumanize other people and make striking out against them easier. It also exaggerates the problem, introduces extraneous considerations, and causes other people to respond to the label rather than to the target behavior. People who play the name-calling game often employ derogatory ethnic labels. Others use regional and family labels. Even adjectives, such as "rigid," "insensitive," "closed," "immature," and "obnoxious," can dramatically confuse and embroil human interaction.

Severance of communication   Cutting off communication may generate increased hostility. You might suppose that noncommunication would at least keep a relationship from worsening, but the reverse is probably true. Research by Sadler and Tesser (1973) suggests that if a person has an opportunity to meditate on an insult or unjust treatment, hostility is often intensified. Most people will indeed find the time to repeat symbolically a disagreement, especially when the door to communication is closed. We thus recommend that you continue to talk even when you may disagree with a person on some points. Continued interaction will at least give you a chance to resolve your differences. Our first objective in counseling a married couple is usually to increase the amount of communication between them. Very frequently, real communication between the two has practically ceased. They engage in conversation only about the most superficial issues, while frustration regarding their problems builds toward a cataclysmic eruption. So just being able to talk about their problems, no matter how awkward that talk might seem, represents real progress.

Changing Others' Behavior

Now that we have suggested how *you* should behave in order to resolve conflicts, what about the other person? It has no doubt occurred to you that sometimes the other person is primarily at fault. He/she may be the one who is being defensive or making unfair judgments. Another person can sometimes make your life very difficult. You cannot always be expected to change every time a conflict develops.

We are not suggesting that you can always alter the behavior of others. In fact, there is no need to change others' behavior merely because they disagree with you or because their philosophy is different from yours. People have a right to their own views. Disagreements need not lead to disagreeableness. You can often express your own opinions without having to change the views of others. Likewise, you can permit others to express their beliefs without feeling that your views are under attack. Nevertheless, situations do arise when your interests and others' interests conflict. Changing their behavior may be essential for you to function adequately. We cannot guarantee results, but we believe that the following suggestions may be helpful in changing others' inappropriate behavior.

Working cooperatively   One of the surest ways of reducing another's conflictual behaviors is to work with that person on a cooperative venture. People who work together have the opportunity for increased interactions, can experience the rewards of achieving a common goal, and can observe each other's helpfulness. Hopefully, working together on one venture will bring them closer together on other issues. The problem is to arrange for cooperation with someone with whom you are in conflict. This can be achieved in several ways. If the other person has evidenced an interest in a project in which you are presently involved, you might ask him/her to work with you on that project. Or, you might volunteer to work on a project in which the other person is already involved. The indication that you are willing to work with other people can have a profound effect on their behavior.

Demonstrating similarity to another   A second method of altering another's negative behavior is to demonstrate your similarity to that person. Berscheid and Walster (1969) indicate in their summary work on interpersonal attraction that people like those who have attitudes similar to their own. Thus, we recommend that you diligently look for points of similarity between you and those who are causing you problems. After you have identified sources of similarity, find opportunities for helping the other person see the likenesses. Such opportunites often arise in group discussions. Possibly you will see the chance to comment, "I agree with ———— on that," "It seems that

——— and I have a lot in common," or "You made a good point; I agree with you." Seeing that another person is similar to you in one area may cause that person to be less resistant in other areas.

Reversing obligations   Conflicts sometimes result from another person's domineering behavior. A favorite tactic of domineering people is to make you feel obligated to them. "What are you doing to earn your keep in this household?" "Don't forget that I'm the boss and I pay your salary," and "I'm the teacher, so if you want to pass this course you'll . . . " Such statements illustrate this tactic. In dealing with a rebellious adolescent, Masters (1970) had the adolescent initiate activity that would make his parents feel obligated to him. The adolescent had rebelled previously against parental dictates, which were often enshrouded with such statements as, "I pay for the food in this house; you earn your keep by mowing the lawn." By doing the task before he was commanded, the adolescent reversed the direction of control. Because he voluntarily mowed the lawn, his parents now felt obligated to do something nice for him. Eventually, he began to view his parents more positively, since he was now controlling their behavior. His parents began to view him more positively, since he was assuming responsibility without their having to prod him. The essence of this strategy is to do things that are expected by the other person before he/she has a chance to direct you to do them.

Expressing criticism   Criticism is sometimes the only avenue for changing another's bad behavior. However, you must be especially cautious about the manner in which you give criticism. First, make your criticism very specific. Few things are more frustrating than being criticized and not being able to determine exactly what the other person is objecting to. Second, criticize in private whenever possible. People become defensive when put on the spot in public. Third, attempt to restrict your criticism to occasions when it is requested. A person is more likely to listen to criticism under these circumstances than when it is arbitrarily imposed. Individuals often ask for feedback on specific behaviors that affect their interpersonal relations with you. If they do this, you should respond without overwhelming them with an avalanche of past iniquities. Stay in the present and on the precise issue mentioned by the solicitor of criticism. Finally, sandwich criticism between positive statements. This practice makes criticism more palatable.

Responding to feelings   Some behaviors that might appear to call for criticism can better be changed by active listening. Lazarus (1973) provides an example of this possibility. While being waited upon by an abrasive sales clerk, he considered three possible negative responses to the individual: (1) personally chastizing him, (2) using one-upmanship (i.e., insulting him), or (3) reporting him to the manager. However, instead of verbally attacking him, Lazarus decided to respond emphatically: "You seem to be having a hell of a bad day. Is something wrong?" The sales clerk proceeded to explain that his wife was in the hospital and he was very anxious about her condition. What followed was a significant conversation focusing on the man's feelings about his wife's illness. Undoubtedly, both men felt substantially better as a result of this positive, supportive interaction.

Reinforcing constructive behaviors   We must not conclude our analysis of changing others' undesirable behavior without a word about reinforcement. Perhaps the best way to reduce people's bad behaviors is to reinforce their constructive responses. We have yet to meet the person who does not exhibit at least some good behaviors—probably many more than we presently recognize. If you are quick to respond to those behaviors, while giving little attention to undesirable responses, you can be sure that the person's behavior will become more constructive.

Self-Management Checklist

This section emphasized that the best way to deal with interpersonal conflicts is first to evaluate your own behavior. Then and only then should you consider changing the behavior of others. "Cast out the beam in your own eye before beholding the mote in your brother's eye." The following checklist should help you determine whether you need to undertake a self-management project related to issues in this section.

___I do not usually react to confrontative situations in a defensive manner.

___I seek out opportunities to be exposed to viewpoints other than my own.

___I seldom engage in competition with others.

___When in doubt about a person's intentions, I investigate the meaning of his actions.

___I always avoid name-calling or labeling of persons with whom I disagree.

__ When involved in controversies, I stick to the observable facts rather than imputing motives.

__ To resolve conflicts I occasionally search for ways of cooperating with the other party to the dispute.

__ I have no acquaintance to whom I cannot sometimes be reinforcing.

Behaving Assertively

To apply many of the suggestions of this chapter requires what psychologists now call assertive behavior. This is especially true of such negative responses as criticizing and complaining. However, many of us also have difficulty with positive behaviors: meeting new people, exhibiting nonsexist behaviors, and expressing affection to others. People who behave assertively act on their feelings. If they are upset about something, they let appropriate other people know about it. If they want to meet a certain person, they do so. If they wish to convey affection, they do so. We suspect that assertive behavior prevents many of those hurt and depressed feelings that result from human interactions. When you are unable to express the affection that you have for a person, you do not feel very good about yourself. When you are unable to tell someone that he/she is criticizing you unfairly, you are likely to feel hurt and hostile.

Before proceeding with our discussion of assertive behavior, we must stress the distinction between assertive responses and aggressive responses. Aggressive behavior connotes attack. Being aggressive puts people on the spot, impugns their motives, blames them for your problems, or threatens them. Assertive behavior, on the other hand, consists of asserting one's worth and one's rights as a human being. Assertive people look you in the eye, move their bodies freely, speak openly of their feelings, readily accept compliments, periodically talk about themselves, and disagree with you on occasion. When assertive people get upset, they focus on their own feelings rather than impugning yours; they identify the specific behaviors or circumstances to which they object rather than issuing broad indictments; and they specify the changes they desire rather than dwelling on who is to blame for past mistakes.

Expressing Grievances

Let us present an example of how an assertive person would express dissatisfaction with another's behavior. For quite some time, you and

Barbara have been close friends. You play tennis together, go to lunch together, go to the library together, and frequently go out on the town together. There are many things about Barbara that are attractive, but one of her behaviors is increasingly irritating you: Barbara is habitually ten to fifteen minutes late for your appointments. You have decided to confront Barbara with her behavior. This confrontation would probably involve the following behaviors: telling Barbara that having to wait has come to be a source of irritation to you, identifying specific inconveniences that have resulted from her tardiness, and requesting that both of you stick to the appointed times. Notice that there is no tirade in this scenario, no questioning of Barbara's integrity, and no skirting of the real cause of your dissatisfaction.

We could not discuss expressing grievances without mentioning the classic restaurant scene. You have looked forward all week to going to a particular restaurant on Saturday night. You practically have picked out your steak ahead of time. Although the restaurant has an excellent reputation and you have eaten there many times, the steak you get this particular evening is a loser. As soon as you have established that the steak is of low quality (two or three bites), you motion for the waiter. Nothing more is required than simply indicating that you have been served a bad piece of meat and would like to exchange it for another. There is no shouting, no blaming of the waiter or chef, and certainly no attempt to embarrass anyone. Instead, there is simply a calm statement of what is wrong and what should be done to correct it.

Becoming Assertive

Our examples of assertive behavior may sound quite acceptable to you, but that does not mean that you will be able to exhibit those responses. Where does one begin to increase one's assertive behavior? As with all behavioral goals, you start only slightly above where you are presently operating. If you have never said a word in group meetings, challenging the company president in a board meeting probably would not be a good first goal. It is imperative that your initial goal represent a behavior that will produce immediate reinforcement. Selecting an initial goal that will bring punishment is an effective way to make you forever nonassertive. Before you designate that initial goal, look around and see which individuals usually welcome candid feedback. If you are upset (even mildly so) about one of their behaviors, express your feelings to them in the manner we have previously described. This arrangement will maximize your chances for reinforcement.

If behaving assertively in real situations is initially too threatening, there are other ways of practicing assertiveness.[2] Suppose you are unable to state your viewpoints very emphatically and generally speak softly and emotionlessly. A good exercise is to read some passage in a manner that conveys anger, sadness, or elation. Tape-record those readings and see if someone else can correctly identify the emotion intended in each. Keep practicing until others can easily discern that you sound upset, sad, or happy in the various readings. Some shouting exercises might also be helpful. Pick out a neutral phrase and repeat it several times, each time slightly louder than before. Continue until you are shouting at the top of your lungs. (This also ought to improve your thought-stopping skills.) This exercise will allow you to become adjusted to hearing yourself speak up. A public park is probably not the best place for engaging in this exercise.

Role playing is another effective way of preparing for the real thing. Perhaps you have friends who are sensitive to your problem and who would be willing to role-play troublesome situations with you. Or, you might ask others who are nonassertive to work with you in role play. With this arrangement, all parties would directly benefit from the experience. There is great virtue in getting the feel for a behavior before attempting that behavior in an actual situation. If role play is too advanced, you can always engage in covert reinforcement exercises. You can imagine yourself meeting new people, expressing grievances, and conveying affection; then imagine positive social consequences: people are friendly, they graciously correct their mistakes, and they provide counteraffection. These exercises should get you in the habit of visualizing yourself being assertive.

A principal deterrent to assertive behavior appears to be anxiety. Several therapists (Wolpe, Lazarus) have viewed anxiety and assertive behavior as incompatible responses. If this is true, dealing with that anxiety is essential. Perhaps the best way of attacking your anxiety is through self-directed relaxation. First, formulate a hierarchy of assertive behaviors that you have difficulty emitting. A hierarchy related to group interaction might include (1) volunteering a

---

[2]If you want explicit directions on how to become assertive, you could order Lazarus' tape on assertive behavior from Instructional Dynamics, Inc. 166 East Superior Street, Chicago, Illinois 60611.

comment during group discussion, (2) expressing your feelings about an issue, (3) asking another person why he/she holds a certain view, (4) changing the discussion topic, and (5) verbally disagreeing with another viewpoint expressed in the group. Next, apply your relaxation strategy to the visualization of each response and then to the actual response.

Modeling is a behavioral strategy that therapists frequently use in helping people behave more assertively. You usually can find appropriate models among your acquaintances. Look for people who not only articulate their feelings but who also get positive reactions to those feelings. What distinguishes their behavior from that of others who appear to be just as assertive but who usually get poor results (e.g., others become upset)? The answer may be found in the distinction between assertive and aggressive behaviors. If a complaint includes an attack on another's competence or integrity, you can count on an abrasive counterresponse. If your circle of acquaintances lacks appropriate role models, you may want to obtain a commercially available tape or film portraying assertive behavior.[3]

Another means of shaping assertive behavior is through feedback. Behavior therapists often videotape group sessions so that people can see themselves in action. If that is not feasible in your case, you can practice assertive behavior in front of a mirror or have a friend provide feedback relative to your assertive responses. If you are quite unassertive at this point, you are probably very sensitive to social criticism. In that case it may be best to ask your friend initially to identify the positive features of your behavior.

If you rarely verbalize your feelings, we doubt that our brief suggestions will make you an assertive person. Under those circumstances we recommend that you seek assertive training through your college counseling center. However, if you are able to express your feelings in some situations, our suggestions may help you expand the number of those situations.

Self-Management Exercise

Since criticizing or complaining is probably the most difficult assertive behavior to emit, you may find that a self-management project in

---

[3]Audiovisual materials of this nature can be obtained from Instructional Dynamics, Inc.

this area would be helpful. Even if you are a perpetual complainer, you can still profit from this experience, because if you are complaining that much, you must be complaining ineffectively.

1. *Selecting a goal:* If you complain very infrequently, your first goal might be simply to increase the frequency of your complaints. You do not want to become a cantankerous person, but you do want to be able to let others know when you are upset. If you presently complain a great deal, an appropriate goal would be to increase the percentage of complaints that produce positive actions from others.

2. *Recording quantity and circumstances of behavior:* You should record the frequency of your complaints. But you should also monitor the quality of those complaints. (Did you specify the behavior to which you were objecting? Did you attack the other person's competence or integrity?) You also should record setting events. Was the complaint given privately or publicly? Was the complaint given while sufficient time remained to solve the problem? Whatever your goal, you should record the occasions on which you complain, the nature of your complaints, and the effects of your complaints.

3. *Changing setting events:* If you have extreme difficulty complaining, you can first arrange a role-play situation. Following that, you should attempt to complain in private rather than in public. You might also join an assertiveness training group in which the accent is on interpersonal candor. If you want to alter the quality of your complaints, first try complaining to a person that you really like— assuming that that arrangement would decrease the belligerence of your complaints.

4. *Arranging consequences:* Since you want feedback and support when you behave assertively, you might try complaining when you are with someone who will evaluate your complaints and praise you when you complain appropriately. Complaining behavior is ideally suited for a point system. If you now complain infrequently, give yourself points for complaining and additional points for complaining effectively, specifying a certain number of points required for a high-priority privilege.

5. *Focusing on contingencies:* At the critical moment, you can think of a thousand excuses for not complaining (e.g., you do not want to hurt the other person's feelings, it probably would not do any

good anyway). Instead, try reminding yourself of the positive benefits of complaining. You could make a list of these benefits, e.g., correcting bad situations, getting things off your chest, feeling more adequate. You might even write these benefits on a small note card, to which you could inconspicuously refer in situations where complaining might be appropriate.

6. *Applying covert control:* You can use covert reinforcement by imagining the complaining responses and positive reactions to those responses. If you are exceedingly anxious about complaining, try to define a hierarchy of situations in which you would have difficulty complaining; then apply relaxation exercises to that hierarchy.

Concluding Comments

We believe that all relationships are potentially changeable. Naturally, you cannot always control the factors that would produce change. It is improbable that any person will like or be liked by all human beings with whom he/she comes in contact. However, every person can establish positive relationships with certain other people. These may be people with whom you work, members of your family, or social acquaintances. Hopefully, the suggestions in this chapter will enhance those relationships. One's subjective sense of meaning in life is largely dependent on the quality of one's interpersonal contacts. Without at least some human support, life would be intolerable. But who can measure the value of a life filled with love and friendship?

References

Berscheid, E., and Walster, E. H. 1969. *Interpersonal attraction.* Reading, Mass.: Addison-Wesley.

Byrne, D. 1971. *The attraction paradigm.* New York: Academic Press.

Griffitt, W. 1968. Attraction toward a stranger as a function of direct and associated reinforcement. *Psychonomic Science 11*(4), 147-148.

Lazarus, A. A. 1973. On assertive behavior: a brief note. *Behavior Therapy 4,* 697-699.

Lott, B. E., and Lott, A. J. 1960. The formation of positive attitudes toward group members. *Journal of Abnormal and Social Psychology 61,* 297-300.

Masters, J. C. 1970. Treatment of adolescent rebellion by the reconstrual of stimuli. *Journal of Consulting and Clinical Psychology 35,* 213-216.

Mehrabian, A. 1969. Significance of posture and position in the communication of attitude and status relationships. *Psychological Bulletin 71*(5), 359-372.

Miller, M. L., and Siegel, P. S. 1972. *Loving: a psychological approach.* New York: John Wiley and Sons.

Sadler, O., and Tesser, A. 1973. Some effects of salience and time upon interpersonal hostility and attraction during social isolation. *Sociometry 36*, 99-112.

Walster, E., Walster, G. W., Piliavin, J., and Schmidt, L. 1973. "Playing hard to get": understanding an elusive phenomenon. *Journal of Personality and Social Psychology 26*, 113-121.

. . . if one is exploring the possibility of behaving differently, that person
should receive group support.

"Hold me" frequently comes from the lips of a child who has just experienced physical or emotional hurt. We adults sometimes make the same request, although probably not as often as we would like. This request depicts a fundamental reality of the human condition— we all, periodically, need assistance, support, and comfort from others.

When you initially think of self-management, you may have visions of people independently controlling all their behavior. That is a misconception, because our behavior is always affected by the reactions of others. Self-management simply implies that you make the final decisions with respect to your behavior. There are times when others can assist you in reaching decisions or in attaining goals you have set for yourself. You may solicit feedback from others as a means of altering your behavior; you may work out a behavioral contract with those involved in a problem situation; you may seek the support of a self-help group; or you may want assistance from someone who has professional expertise in the area of concern.

Feedback

As we use the term, feedback means information communicated from others showing how they perceive your behavior. It can be extremely helpful as you attempt to alter a variety of responses. For example, you may find that you have difficulty controlling a distasteful idiosyncrasy during conversations. You might want someone to log the behavior and tell you exactly when it occurs. Or, you may find that you are too involved emotionally with a problem to make an objective analysis of your own behavior. In many instances we cannot even identify our problem behaviors without assistance from others. A new teacher who may be acutely aware of the tumultuous conditions in the classroom may be quite unaware of what he/she is doing to foster that tumult. In cases like these, feedback from others can be indispensable to self-management.

A multitude of interpersonal problems can be solved through feedback. Unfortunately, it is seldom given. How should one behave in order to get useful feedback from others? Obtaining useful feedback is seldom as simple as saying, "I need your help." A number of variables may influence whether you obtain feedback and, even more important, whether that feedback is helpful. Your chances of success depend on (1) your reactions to feedback, (2) the precision of your requests, and (3) the ability of the helper.

Your Reactions to Feedback

Most of us have learned that individuals who ask for help do not always want it. Suppose you ask for feedback but quickly become argumentative when your behavior is challenged. When the other person suggests that you are behaving defensively, you vehemently protest, "I am not being defensive!" Under such circumstances others would conclude that you are seeking confirmation of your present behavior rather than attempting to evaluate that behavior honestly. Consequently, your husband, wife, or good friend may tell you what he/she thinks you want to hear. Why should anyone give you honest feedback if the reward for previous attempts has been a rebuff?

To let others know that you genuinely want feedback, we suggest that you listen carefully to whatever is offered. Do not interrupt or become argumentative. You asked for feedback; therefore, hear out the person who is trying to help. If you are not sure what that person is telling you, ask for clarification. This can best be achieved by using some of the nondirective strategies described in the previous chapter; e.g., "Are you saying . . .?" "You feel that I've . . .?" If you disagree with the feedback that is given, do not express your disagreement at that time. Thank the other person for the feedback and indicate your willingness to consider it. We sometimes find that we initially disagree with a person's feedback but later see its wisdom. Seldom are we able to assimilate fully negative feedback at the moment it is given. If a person's feedback proves exceedingly helpful to you over a period of time, let the person know. We have had people come to us several days after a candid interchange and express their appreciation for our comments. This reaction makes us far more likely to offer candid feedback again.

Precision of Requests

Your success in achieving feedback may also be affected by the precision of your requests for help. Suppose you ask a friend to evaluate a speech that you are preparing. Is your friend to concentrate on your delivery, the content, the logic of your arguments, or the length of the speech? Lack of specificity in requesting assistance may lead others to be equally imprecise in the information they give. While counselors and other trained helpers may be experts at identifying your problems, most people are not. Whenever possible, precisely identify the problem behavior with which you are seeking assistance. (Remember Step 1 in the model.)

You undoubtedly know that the kind of feedback you receive, not just the amount of feedback, is the variable that most affects your future behavior. Therefore, you should solicit the type of feedback you know you can handle. If you are not aware of how you respond to various forms of feedback, maybe it would be worthwhile for you to record your performances following, say, praise, reproof, or a combination of the two, from different individuals. If you determine, for example, that criticism usually has a debilitative effect on you, ask the other person to identify the better features of your paper, speech, or athletic performance. If you want negative feedback, ask the person how the behavior being criticized could be improved. We mentioned in Chapter One that negative feedback probably serves as an impetus to change. If you ask a person how your behavior could be improved, you not only have an impetus to change but also some direction for change.

Ability of the Helper

Do not make the mistake of depending on feedback from individuals who lack the ability to help you with the designated problem. A person who has never been to graduate school might have difficulty appraising your adequacy for graduate study. An individual whose social life is in shambles could hardly be counted on to provide useful feedback regarding your social behaviors. A person who has just flunked out of school might be unable to tell you how to study more effectively. We are not saying that you should never ask a nonprofessional for feedback. However, you should seek feedback from those who have enjoyed some success in the problem area. You should seek feedback from several different sources—casual acquaintances as well as close friends. In fact, we have often heard that if you want your behavior thoroughly criticized, ask your worst enemy for an assessment.

Applied Exercise

Although feedback provides a valuable source of information for changing behavior, few people capitalize on that source. We feel that the application of our suggestions on how to ask for feedback, whom to ask, and how to respond once it is given can have a positive impact on your behavior. You might think for a moment of some interpersonal domain where you are experiencing frustration. How can you obtain precise feedback regarding your interaction with others in that situation?

1. *Defining a goal:* Instead of seeking feedback indiscriminately, seek specific feedback regarding specific behaviors. For example, you may want feedback on your listening behaviors, your reinforcing responses, or your sexist behaviors.

2. *Recording quantity and circumstances of behavior*: You should record the frequency of feedback, the focus of feedback, whether feedback was negative or positive, and what preceded and followed it.

3. *Changing setting events*: By first admitting that you are having problems, you indicate a willingess to examine your behavior. The amount and quality of feedback obtained may also be affected by whether that feedback is requested in a private or group setting. Surprisingly, some individuals are more inclined to give feedback in a group setting than in a one-to-one situation. When others share their perceptions, they probably feel more comfortable about expressing those perceptions to you.

4. *Altering consequences of behavior*: Once you have received feedback, you can first indicate through paraphrases that you understand what the person is saying to you. You can also convey your appreciation for the person's candor. Perhaps most importantly, you can tell the person a few days later how helpful the feedback has been. Most of us become anxious about the long-range effect of negative feedback on our interpersonal relationships. It is reassuring to know that all is well.

5. *Focusing on consequences*: Make a list of the potential benefits of getting honest feedback from others. Survey the list just before meeting the people from whom you plan to solicit feedback. This will help you keep the purpose of the interaction clearly in focus.

6. *Applying covert control*: Our anxiety sometimes gets in the way of soliciting feedback. We may be terribly apprehensive about the prospect of negative feedback. Formulate a hierarchy of criticism you might receive and then apply your relaxation strategy to that hierarchy.

Mutual Agreements

Sometimes the resolution of problems requires more than feedback from others. Your behavior may become so intertwined with others' behavior that you find it difficult to change unless they also change. Such is often the case between teacher and student, parent and child, husband and wife, and friend and friend. What frequently happens in these relationships is that the parties fail to reinforce the behaviors they want from each other. When the unreinforced behaviors begin to decline in frequency, one person may harass, criticize, or cajole the other into emitting the desired responses. The result is resentment or withdrawal.

An effective means of resolving many interpersonal problems is behavior contracting. A behavior contract is a mutual agreement between two or more parties to do or not to do certain things. While making contracts is not new in the business world, it is relatively new to the interpersonal domain. The purpose of contracts, whether in business or private relations, is to assure both parties that they will get something of value if they in turn give something of value. A contract explicitly states what both parties want and what they will pay to get it. It is a far kinder method than a cold shoulder or the back of a hairbrush. So, let us examine the role of contracts in primary relationships, such as marriage, and the application of contracts to friendships.

Contracting Between Husband and Wife[1]

Contracting is not new to marriages. In fact, marriage itself is a legal contract. Beyond the legal dimension of marriage, there is a great deal of informal contracting that occurs in this relationship. A husband may prepare his wife's favorite meal and accompany her to a movie with the implicit understanding that he will receive something in return. Of course, he may derive much personal satisfaction from showing kindnesses to his wife, but would he exhibit these kindnesses without regard to her behavior? Similarly, would a wife assist her husband with a difficult work assignment regardless of how he be-

---

[1]Our suggestions regarding marriage contracting could be applied to any type of relationship where people live together and attempt to achieve their primary satisfaction from each other.

haved towards her? The number of divorces in this society implies that the answer to our questions is no. We simply cannot take others for granted and expect them to remain devoted to us. Of course, many marriages do not end in divorce when there is a dearth of positive reinforcement in the relationship; this state of affairs is typically perpetuated by negative reinforcement—avoidance of adverse financial and social consequences.

Psychologists who do marriage counseling (Rappaport and Harrell, 1972; Stuart, 1969) have developed contracting models for resolving marital discord. Their contracts focus on such behaviors as time spent in conversation, positive comments, sexual interaction, and sharing of household chores. Figure 9-1 is an example of a contract formulated by two of Rappaport and Harrell's clients. The results of contracts negotiated by four of Stuart's couples show that as conversation increased, sexual intercourse also increased. The wives in those cases had wanted more positive conversations with their husbands; both husbands and wives wanted more sexual interaction. The con-

---

Mr. and Mrs. X
Behavioral-Exchange Contract No. 1
February, 1971

CONTRACT

It is hereby agreed that: (A) Mr. X will increase the number of unqualified compliments paid to his wife, if, in return, she spends a half-hour per day with her husband. During this time, Mr. X is to have his wife's undivided attention to discuss pleasant activities.   (B) Mrs. X will spend a half-hour per day providing her husband with her undivided attention for the discussion of pleasant activities, if, in return, Mr. X provides her with an increase in unqualified compliments. This contract is to go into effect on (date).

Husband

Wife

Counselor (Witness)

Figure 9-1   From Rappaport and Harrell, 1972.

tractual agreement permitted the husbands to earn tokens for positive conversations. The accumulation of a requisite number of tokens could then be exchanged for various levels of sexual activity. Talking and listening to each other probably embellished the reinforcement that each partner received from sexual interaction.

While Rappaport, Harrell and Stuart helped couples set up contracts, we believe marriage partners who are familiar with behavior principles can apply contracting to many of their own problems. Remember, your spouse is not clairvoyant. He/she cannot read your mind to determine what you want from him/her. This is especially true in this era of sex-role changes. The written contract makes your expectations known to each other. Because people forget what they have said, the written contract is usually superior to an oral agreement. Contracting is simply an attempt to achieve through positive means what you could not achieve by coercive means.

Contracting Between Friends

In Chapter Eight we noted that many psychologists believe friendships are based on reciprocal reinforcement. The behavior of friends, however, sometimes ceases to be mutually reinforcing. Frequently, one person is operating under an old set of assumptions as to what is reinforcing, while the second person has changed reinforcement priorities. Your friend may keep inviting you to go to hockey matches, while you would now prefer to attend flower shows. You cannot expect another person magically to know what you prefer. If you consider the friendship worth saving, contracting is one way to clarify the expectations you have of each other and to identify appropriate reinforcers for meeting those expectations. If you have a friendship in trouble, think of explicit agreements you might reach to ease the strain. You could agree on study time, lights-out time in the dorm room, time when each gets private use of a shared apartment, or plans for the sharing of jointly purchased property.

Contracts with friends are not solely for the purpose of preserving friendships. Contracts can be directed toward changing behaviors that are quite unrelated to the friendship. If the other person possesses significant reinforcers, there is no reason why these payoffs should not be applied to behaviors you want to change. This arrangement works particularly well when the two people are working on a similar behavior (e.g., smoking, eating, project completion). Both can operate under essentially the same set of contingencies. A person who has consequences applied to his/her own behavior will be more faithful in applying these consequences to the other person. So if you and a friend have a similar problem, draw up an agreement as to the reinforcers (privileges, praise, lunch) you can expect from the other for exhibiting appropriate behavior.

Although we recognize that contracting may sound a bit mechanical, it has a philosophical tone that we like. A contract implies that two people are mutually committed to preserving their relationship or to helping each other deal with an important problem. A written contract simply specifies the logistics for actualizing that commitment.

Self-Management Checklist

How do you determine whether an interpersonal contract would be appropriate for a given problem? The more checks you give to the following items, the more appropriate a contract would be.

__The problem involves another person's behavior.

__The other person is not fulfilling my expectations.

__I do not know what the other person expects from me.

__ I am using pressure to get the other person to behave in a more appropriate way.

__The other person has a problem similar to mine.

Joining a Self-Help Group

Many people find that belonging to a group gives them the support they need to resolve problems they have not solved on their own. Self-help groups have been formed by people interested in losing weight, exercising, reducing smoking, developing athletic skills, studying more effectively, gaining political power, and solving community problems. Such groups no doubt exist in your community.

A reinforcer that is used by practically all groups is social attention. Social attention in the form of approval can alter a wide variety of behaviors. A group of individuals with common goals will offer social support for achievements to which others would be oblivious. The obese person who describes resisting a piece of pie may receive a standing ovation from a group of dieters; the same story told to a group uninterested in dieting might result only in a few raised eyebrows.

The group itself may never talk about social attention and how attention affects the members, but that does not negate the reality of this phenomenon. When members listen, nod approval, applaud successes, and offer words of encouragement, social attention is at work. People talk because others listen. People persist in striving toward goals because others care about the results that are obtained. And we have already shown the aversive value of having to face others when you state a goal and then show no progress. Social attention is thus a double-barreled approach with both praise and reproof serving as potential helpers.

Weight Watchers

The far-reaching impact of self-help groups is epitomized by the Weight Watchers society. Jean Nidetch (1972), a founder of Weight Watchers, reports that she initially invited a group of six fat friends over to her house to talk to them about the difficulties and successes she was having with a new diet. She thought her fat friends might give her the support she needed to reach her goal, and she was right. They listened to her story and began to talk about ways they could help one another. In subsequent meetings, the group shared experiences and applauded each other's successes. Under Nidetch's guidance Weight Watchers soon became an international business that has helped millions of overweight persons. People meet in small groups where they hear lecturers tell how they have successfully lost weight, and where members discuss their problems and receive encouragement for their efforts to change. The group, of course, has a diet plan and methods to control eating behavior, but social attention continues to be a major reinforcer. Without reinforcement from some source, dieting behavior would not be sustained. People generally do not lack knowledge as to what they should or should not do; often, however, they lack the necessary social support actually to alter that behavior.

Smoke Watchers Incorporated

Weight Watchers is not the only organization to use social attention to modify behavior. Smoke Watchers Incorporated (1970) suggests that you associate with a benevolent pressure group of other smokers who are trying to reduce their smoking. Smoke Watchers contends that social pressure started you smoking and can help you stop. We agree. If you cannot join a Smoke Watchers group, groups formed by the American Cancer Society, a municipal government agency, or some health group may assist you in controlling your smoking. If you cannot join any organized group, Smoke Watchers recommends that you at least seek out others who are trying to quit smoking. Perhaps you know that a fellow commuter, colleague, or a person who you meet frequently on campus is also trying to quit. You could develop an informal group comprising those individuals. People who share your problem will know the significance of each effort you make. You can give encouragement to others, tell them about your plans, and, in return, get encouragement and additional ideas.

Alcoholics Anonymous

The best-known self-help group is Alcoholics Anonymous (A.A.). Although A.A. has a strong religious character and appeals to spiritual resources in changing behavior, it also makes extensive use of social support. The group is defined as a "fellowship of men and women who share their experiences, strength and hope with each other that they may solve their common problem and help others to recover from alcoholism" (Norris, 1970, p. 155). Alcoholics are welcomed into A.A. by fellow alcoholics who stand ready to assist them twenty-four hours a day in their efforts to maintain sobriety. Such help comes at a time when individuals may be experiencing rejection from their closest friends and associates. The members listen to one another's efforts to effect change, and they applaud those efforts. This is social attention at its best. Not only do alcoholics get help, but they also give help by telling their own success story and offering encouragement to others. Getting and giving is what social attention is all about; it adds meaning to all our lives, whether we are alcoholics or teetotalers. Perhaps the religious character of A.A. and its emphasis on total sobriety is not appropriate for everyone, but few approaches can claim universal appeal. The point is that groups can use social attention as a powerful tool for changing behavior, no matter where the emphasis is placed.

Synanon Foundation

One of the most widely publicized treatment groups for drug addiction is the Synanon Foundation. This foundation was established in

1958 as an offshoot of a local A.A. chapter in Ocean Park, California. Its original mission was to help narcotics addicts transcend their addiction; more recently the foundation has accepted alcoholics, emotionally troubled persons, and those who simply want to live in a drug-free society. Synanon is now a multimillion-dollar operation; it includes large live-in complexes, interviewing centers, service stations, its own school system, and the Synanon Fair.

Synanon's methods differ substantially from the strategies of the other self-help groups. A visitor to Synanon would be impressed more with the brutal candor that characterizes interaction than with social approval for appropriate behavior. The major treatment activity is the Synanon Game. The game (group) comprises about a dozen people and demands that people admit weaknesses and take responsibility for their own behavior. Group members frequently yell and swear at each other—particularly when someone is making excuses for behavior or blaming problems on family and society. The goal of the group is for all members to bare their souls and to rebuild their personalities.

Although the methods of Synanon sound terribly harsh, the society is also very protective. In a sense one enjoys total immunity from the problems and temptations of the larger society. One is constantly surrrounded by those who share a commitment to a drug-free life. In contrast to the world outside, setting events and reinforcement contingencies strongly favor nonuse of drugs. Perhaps this is why recidivism is ostensibly much lower in Synanon (no exact data are available) than in more conventional treatment centers (Davidson, 1970). However, one must remember that Synanon is essentially a communal existence. Synanon does not necessarily prepare a person to live a drug-free life in our larger society.

Consciousness-Raising Groups

Many advocates of the human liberation movement see consciousness-raising groups as major vehicles for eliminating sex-role behaviors. Since sex-role stereotypes are so deeply entrenched in our culture, one may experience little support for nonstereotypic responses among one's usual associates. Joining a consciousness-raising group can be an ideal way to mobilize support for those responses.

So far, men and women have generally met in separate groups. The rationale has been that the presence of the opposite sex might impede exploration of more sensitive areas. Women will be attuned to problems of womanhood unknown to men, just as men will have perceptions of manhood unknown to women. At the outset of consciousness raising, men and women should therefore be most sympathetic and approving toward members of their own sex. The approval in a consciousness-raising group should mainly be directed toward "exploring" behaviors. An individual can have a plethora of stereotypic responses, but if one is exploring the possibility of behaving differently, that person should receive group support. The housewife who is just beginning to explore possibilities outside the home ought to be supported just as much as the radical feminist. Only the individual who refuses to examine his/her own behavior or to consider alternative behaviors meets with group disapproval.

Activist Groups

Groups committed to changing laws, job opportunities, work conditions, housing regulations, and political parties have made a tremendous impact on this society in the last two decades. The impact of such groups is most dramatically seen in the civil rights organizations of the 1960s. Large, cohesive groups can produce changes in society that a single individual would be powerless to make. If societal conditions are preventing you from realizing important personal aspirations, we strongly recommend that you become aligned with an appropriate activist group. Although societal changes will probably come slower than you would like, you can still derive tremendous satisfaction from working with people who share your goals.

As with the other groups that we have discussed, social approval is a powerful means of controlling behavior within activist organizations. In fact, a major danger we see in such groups is that group approval will become too important. We generally support activist organizations committed to social change. Sometimes, however, these groups almost demand that people abdicate their personal identities. In other words, one is expected to support group norms unconditionally. We feel that groups are strengthened when their members can question group goals, deviate from group norms, and, in essence, be unique individuals. Probably the best way to destroy the vitality of a group is for group members to accept unconditionally the actions of the group.

A Word of Caution

We have emphasized the role of group attention in altering your behaviors. However, group attention is not always directed toward self-improvement. You might find yourself a bona fide member of the Mutual Crying Society. Members of that society—some of whom are found in every group—reinforce one another in complaining about their problems, blaming their difficulties on others, and bemoaning their fate. They thus accomplish little. If others begin complaining rather than seeking ways to change, ask them, "How do you feel you could improve the situation?" "What do you have planned as a remedy?" You could then reinforce positive actions with words of commendation.

Self-Management Within a Group

Joining a group or trying to obtain the benefits of a group may require some self-management on your part. In fact, just getting to the meetings may require self-management. Once you are an active member, you may have to employ additional self-management procedures to obtain the group support needed to reach personal goals.

1. *Selecting a goal:* Is your goal to attend meetings, participate in meetings, or assist others in the group?
2. *Recording the quantity and circumstances of behavior:* What was the level of your behavior before joining? In what ways are you improving? To what extent are you improving?
3. *Controlling setting events:* Has the group given you any suggestions for altering the circumstances that typically precede your unwanted behavior?
4. *Establishing effective consequences:* For what behaviors does the group offer social attention?
5. *Focusing on contingencies:* Does the group teach you about the benefits or aversive consequences of certain actions? Does the group make suggestions that make you more aware of your behavior? Is a group member observing your behavior or cuing you to certain behaviors that you spontaneously exhibit?
6. *Applying covert control:* Have you thought about using covert processes to help you attend meetings, share your experiences, or become less anxious about any aspect of group interaction?

Seeking Professional Help

The time may come when you feel that your own efforts and those of your friends have failed to resolve your problems. You may then turn to a professional person for assistance. Self-management does not end here, however, because you permit only certain people to help. Some treatments you will readily accept; others you will reject. Getting professional help means just that—help. Professionals do not solve your problem; they help *you* to solve the problem. You cannot give your problems away by going to a professional helper. Even with the most severe problems, the goal of those who offer help is re-establishment of self-management skills in the person seeking help. So there is no escape from self-management, not even when getting professional assistance.

The helpers most readily available in the college setting are clinical psychologists and counselors. Clinical psychologists hold a doctoral degree in psychology with special training in research, assessment (testing and diagnosis), and techniques of therapy. Counselors generally hold a master's, or doctoral degree in counseling psychology; they also have training in research, assessment, and therapy. Counselors sometimes refer serious problems to clinical psychologists, whose training may be more extensive than the counselor's, or to psychiatrists or psychoanalysts, whose medical expertise may be required.

There is no single accepted way for a therapist to help a troubled individual. The kind of help therapists offer is a function of their previous educational training, experience, and philosophy about human nature. We do not accept the hypothesis that the "doctor knows best" and that you must take whatever is offered. You do not surrender your rights when you ask for help. Most helpers realize this, and if they cannot offer assistance that is suitable to you, they will refer you to a colleague who can. College counseling centers frequently employ persons with different kinds of helping orientations; however, the most widely used approaches are nondirective counseling and behavior therapy. In addition, most counseling centers provide group experiences that include a combination of several approaches.

Nondirective Counseling

Client-centered, or nondirective, therapy is probably the most prevalent approach offered in the college setting. This approach grew out of the writings of Carl Rogers in the early 1940s and has continued to flourish under his leadership. Rogers believes that individuals need insight into their present feelings rather than past experiences. He contends that when people are unaware of their own feelings, they are less than fully functioning persons. The role of the Rogerian, or client-centered, therapist is to help clients see their real feelings. To accomplish this goal, the therapist acts something like a mirror, reflecting back in nonjudgmental phrases what the client has expressed verbally and nonverbally. The therapist may reflect back by commenting, "I hear you saying . . ." "You are upset because . . ." "You feel angry at your boss because . . ." "You wish you could . . ." The therapist does not make judgments about the acceptability of the client's behavior and does not tell the client what to do. The objective of client-centered therapy is increased self-awareness and self-acceptance.

Client-centered therapy generally involves no more than one one-hour session per week and seldom lasts more than forty weeks. The approach has considerable merit because clients are provided with a friendly, accepting environment in which to explore their problems. The major difficulty for some people, however, is that the therapist provides a minimum of direction and information. If you want specifics on how to resolve such problems as overeating, inefficient study habits, smoking, or drinking, you might not be interested in the idea of talking about your feelings. That is not to say that overt behaviors cannot be changed once you understand how you feel, but you may prefer a more direct attack on the behaviors themselves.

Behavior Therapy

This approach is based on the belief that behavior is learned. An individual learns to behave, think, and feel as a function of what is associated with behaving, thinking, and feeling. Consequently, the behaviorally oriented therapist tries to change or help the client change what happens before or after various actions. In helping individuals rearrange their environments, behavior therapists use many of the techniques described in this book. They help you define your problem in behavioral terms, devise a means of monitoring the problem behavior, arrange appropriate setting events, specify reinforcers for the desired response, identify ways to focus on behavioral contingencies, and, where appropriate, apply covert control. Since behavior therapists frequently treat anxiety reactions, systematic desensitization is one of their most commonly employed techniques. Thus, the behavioral approach is oriented toward alleviating specific problem behaviors rather than attempting to alter a person's entire being. The research literature indicates that this approach has been highly successful in producing specific behavior changes in relatively short periods.

Group Therapy

Group therapy has been used with any number of therapeutic approaches. Individuals may be asked to come together in groups of perhaps eight to twelve persons to explore their past, talk about their present feelings, report behavior changes, confront one another, or undergo group desensitization. People find interaction with other group members to be a closer approximation of real life than interacting only with the therapist. Therapists, of course, provide guidance for groups and it is their presence as professionals that distinguishes group therapy from other self-help groups.

Among the group approaches currently used on college campuses, perhaps the most notable are sensitivity groups and encounter groups. Sensitivity groups grew out of attempts to provide leadership and human relations skills to the business community. Today, sensitivity groups continue to be interested in human relations skills. They tend to emphasize honesty, openness of expression, trust in others, and the development of positive feelings towards oneself and others. Exercises designed to create verbal and nonverbal interactions among group members are an important part of sensitivity training. Feedback from the group provides pressure for individuals to change the way they interact with others.

In encounter groups, members are confronted with their behaviors. A person may be told by a fellow group member, "You are only making excuses for your actions," or "You are hiding behind your big words." That person may then be asked how he feels about being confronted. The theoretical aim of encounter groups is to help people become more aware of their behaviors and feelings. Through confrontation individuals are helped to break down pretenses and defenses that undermine interpersonal relationships. There is little time for planning a reaction when one is confronted and must respond immediately. Individuals are presumably helped to realize that they can form meaningful relationships based on honesty and sensitivity to themselves and to others.

In our opinion, group therapy provides an excellent opportunity for people to learn appropriate modes of interacting with others. The behaviors learned within the group may or may not generalize outside the group setting. However, personal growth probably can better be achieved in an accepting and reinforcing group atmosphere than in an attacking one. This does not mean that one's behavior should not be challenged. But the emphasis should be on helping people learn more effective modes of behavior, rather than chastizing them for present behaviors.

Concluding Comments

Two extreme and equally erroneous ways to perceive the resolution of your problems are as follows: (1) Others are responsible for solving my problems; (2) I can solve my problems totally by myself. The first perception usually leads to a great deal of self-pity, because others simply will not assume total responsibility for your problems. The second perception may lead to what is commonly described as beating your head against a wall. There are problems that demand more than your personal resources can provide, and no matter how hard you try, you cannot solve these problems by yourself. It is a pathetic individual who laments that he/she has no resources for dealing with problems; it is a very unwise person who claims to be self-sufficient in all areas of life. All of us can profit from regular feedback from others. Many of us could benefit both personally and interpersonally from contracting with others. Some of us, at least for a portion of our lives, will need the support and direction offered by self-help groups or professional helpers. Knowing when and how to get that help is as much a part of self-management as changing setting events to correct a minor eating problem.

References

Davidson, B. 1970. They shared a victory over heroin. *Good Housekeeping,* October, 102-3.

Nidetch, J. 1972. *The story of weight watchers.* New York: New American Library.

Norris, J. 1970. Alcoholics anonymous. In *World dialogue on alcohol and drug dependence,* ed. E. D. Whitney. Boston: Beacon Press.

Rappaport, A. F., and Harrell, J. 1972. A behavioral-exchange model for marital counseling, *Family Coordinator,* April, 203-212.

Rogers, C. 1942. *Counseling and Psychotherapy.* Boston: Houghton Mifflin.

_____ 1951. *Client Centered Therapy.* Boston: Houghton Mifflin.

_____ 1961. *On Becoming A Person.* Boston: Houghton Mifflin.

Smoke Watchers International, Inc. 1970. *The smoke watchers' how-to-quit book.* New York: Bernard Geis.

Stuart, R. B. 1969. Operant-interpersonal treatment for marital discord. *Journal of Consulting and Clinical Psychology 33*(6), 675-682.

Now that you have concluded the book, it would be nice if we could get together over a cup of coffee to discuss where you go from here. Since that will not be possible unless we have a chance meeting, let us simply offer a few parting thoughts. Most people have the potential for resolving most of their personal problems. This text hopefully has provided the techniques for you to actualize that potential. Until you have consistently applied these techniques, you cannot judge the extent to which self-management can affect your life.

But self-management is more than just a collection of techniques; it is a life style, a way of looking at yourself and at life. We may not have discussed the behaviors of greatest importance to you or the setting events and reinforcement contingencies necessary to alter your target behaviors. But if our message has taken hold, you now can assume these responsibilities for yourself. You can describe your problems in behavioral terms, and you can rearrange the environment to produce the behaviors you desire.

Do not conclude from our book that you need to spend the rest of your life recording and charting behavior. Behavior recording is most indispensable when you are just beginning self-management endeavors. When the self-management approach becomes habitual, you can analyze and resolve many problems without putting anything on paper. For example, we used a multitude of self-management strategies in writing this book. However, very few of these were ever formalized. From our previous writing experiences, we knew what setting events and reinforcers were necessary to maintain writing behaviors. These were applied abundantly, but inconspicuously, throughout the project.

We are committed to partaking of life's happier moments. Although we therefore devote little time to self-pity, we realistically accept life's insolubles. The song, "If I Ruled the World," reflects our sentiments about such problems. But most of our time is devoted to problems over which we have some control. It is our ability to deal with these problems that primarily determines the quality of life. Our thesis is that people must be true to themselves before they can be true to others. Live the fullest life you can and you will have something to contribute to the rest of us.

Anxiety hierarchy. Identification and low-to-high ranking of anxiety-producing stimuli. Usually there are a number of stimuli (settings, persons, events) related to a particular kind of anxiety, and these stimuli produce different degrees of uneasiness. For example, you may be anxious about public speaking, but speaking before one or two persons may create less anxiety than speaking before ten or twelve persons. Typically, one visualizes the stimulus situations (beginning with the least threatening) while in a relaxed state.

Aversive stimulus. Any event that you seek to avoid or terminate. Because aversive stimuli are consequences, they can be used to suppress unwanted behavior or to increase desired behavior. Social reproval, an electric shock, the flip of a rubber band, or any pain-producing stimulus can qualify as an aversive stimulus.

Back-up reinforcer. A reinforcer that can be obtained by cashing in other items such as points, physical tokens, stars, money. Back-up reinforcers give value to such items as points, which can be given immediately for desired behavior. For example, you might award yourself one point for each five minutes of study. Subsequently, you could cash in a specified number of points for a night out.

Baseline. Level of behavior before any attempt at modification. Baseline data can be used to determine whether a change is needed and as a reference point for measuring the effects of modification procedures. Ordinarily, a baseline is established over a period of several days.

Behavioral goal. The results one seeks to achieve in using a behavior management plan. Behavioral goals typically include the process (e.g., decrement in snacking) one will use as well as the results (e.g., weight reduction) one hopes to achieve through self-management. Behavioral goals may involve changing covert behavior, such as feelings or thoughts, overt behaviors, such as speaking before groups, or both.

Behavior contract.   An agreement between two or more persons to do or not to do certain things. Contracts, long used in the business world, are now proving effective in improving interpersonal relations. Contracting between husband and wife, parent and child, or teacher and pupil, for example, can lead to greater clarity and fulfillment of what people expect from each other. Contracts usually specify appropriate and inappropriate behaviors and the consequences of each.

Chain.   A series of responses that follow in close succession and thus form a more complete behavior. For example, the complete act of hitting a tennis ball requires running to the ball, getting your racket back, bending your knees, watching the ball, and swinging through the ball. Normally, completion of one response in a chain constitutes the stimulus for the next response. Thus, when one response is disrupted, the entire behavior chain is likely to be disrupted.

Conditioning.   The process of changing behavior by systematically manipulating environmental events. In self-management, conditioning is typically accomplished by an individual's manipulating events that immediately precede and follow behavior.

Contingency.   A behavioral condition under which a reinforcer or punisher is administered. For example, if you required yourself to engage in a specific amount of exercise before you attend a certain theatrical performance, the exercise requirement would constitute a reinforcement contingency (i.e., a condition for reinforcement). On the other hand, if you flip yourself with a rubber band whenever you have a specified thought, having that thought would be considered the contingency (condition) for self-punishment.

Controlled responses.   A target behavior that a person wants to change through self-management strategies. Controlled responses are products of our actions and/or other environmental influences and are thus legitimate targets for behavior change. For example, eating, exercising, smoking, and talking might be considered controlled responses.

Controlling responses.   Behaviors that people emit to change target behaviors. Developing a time schedule, keeping a clean study area, recording all assignments, making a reward contingent upon a specified amount of study, and controlling other situations to facilitate study illustrate controlling responses. These actions partly control people's study behavior.

Coverant pairs. Coverant is a contraction for *covert operant.* It applies to thoughts that have an effect on the environment. When a person initially thinks about emitting an undesirable behavior, he/she should first emit a negative coverant (a thought focusing on the negative consequences of exhibiting that behavior) and then a positive coverant (a thought related to the positive consequences of not exhibiting that behavior). These two coverants constitute a coverant pair and should be followed by an overt reinforcing activity.

Covert negative reinforcement. Unpleasant imagery that by its termination strengthens thought or behavior. For example, you might imagine that you are about to be bitten by a poisonous snake and then abruptly focus your thought on a behavior, such as speaking in groups, that you want to strengthen. Because thinking about the latter behavior terminates visualization of the unpleasant scene, that thought ("speaking in groups") is said to be negatively reinforced.

Covert positive reinforcement. Imagery that strengthens the thought or behavior immediately preceding it. For example, if thinking about a sandy seashore is pleasant imagery, that imagery could be used to reinforce visualization of a desired behavior.

Covert sensitization. Learning to avoid an undesirable stimulus by imagining a negative event (e.g., nausea) following approach responses to that stimulus. For example, you might first imagine yourself pouring an alcoholic beverage, picking up the glass, bringing the glass to your lips, and then feeling nauseated. The nausea should prevent the consummatory response (drinking the liquor) from occurring.

Desensitization. Elimination of an anxiety response to certain stimuli. The therapist first asks the individual to visualize each stimulus situation (beginning with the least threatening) while in a relaxed state. Because muscular relaxation presumably is incompatible with anxiety, the pairing of these stimuli with relaxation responses should weaken anxiety. If the individual begins to get anxious while visualizing a stimulus situation, that visualization is stopped and relaxation re-established; then, visualization of the stimulus is continued.

Extrinsic reinforcement. Reinforcement that is part of a person's external environment, as opposed to reinforcement coming from inner thoughts and feelings. Money, food, and praise are examples of extrinsic reinforcement. What is external may eventually be internalized. For example, you might start praising yourself for behaviors for which you have been externally praised.

Frequency count.   A tabulation of the number of times a particular behavior occurs. Any behavior, such as a sarcastic comment, a smile, or an exercise, that has a readily identifiable beginning and end can easily be recorded by means of a frequency count.

Functionalism.   A school of psychology that sought to determine the functions for behavior and mental processes, not just their structure. Functionalism was a part of the evolutionary movement in psychology that led to today's behaviorism, which is primarily concerned with observable, measurable behavior.

Generalized reinforcer.   A reinforcer that has acquired the capacity to strengthen a wide variety of behaviors under diverse conditions. A stimulus, such as money or social approval, that frequently gets paired with other known reinforcers (e.g., food, entertainment, accomplishments) may very well become a generalized reinforcer. You could become a generalized reinforcer for others by being paired with a variety of pleasant circumstances.

High probability behavior.   A behavior in which an individual frequently engages when there are no external consequences (such as positive or negative reinforcement) for engaging in that behavior. Such behavior can be used to reinforce low probability or infrequent behavior by making access to the high probability behavior (e.g., socializing) contingent upon performing the low probability behavior (e.g., studying). See *Premack principle.*

Imagery.   Mental images. Used in conjunction with covert strategies such as covert reinforcement and covert sensitization. The mental image of a behavior or situation should include all the sensations of the actual behavior or situation.

Incompatible behavior.   A behavior that is inconsistent with and cannot occur simultaneously with another behavior. Cooperation, for example, is incompatible with aggression. One way to reduce aggression in a given setting would be to reinforce cooperative behavior.

Interest inventory.   An instrument, such as the *Kuder Occupational Interest Survey* or *Strong-Campbell Interest Inventory,* that compares your interests in various activities with those of people who are successfully engaged in a variety of occupations. The assumption is that the more closely your interests match those of successful persons in a given occupation, the more likely you will find satisfaction in that occupation.

Internal events. Responses, such as depression, troublesome thoughts, or anxiety, that occur within the individual. One way to alter internal responses is to change overt behaviors that are associated with thoughts and feelings. Or, an individual may wish to focus directly upon internal responses through the use of such strategies as muscular relaxation, desensitization, or thought-stopping.

Internal kinesthetic feedback. Sensory feedback regarding your muscle movement, which indicates whether a behavior has been executed appropriately. In this case, appropriateness is defined primarily in terms of process. For example, when a tennis player feels a sense of rhythm in his strokes, internal kinesthetic cues suggest that he is stroking the ball correctly. Because of these cues, the experienced tennis player can usually determine from the moment of impact whether a ball has been hit correctly.

Intrinsic information feedback. Feedback inherent to a sport, which indicates whether a behavior has been performed adequately. In this case, adequacy is defined in terms of product rather than process. Determining whether a basketball goes through the hoop or whether a tennis serve lands within the service court illustrates this kind of feedback.

Intrinsic reinforcement value. The extent to which an activity will be engaged in without additional reinforcing consequences. An activity that has high intrinsic reinforcement value is inherently enjoyable. Watching a good movie undoubtedly has higher intrinsic reinforcement value than cleaning your room.

Modeling. Acquisition of a new behavior by observing and then reproducing the behavior of another person. If you are interested in acquiring a particular skill by this approach, identify someone who effectively performs the skill, observe that person's behavior, and then practice doing what he/she has done. You might learn a golf swing, a social grace, or any number of other behaviors in this manner.

Noncontingent.   Unconditional, not dependent on the occurrence of any specific behavior. For example, you might identify certain reinforcing activities that you make an integral part of your daily schedule. Since you are not required to earn these reinforcing activities, they are considered noncontingent.

Operant behavior.   Behavior that produces a change in the environment, such as rewards or escape from punishment. Individuals operate on their environment to test what consequences their behavior will produce. Behaviors that produce pleasant consequences tend to be repeated, while behaviors that produce unpleasant consequences tend to be eliminated. What is pleasant or unpleasant, of course, varies from person to person.

Overt behavior.   Any observable, measurable action. Talking, smiling, walking, crying, smoking, and eating are examples of overt behavior. Behavior management primarily involves changing overt rather than covert responses.

Positive reinforcer.   Any stimulus that strengthens (maintains or increases) the behavior it follows. What is a positive reinforcer may vary from person to person and from time to time. Positive reinforcers usually take the form of approval, pleasant activities, and tangible payoffs.

Premack principle.   Given two behaviors of different probabilities, the more probable behavior can be used to reinforce the less probable. For example, if an individual studies infrequently but socializes frequently, he could reinforce study by making socializing contingent upon study. In other words, first work, then play.

Process assessment.   Assessment of behaviors (e.g., snacking, socializing) that are contributing to a behavior product (e.g., overweight, incomplete academic assignments). Process assessment focuses on behaviors that must be changed to achieve desired outcomes.

Product assessment.   Examining the results (products) of behavior to verify the effectiveness of self-management. Body weight, for example, can be used to verify the effectiveness of a weight-loss program. Similarly, the number of problems successfully completed can be used to verify the effectiveness of a study technique.

Programmed instruction.   Instructional material that is arranged in small segments, from easiest to most difficult, in order to insure maximum success for the learner. Typically, on each segment the learner must respond overtly (e.g., fill in a blank) before proceeding to the next segment. The learner also receives immediate feedback by comparing the response with the correct response.

Punisher. See *aversive stimulus.*

Reciprocal reinforcement. Reinforcement exchanged between parties. Reinforcement is seldom a unilateral process. Individuals tend to receive about as much reinforcement as they give. So, to increase reinforcement received, increase the amount of reinforcement you give.

Reinforcer. See *positive reinforcer* and *negative reinforcer.*

Reward. See *positive reinforcer.*

Satiation. A strategy of repeatedly indulging in a reinforcing activity until the activity is no longer reinforcing. For example, some people have found that smoking one cigarette after another can cause them to tire of cigarettes. In using this strategy, you must be sure that satiation is reached or else the behavior may become even more resistant to change.

Self-reinforcement. Administering a reinforcer to oneself. Typically, the individual also controls the requirements for reinforcement. However, these requirements may be highly consistent with contingencies that initially were externally imposed. Praising yourself, awarding yourself tokens, or allowing yourself to partake of a particular privilege are examples of self-reinforcement.

Self-verbalization. Talking to oneself. This technique can be used at either a covert or overt level. Self-verbalization may involve directing oneself to emit certain behaviors or making positive statements about oneself.

Stimulus control. A strategy for controlling behavior by altering the stimuli that precipitate behavior. For instance, if you limit the places (stimuli) where you eat you may eventually be better able to control your eating.

Symptom. Any sensation, behavior, or occurrence thought to be indicative of a larger problem. Some psychologists suggest that behaviors are symptoms (signs) of internal events (thoughts, feelings). For example, some believe that overeating, excessive sleep, and alocholism are indicators of a much larger problem, such as a feeling of rejection. Behaviorists, however, generally contend that symptoms are real problems and that individuals can be helped by dealing directly with behavior.

Target behavior. The behavior an individual aspires to alter with a behavior management plan.

Token. A tangible (e.g., poker chips) or intangible (e.g., point) item that can be exchanged for back-up reinforcers. Money is perhaps the best example of a token in our society. Tokens serve a useful function in that they can be immediately dispensed for appropriate behavior and can thus bridge the gap between behavior and valued reinforcers. Tokens may themselves acquire reinforcement value through association with back-up reinforcers.

Token economy. A system in which tokens are given as immediate reinforcers for appropriate behavior. A specified number of tokens can subsequently be cashed in for back-up reinforcers.

Ultimate aversive consequence. The long-range punitive effect of engaging in an undesirable behavior. Obesity, loss of friendship, and cancer may be the ultimate aversive consequences of overeating, sarcasm, and smoking, respectively. Thinking about personally meaningful ultimate aversive consequences may reduce undesired actions.

Visualization. See *imagery*.

Will power. Not some mysterious inner repository of strength, which some persons have and others do not. On the contrary, will power is the manipulation of conditions that will produce a given behavior. However, some individuals are not aware of what they do to produce a behavior change. Thus, will power often refers to unspecified self-management procedures. Individuals need to discover what conditions control what behaviors so that they exercise "will power."

Index